maranGraphics ™
Simplified Computer Guide for
WORDPERFECT® 5.1 for Windows™

Ruth Maran

maranGraphics Inc.
Mississauga, Ontario, Canada

maranGraphics™ Simplified Computer Guide
WordPerfect® 5.1 for Windows™

Copyright© maranGraphics Inc., 1992
5755 Coopers Avenue
Mississauga, Ontario, Canada
L4Z 1R9
Telephone: (416) 890-3300
Fax: (416) 890-9434

Screen shots ©1992 WordPerfect Corporation. Used with permission of WordPerfect Corporation.

Published 1992.

Canadian Cataloguing in Publication Data

Maran, Ruth, 1970-
 MaranGraphics simplified computer guide WordPerfect 5.1 for Windows

Includes index.
ISBN 0-9694290-6-1

1. WordPerfect (Computer program). 2. Word processing - Computer programs. 3. Windows (Computer programs). I. Title.

Z52.5.W65M3 1992 652.5'536 C92-093923-6

All rights reserved. No part of this publication may be used, reproduced or transmitted, in any form or by any means, electronic, mechanical, photocopying, recording or otherwise, or stored in any retrieval system of any nature, without the prior written permission of the copyright holder, application for which shall be made to: maranGraphics Inc., 5755 Coopers Avenue, Mississauga, Ontario, Canada, L4Z 1R9.

This publication is sold with the understanding that neither maranGraphics Inc., nor its dealers or distributors, warrants the contents of the publication, either expressly or impliedly, and, without limiting the generality of the foregoing, no warranty either express or implied is made regarding this publication s quality, performance, salability, capacity, suitability or fitness with respect to any specific or general function, purpose or application. Neither maranGraphics Inc., nor its dealers or distributors shall be liable to the purchaser or any other person or entity in any shape, manner or form whatsoever regarding liability, loss or damage caused or alleged to be caused directly or indirectly by this publication.

Acknowledgements

Special thanks to Saverio C. Tropiano for his support and consultation.

To the dedicated staff at maranGraphics Inc. and HyperImage Inc., including Monica DeVries, Jim C. Leung, Jill Maran, Robert Maran, David Ross and Gavin Yong for their contributions.

To Eric Feistmantl who was always there to solve my technical and operational problems.

To Maxine Maran for providing the organizational skill to keep the project under control.

And finally, a special appreciation to Richard Maran who originated the easy-to-use graphic format of this guide. Thank you for your inspiration and guidance.

Trademark Acknowledgements

WordPerfect®
WordPerfect is a registered trademark of WordPerfect Corporation.

Microsoft and MS-DOS are registered trademarks of Microsoft Corporation.

Windows and the Microsoft Mouse design are a trademark of Microsoft Corporation.

Cover Design:
Jim C. Leung

Art Director:
David Ross

Production:
Jim C. Leung
David Ross

Linotronic L-330 Output:
HyperImage Inc.

Table of Contents

GETTING STARTED

Using this Guide 2
Start WordPerfect 4
Enter Text 6
Select Text 6
Moving Through a Document 8

THE BUTTON BAR

View the Button Bar 10
Change the Button Bar 10
Edit a Button Bar 12
Save a Button Bar 14
Select a Button Bar 14

EDIT A DOCUMENT

Insert and Replace Text 16
Move and Copy Text 18
Delete Text 20
Undo 20
Split and Join Paragraphs 22
Change Text to Upper
or Lower Case 22

SAVE FILES AND EXIT WORDPERFECT

Files and Directories 24
Location of Files 26
Save Files 26
Exit WordPerfect 28

VIEW DOCUMENTS

Open a Document 30
Switch Between Documents 31
Cascade or Tile Documents 32
Close a Document 33
Maximize a Document 33

CHECK A DOCUMENT

Spell Check a Document 34
Thesaurus 36
Word Count 36
Search 38
Search and Replace 38

FORMAT A DOCUMENT

View the Ruler 40
Align Text 40
Change Line Spacing 41
Indent a Paragraph 42
Change Margins 44
Setting Tabs 46
Change Fonts 48
Page Breaks 50
Center Text on a Page 50
Automatic Page Numbering 52
Headers and Footers 54
Footnotes and Endnotes 56

TABLES

Create a Table 58
Join Cells 58
Select Cells 59
Enter Text in a Table 60
Resize Columns 60
Insert a Row or Column 62
Delete a Row or Column 62

GRAPHICS

Retrieve a Graphic Image 64
Size a Graphic 64
Move a Graphic 66
Create a Text Box 66

PRINT

Preview a Document 68
Print a Document 70

MERGE AND SORT FILES

Merge Files Overview 74
Create the Primary File 76
Create the Secondary File 76
Merge Files 78
Print a Merged File 78
Sort Data 80

FILE MANAGER

Open the File Manager 82
View Files 82
Change Directories 84
Change Disk Drives 85
File List 86
Change Layout 86
Copy or Move Files 88
Delete Files 90
Search for a File 90
Exit File Manager 91

HELP 92

INDEX 94

USING THIS GUIDE

This Simplified Computer Guide displays on each page exactly what you see on the screen as you move through WordPerfect® 5.1 for Windows.™

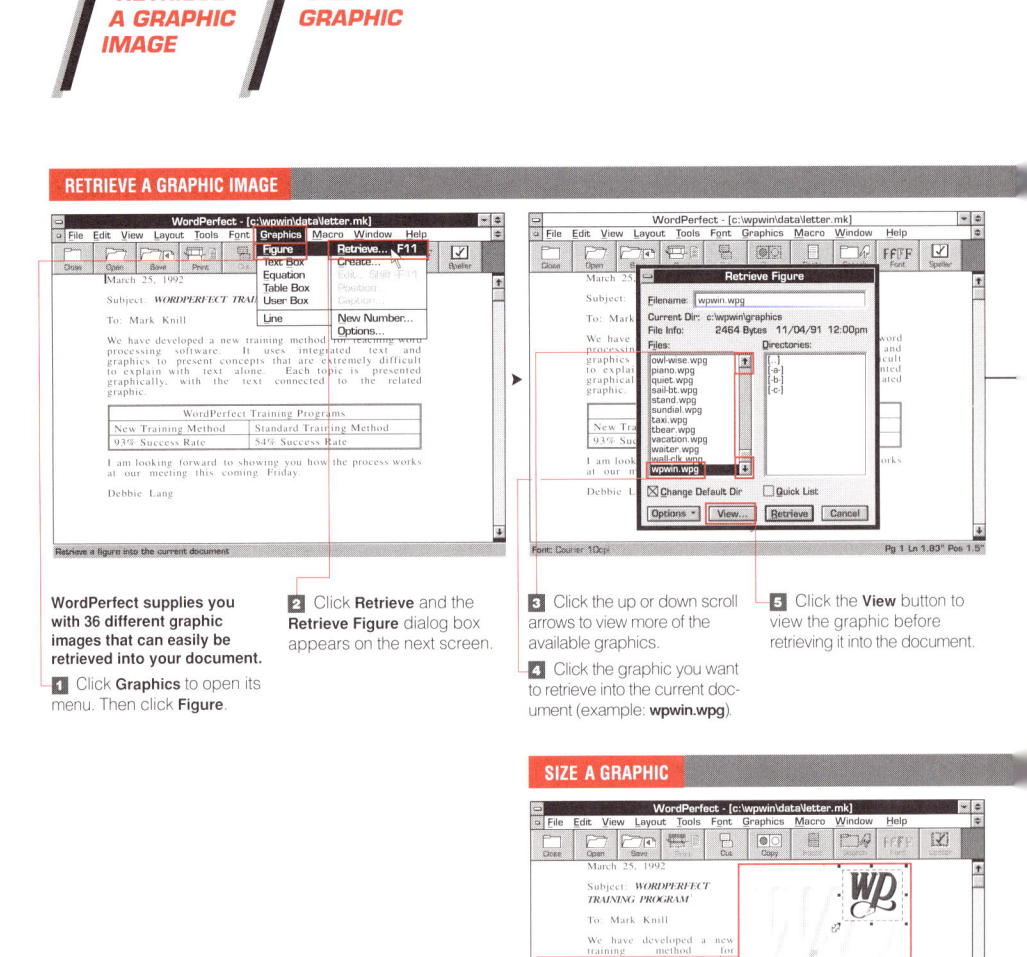

RETRIEVE A GRAPHIC IMAGE

SIZE A GRAPHIC

RETRIEVE A GRAPHIC IMAGE

WordPerfect supplies you with 36 different graphic images that can easily be retrieved into your document.

1 Click **Graphics** to open its menu. Then click **Figure**.

2 Click **Retrieve** and the **Retrieve Figure** dialog box appears on the next screen.

3 Click the up or down scroll arrows to view more of the available graphics.

4 Click the graphic you want to retrieve into the current document (example: **wpwin.wpg**).

5 Click the **View** button to view the graphic before retrieving it into the document.

SIZE A GRAPHIC

1 To select a graphic to be sized, click anywhere inside the box surrounding the graphic.

2 Move the mouse over one corner of the graphic and it turns into.

3 Click and hold down the left mouse button as you drag the edge of the graphic to the desired size.

64

| USING THIS GUIDE | START WORDPERFECT | ENTER TEXT | SELECT TEXT | MOVING THROUGH A DOCUMENT |

■ All topics within the current chapter are displayed. The current topic is highlighted in red type.

RETRIEVE A GRAPHIC IMAGE | SIZE A GRAPHIC | MOVE A GRAPHIC | CREATE A TEXT BOX

■ All chapters in the guide are displayed. The current chapter is highlighted in red type.

GETTING STARTED
THE BUTTON BAR
EDIT A DOCUMENT
SAVE FILES AND EXIT WORDPERFECT
VIEW DOCUMENTS
CHECK A DOCUMENT
FORMAT A DOCUMENT
TABLES
GRAPHICS
PRINT
MERGE AND SORT FILES
FILE MANAGER
HELP

■ The graphic (example: **wpwin.wpg**) is viewed.

6 Click the **Retrieve** button to retrieve the graphic into the document.

■ The graphic is retrieved into the document.

Note: If a box appears with the statement **Fig Box: 1**, the **Graphics** mode is not on. Click **View**, then click **Graphics** to turn on the graphic mode and view the retrieved graphic.

DELETE A GRAPHIC
1 Select the graphic.
2 Press **Delete**.

4 Release the button and the graphic is sized.

◀ 65

◀ 3

START WORDPERFECT

START WORDPERFECT FOR WINDOWS

1 To start WordPerfect® for Windows™ from MS-DOS, type **win** and press **Enter**.

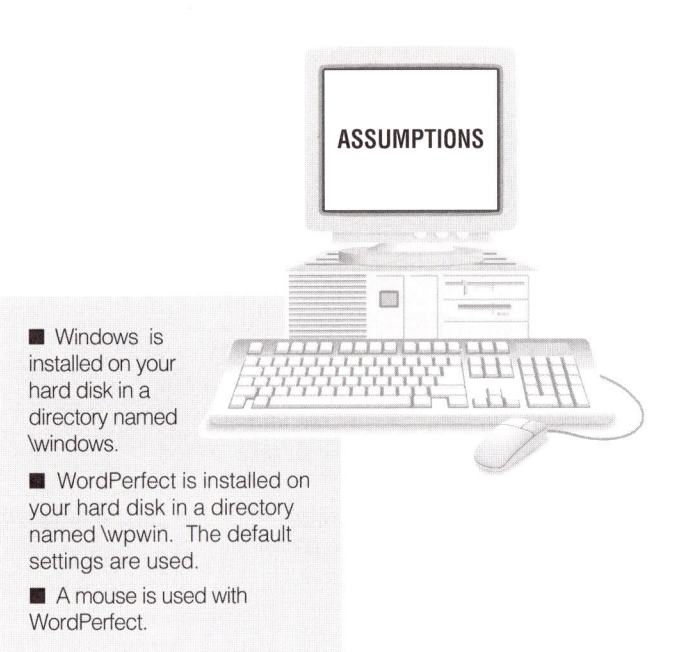

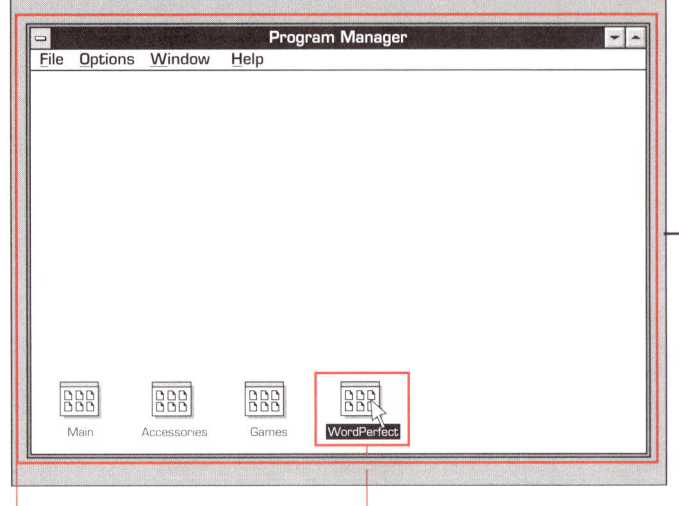

■ The **Program Manager** window is displayed.

All window applications are started from the Program Manager.

The Program Manager window contains icons which represent group applications. Each group icon can be opened into a window to display its related applications or programs (example: the Games group icon contains all the Games programs).

This permits you to organize your applications into groups to make them easier to find and manage.

2 To open the WordPerfect group icon, move the mouse over its icon and click the left button twice in quick succession.

ASSUMPTIONS

■ Windows is installed on your hard disk in a directory named \windows.

■ WordPerfect is installed on your hard disk in a directory named \wpwin. The default settings are used.

■ A mouse is used with WordPerfect.

4

| USING THIS GUIDE | **START WORDPERFECT** | ENTER TEXT | SELECT TEXT | MOVING THROUGH A DOCUMENT |

GETTING STARTED

THE BUTTON BAR

EDIT A DOCUMENT

SAVE FILES AND EXIT WORDPERFECT

VIEW DOCUMENTS

CHECK A DOCUMENT

FORMAT A DOCUMENT

TABLES

GRAPHICS

PRINT

MERGE AND SORT FILES

FILE MANAGER

HELP

■ The **WordPerfect** group window appears.

3 To start the **WordPerfect** application, move the mouse over its icon and click the left mouse button twice in quick succession.

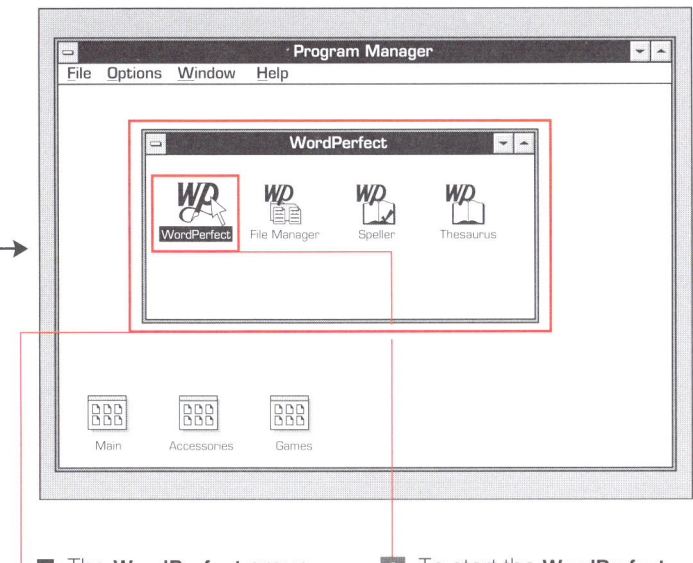

■ WordPerfect displays a new document.

File Manager

The File Manager helps organize and manage your files and directories.
Note: The File Manager is discussed in detail starting on page 82.

Speller

The WordPerfect Speller checks your document for spelling errors.
Note: The Speller is discussed in detail starting on page 34.

Thesaurus

The WordPerfect Thesaurus searches for synonyms and antonyms for a word.
Note: The Thesaurus is discussed in detail starting on page 36.

USING THE KEYBOARD

If key names are separated by a plus sign (**+**), press and hold down the first key before pressing the second key (example: **Ctrl** + ⇥).

USING THE MOUSE

For this guide, the following shortcuts are used:

■ "Move the mouse over **xx** and click the left button" becomes:

Click **xx**

■ "Move the mouse over **xx** and click the left button twice in quick succession" becomes:

Double click **xx**

◀ 5

ENTER TEXT | SELECT TEXT

ENTER TEXT

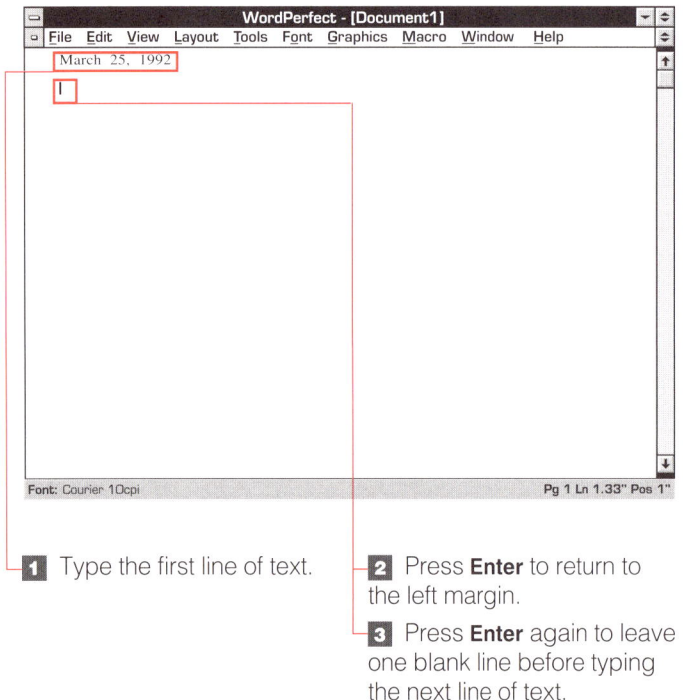

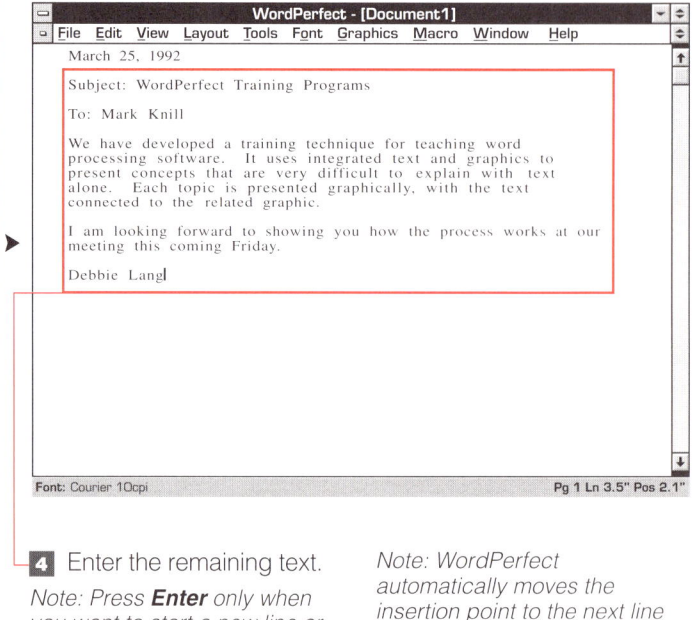

1 Type the first line of text.

2 Press **Enter** to return to the left margin.

3 Press **Enter** again to leave one blank line before typing the next line of text.

4 Enter the remaining text.

*Note: Press **Enter** only when you want to start a new line or paragraph.*

Note: WordPerfect automatically moves the insertion point to the next line as you type.

SELECT TEXT

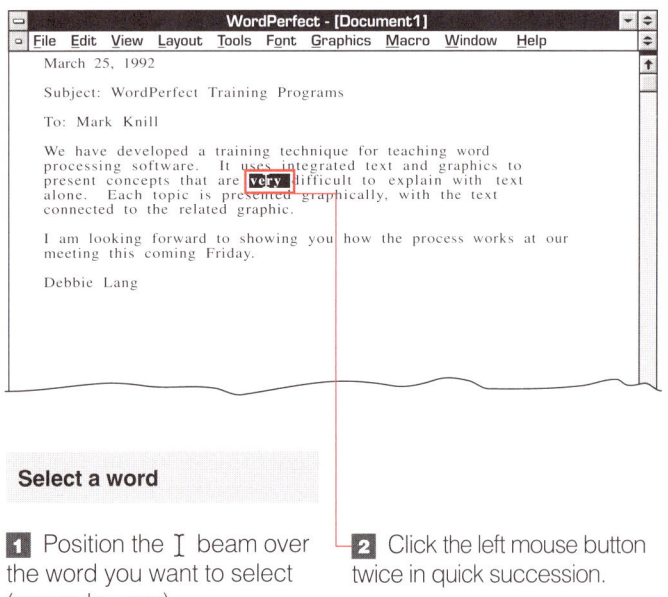

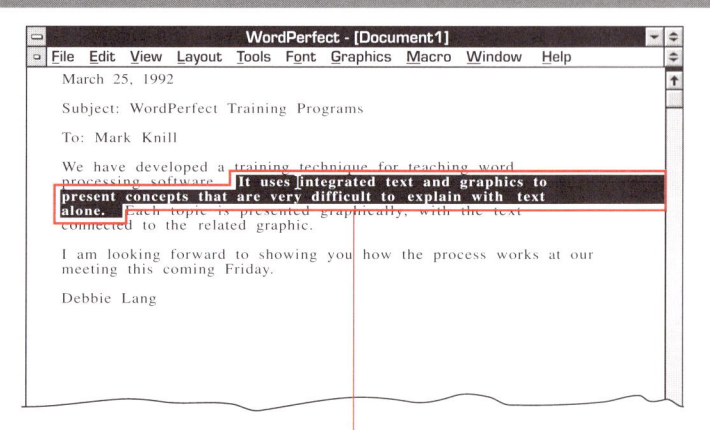

Select a word

1 Position the I beam over the word you want to select (example: **very**).

2 Click the left mouse button twice in quick succession.

Note: To deselect text, click the left mouse button.

Select a sentence

1 Position the I beam anywhere over the sentence you want to select.

2 Click the left mouse button three times in quick succession.

Note: To deselect text, click the left mouse button.

USING THIS GUIDE | START WORDPERFECT | **ENTER TEXT** | **SELECT TEXT** | MOVING THROUGH A DOCUMENT

The position of the insertion point is indicated at the bottom of your screen.

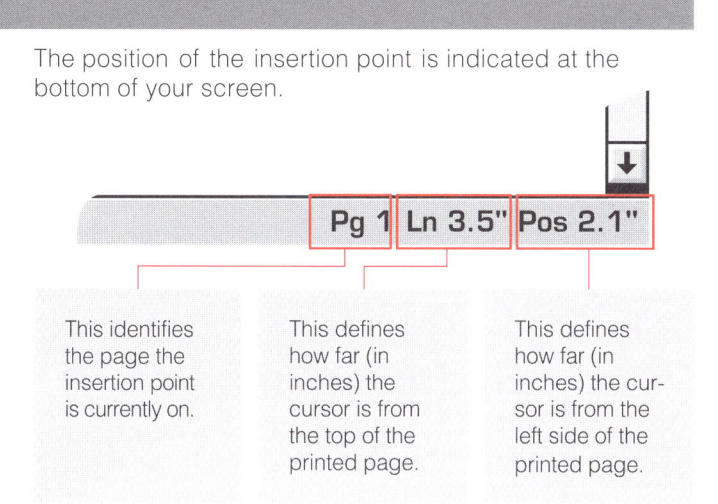

Pg 1 — This identifies the page the insertion point is currently on.

Ln 3.5" — This defines how far (in inches) the cursor is from the top of the printed page.

Pos 2.1" — This defines how far (in inches) the cursor is from the left side of the printed page.

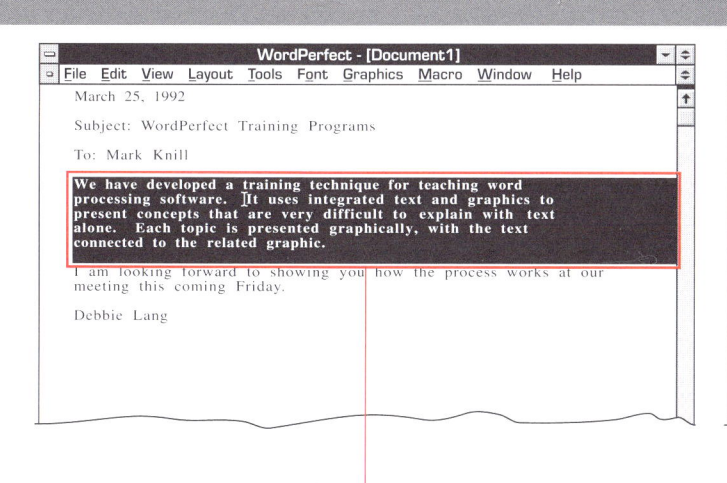

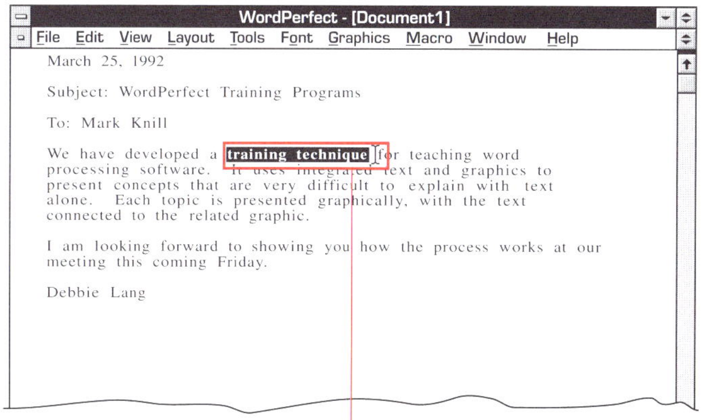

Select a paragraph

1 Position the I beam anywhere over the paragraph you want to select.

2 Click the left mouse button four times in quick succession.

Note: To deselect text, click the left mouse button.

Select by dragging the mouse

1 Position the I beam over the first character of the text you want to select.

2 Click and hold down the left mouse button as you drag the I beam over the text. Then release the mouse button.

Note: To deselect text, click the left mouse button.

GETTING STARTED

THE BUTTON BAR

EDIT A DOCUMENT

SAVE FILES AND EXIT WORDPERFECT

VIEW DOCUMENTS

CHECK A DOCUMENT

FORMAT A DOCUMENT

TABLES

GRAPHICS

PRINT

MERGE AND SORT FILES

FILE MANAGER

HELP

MOVING THROUGH A DOCUMENT

USING THE MOUSE

MOVE TO ANY CHARACTER ON THE SCREEN

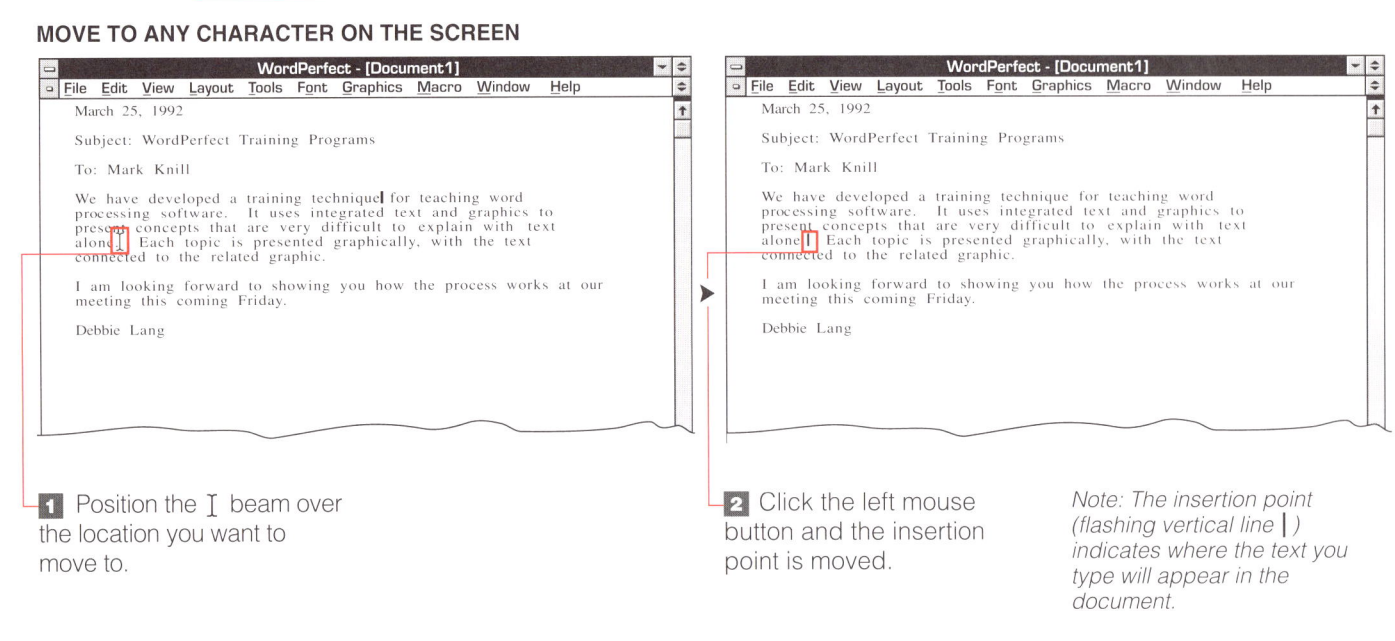

1 Position the I beam over the location you want to move to.

2 Click the left mouse button and the insertion point is moved.

Note: The insertion point (flashing vertical line |) indicates where the text you type will appear in the document.

MOVE TO ANY CHARACTER IN THE DOCUMENT (if the document extends beyond the current window)

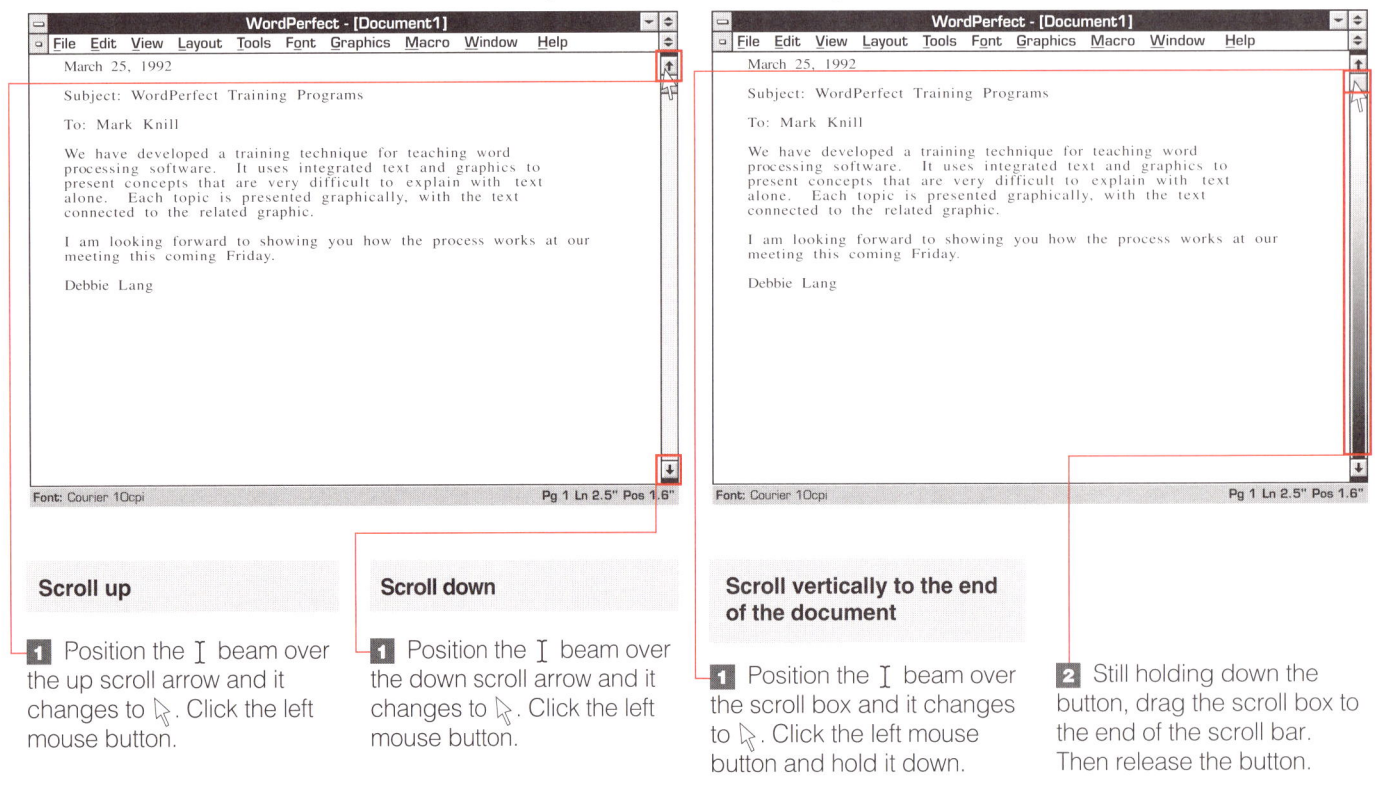

Scroll up

1 Position the I beam over the up scroll arrow and it changes to ↖. Click the left mouse button.

Scroll down

1 Position the I beam over the down scroll arrow and it changes to ↖. Click the left mouse button.

Scroll vertically to the end of the document

1 Position the I beam over the scroll box and it changes to ↖. Click the left mouse button and hold it down.

2 Still holding down the button, drag the scroll box to the end of the scroll bar. Then release the button.

8

USING THE KEYBOARD

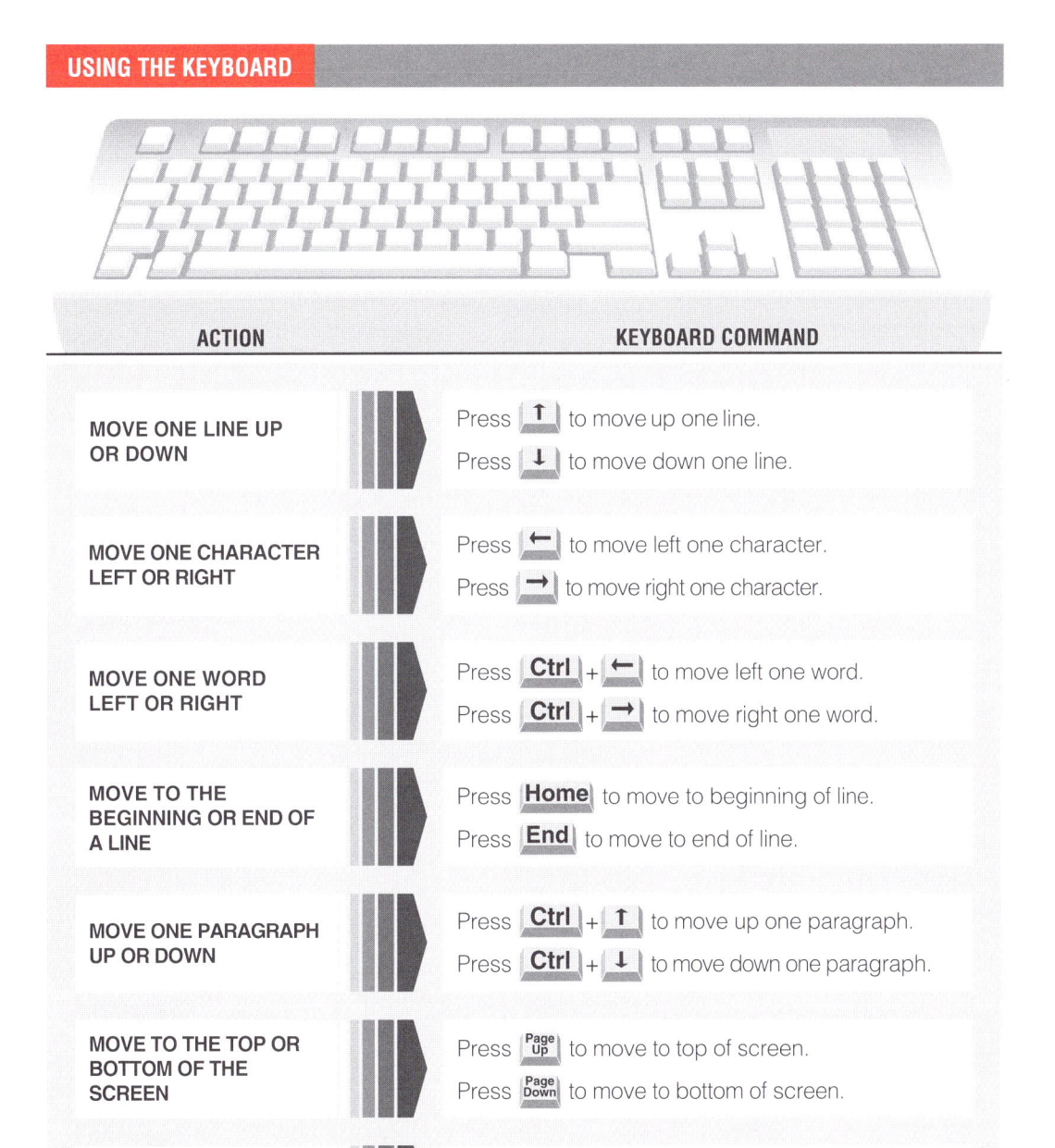

ACTION	KEYBOARD COMMAND
MOVE ONE LINE UP OR DOWN	Press **↑** to move up one line. Press **↓** to move down one line.
MOVE ONE CHARACTER LEFT OR RIGHT	Press **←** to move left one character. Press **→** to move right one character.
MOVE ONE WORD LEFT OR RIGHT	Press **Ctrl** + **←** to move left one word. Press **Ctrl** + **→** to move right one word.
MOVE TO THE BEGINNING OR END OF A LINE	Press **Home** to move to beginning of line. Press **End** to move to end of line.
MOVE ONE PARAGRAPH UP OR DOWN	Press **Ctrl** + **↑** to move up one paragraph. Press **Ctrl** + **↓** to move down one paragraph.
MOVE TO THE TOP OR BOTTOM OF THE SCREEN	Press **Page Up** to move to top of screen. Press **Page Down** to move to bottom of screen.
MOVE TO THE TOP OR BOTTOM OF THE DOCUMENT	Press **Ctrl** + **Home** to move to top of document. Press **Ctrl** + **End** to move to bottom of document.

*Note: You cannot move the insertion point beyond the last character of the last line in a document. To add a line, press **Enter**.*

VIEW THE BUTTON BAR

VIEW THE BUTTON BAR

The Button Bar is a powerful tool that allows for quick and easy access to WordPerfect's most utilized commands.

1 Click **View** to open its menu.

2 Click **Button Bar**.

■ The Button Bar is displayed.

*Note: When buttons are dimmed, they are not currently operational (example: **Cut**).*

*Note: To hide the Button Bar, click **View** to open its menu. Then click **Button Bar**.*

CHANGE THE BUTTON BAR

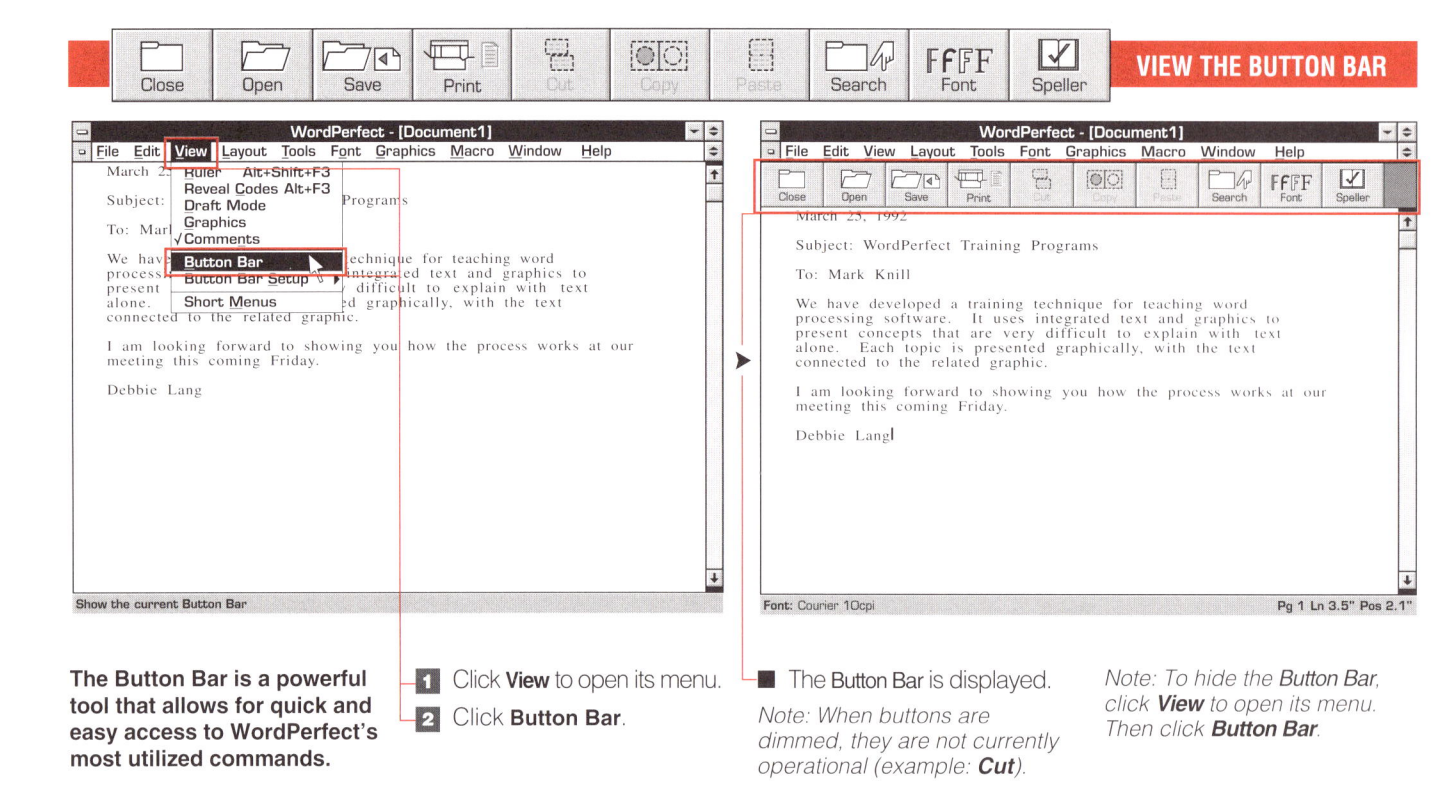

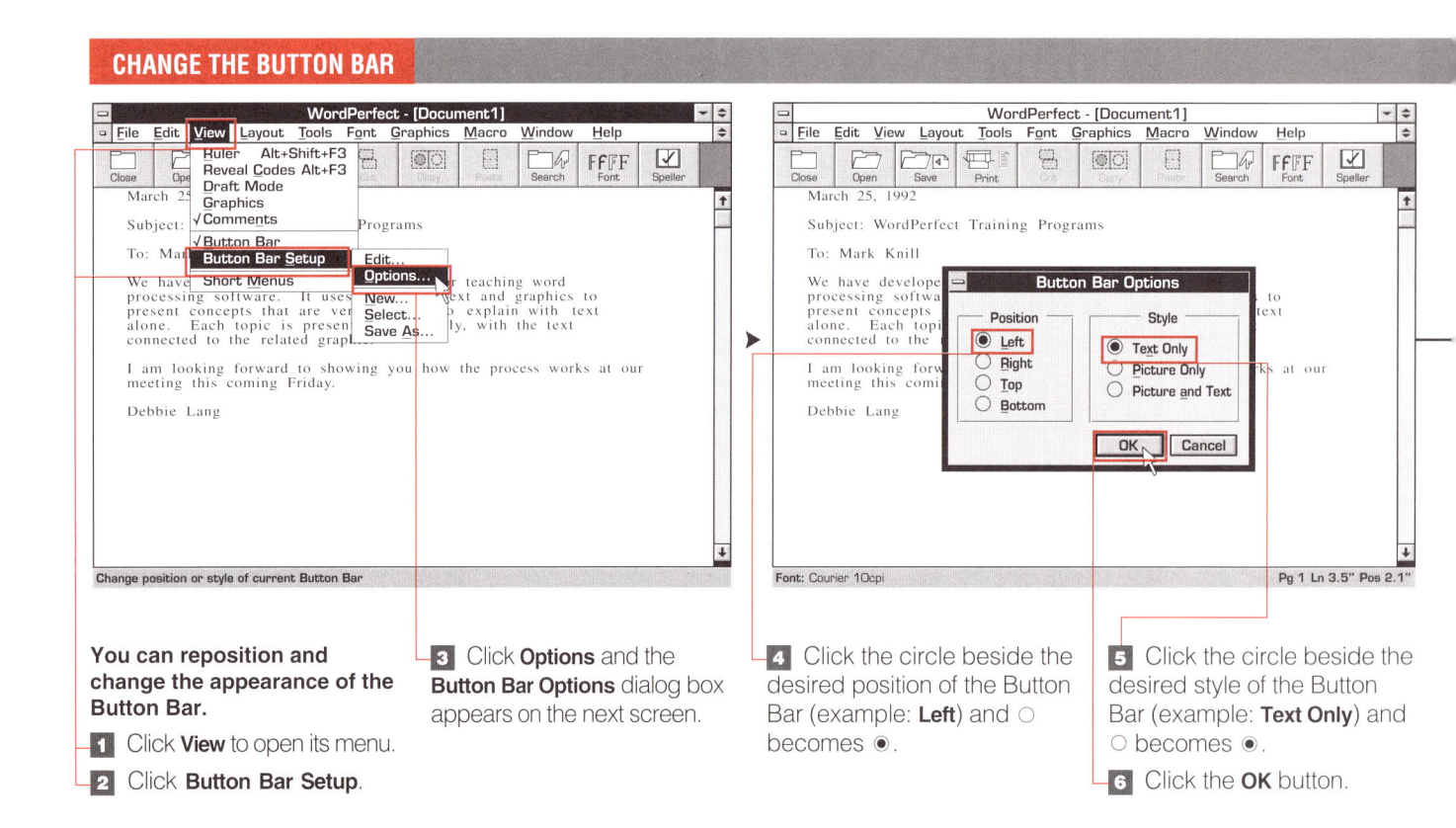

You can reposition and change the appearance of the Button Bar.

1 Click **View** to open its menu.

2 Click **Button Bar Setup**.

3 Click **Options** and the **Button Bar Options** dialog box appears on the next screen.

4 Click the circle beside the desired position of the Button Bar (example: **Left**) and ○ becomes ⦿.

5 Click the circle beside the desired style of the Button Bar (example: **Text Only**) and ○ becomes ⦿.

6 Click the **OK** button.

10

| VIEW THE BUTTON BAR | CHANGE THE BUTTON BAR | EDIT A BUTTON BAR | SAVE A BUTTON BAR | SELECT A BUTTON BAR |

KEYBOARD SHORTCUT TO SELECT MENU COMMANDS

■ To select a menu command (example: **Button Bar**), press **Alt**+**V**+**B**.

V is the underlined letter for the **View** menu,

B is the underlined letter for **Button Bar**.

Note: WordPerfect commands are not case sensitive. You can press **Alt**+**V**+**B** or **Alt**+**v**+**b**.

Note: If a dimmed menu item appears, this means it is not currently operational.

■ Some commands display alternate keyboard shortcuts. For example, to select the **Ruler** command, press **Alt**+**Shift**+**F3**.

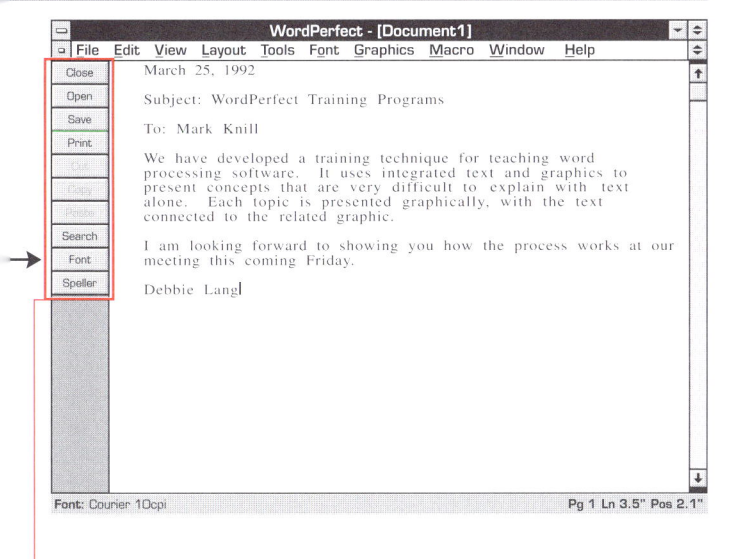

■ The new position and style of the Button Bar is displayed.

Note: To return the Button Bar to its original position and style, repeat steps **1** through **6**, selecting **Top** in step **4**, and **Picture and Text** in step **5**.

GETTING STARTED

THE BUTTON BAR

EDIT A DOCUMENT

SAVE FILES AND EXIT WORDPERFECT

VIEW DOCUMENTS

CHECK A DOCUMENT

FORMAT A DOCUMENT

TABLES

GRAPHICS

PRINT

MERGE AND SORT FILES

FILE MANAGER

HELP

◀ 11

EDIT A BUTTON BAR

DELETE A BUTTON

You can easily remove a button that you rarely use to help tidy your Button Bar workspace.

1 Click **View** to open its menu.

2 Click **Button Bar Setup**.

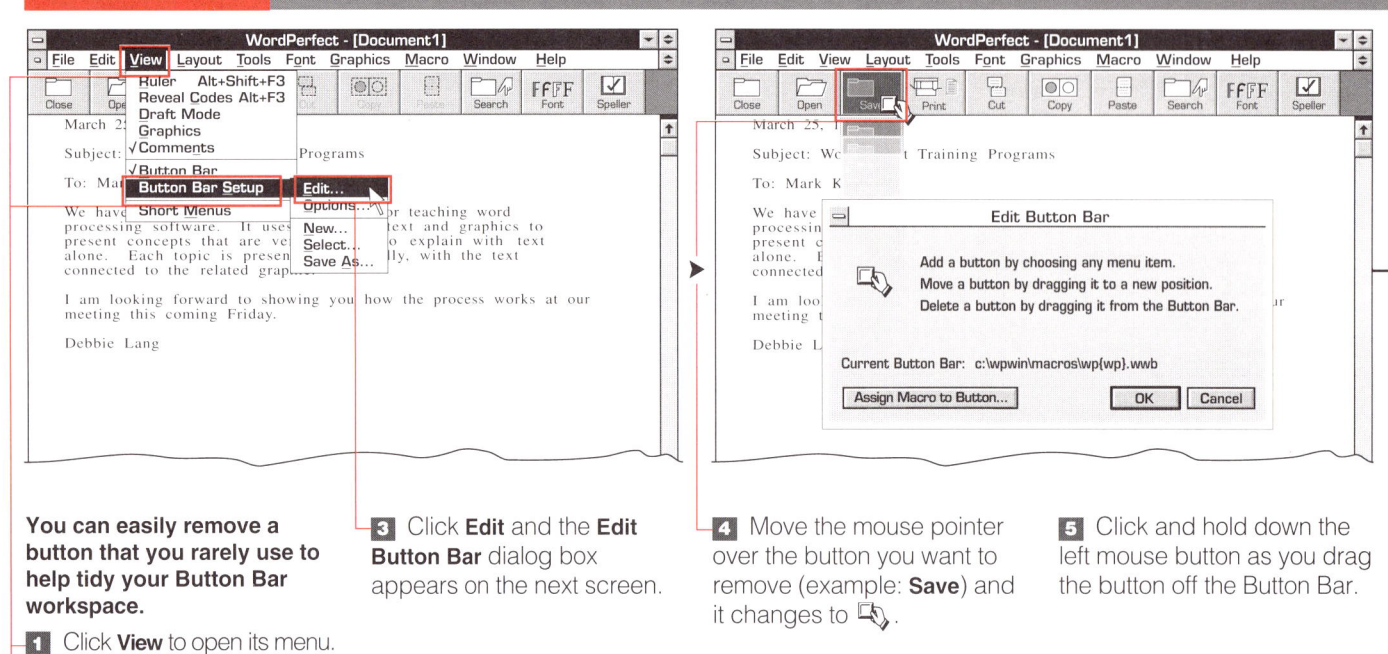

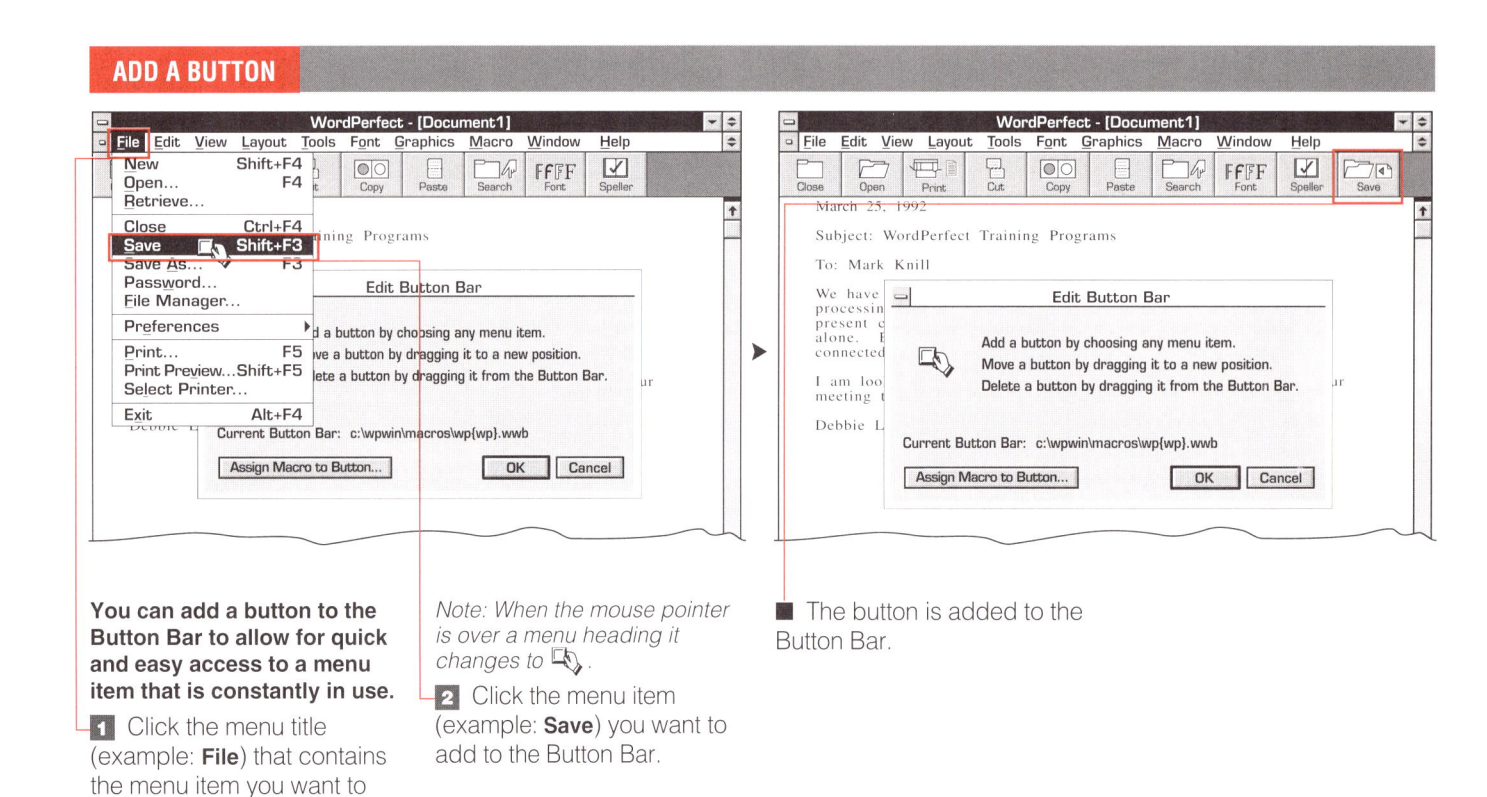

3 Click **Edit** and the **Edit Button Bar** dialog box appears on the next screen.

4 Move the mouse pointer over the button you want to remove (example: **Save**) and it changes to .

5 Click and hold down the left mouse button as you drag the button off the Button Bar.

ADD A BUTTON

You can add a button to the Button Bar to allow for quick and easy access to a menu item that is constantly in use.

1 Click the menu title (example: **File**) that contains the menu item you want to add to the Button Bar.

Note: When the mouse pointer is over a menu heading it changes to .

2 Click the menu item (example: **Save**) you want to add to the Button Bar.

■ The button is added to the Button Bar.

12 ▶

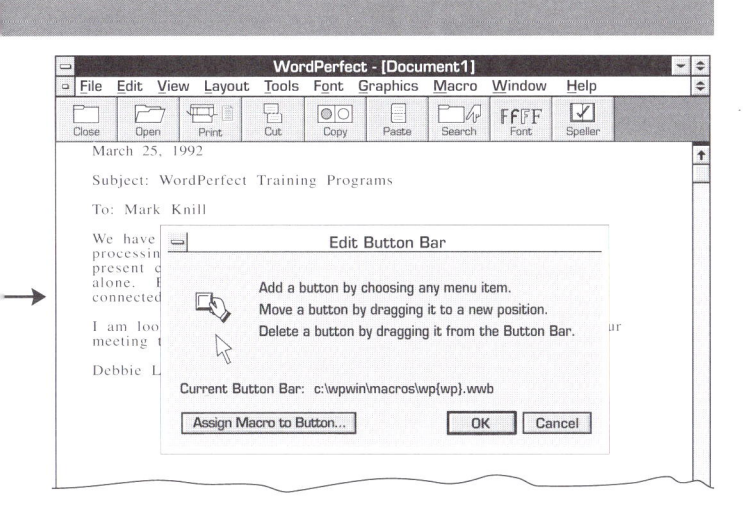

VIEW THE BUTTON BAR | CHANGE THE BUTTON BAR | **EDIT A BUTTON BAR** | SAVE A BUTTON BAR | SELECT A BUTTON BAR

6 Release the mouse button and the button is removed.

MOVE A BUTTON

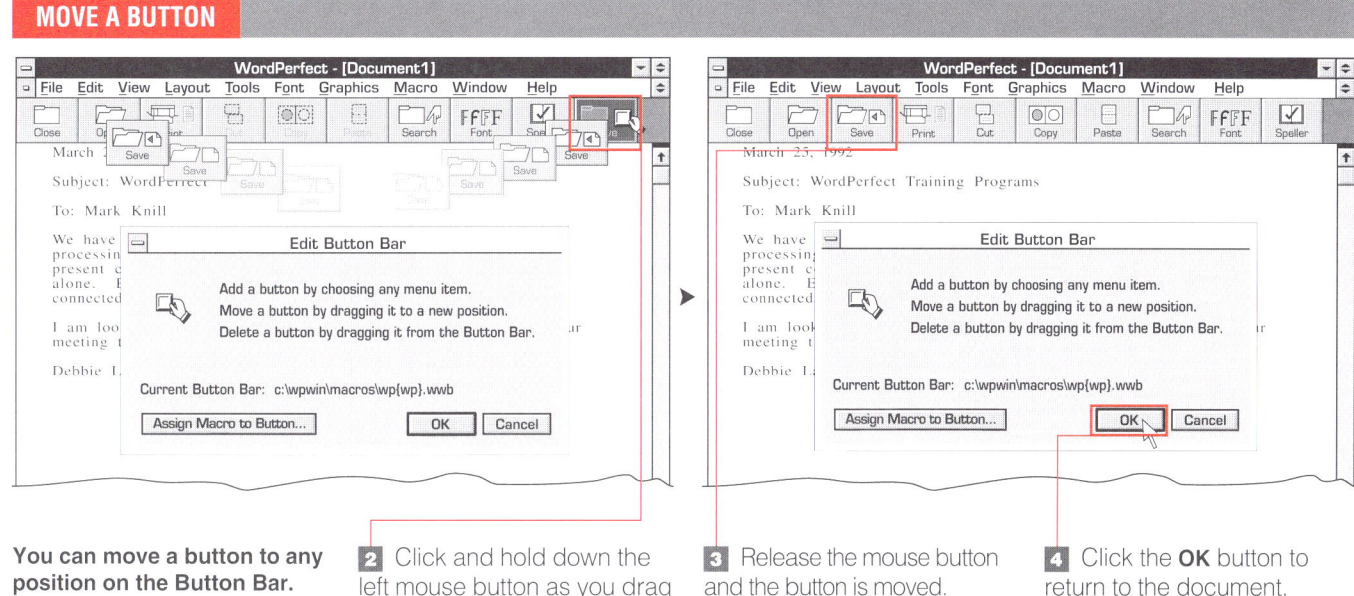

You can move a button to any position on the Button Bar.

1 Move the mouse pointer over the button you want to move (example: **Save**) and it changes to.

2 Click and hold down the left mouse button as you drag the button to its new position on the Button Bar.

3 Release the mouse button and the button is moved.

4 Click the **OK** button to return to the document.

*Note: Click the **Cancel** button to cancel the changes made to the Button Bar.*

GETTING STARTED

THE BUTTON BAR

EDIT A DOCUMENT

SAVE FILES AND EXIT WORDPERFECT

VIEW DOCUMENTS

CHECK A DOCUMENT

FORMAT A DOCUMENT

TABLES

GRAPHICS

PRINT

MERGE AND SORT FILES

FILE MANAGER

HELP

◀ 13

SAVE A BUTTON BAR | **SELECT A BUTTON BAR**

SAVE A BUTTON BAR

Different Button Bars can be created, then saved, for specific tasks you want to accomplish.

Each Button Bar can then be retrieved (selected) when you require it.

For example, you may wish to create a special Button Bar to help you quickly edit a document, or create a table.

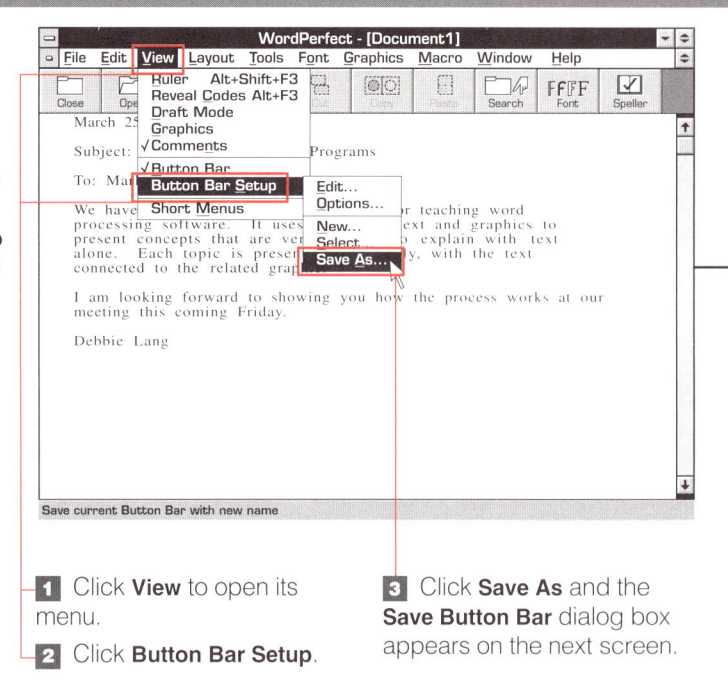

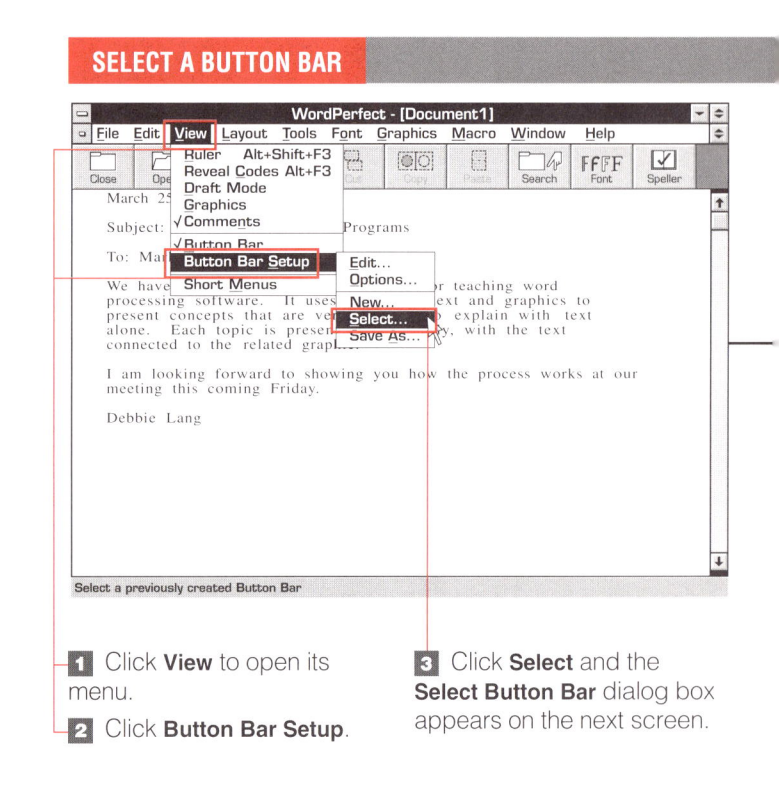

1 Click **View** to open its menu.

2 Click **Button Bar Setup**.

3 Click **Save As** and the **Save Button Bar** dialog box appears on the next screen.

SELECT A BUTTON BAR

1 Click **View** to open its menu.

2 Click **Button Bar Setup**.

3 Click **Select** and the **Select Button Bar** dialog box appears on the next screen.

14

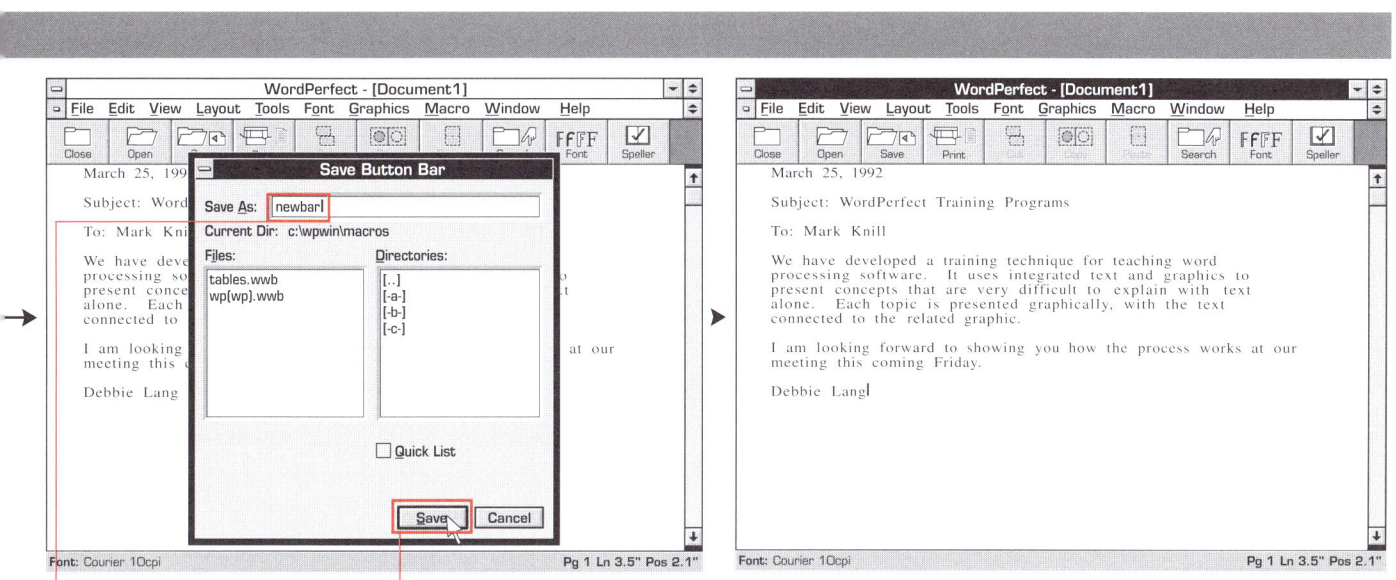

VIEW THE BUTTON BAR | CHANGE THE BUTTON BAR | EDIT A BUTTON BAR | **SAVE A BUTTON BAR** | **SELECT A BUTTON BAR**

GETTING STARTED

THE BUTTON BAR

EDIT A DOCUMENT

SAVE FILES AND EXIT WORDPERFECT

VIEW DOCUMENTS

CHECK A DOCUMENT

FORMAT A DOCUMENT

TABLES

GRAPHICS

PRINT

MERGE AND SORT FILES

FILE MANAGER

HELP

4 Type the name that you want to save the Button Bar as (example: **newbar**).

5 Click the **Save** button.

■ The Button Bar is saved.

Note: WordPerfect automatically adds an extension of **wwb** to the name (example: **newbar.wwb**).

Note: In this example, the **newbar** Button Bar contains the same buttons as the default Button Bar **wp{wp}.wwb**.

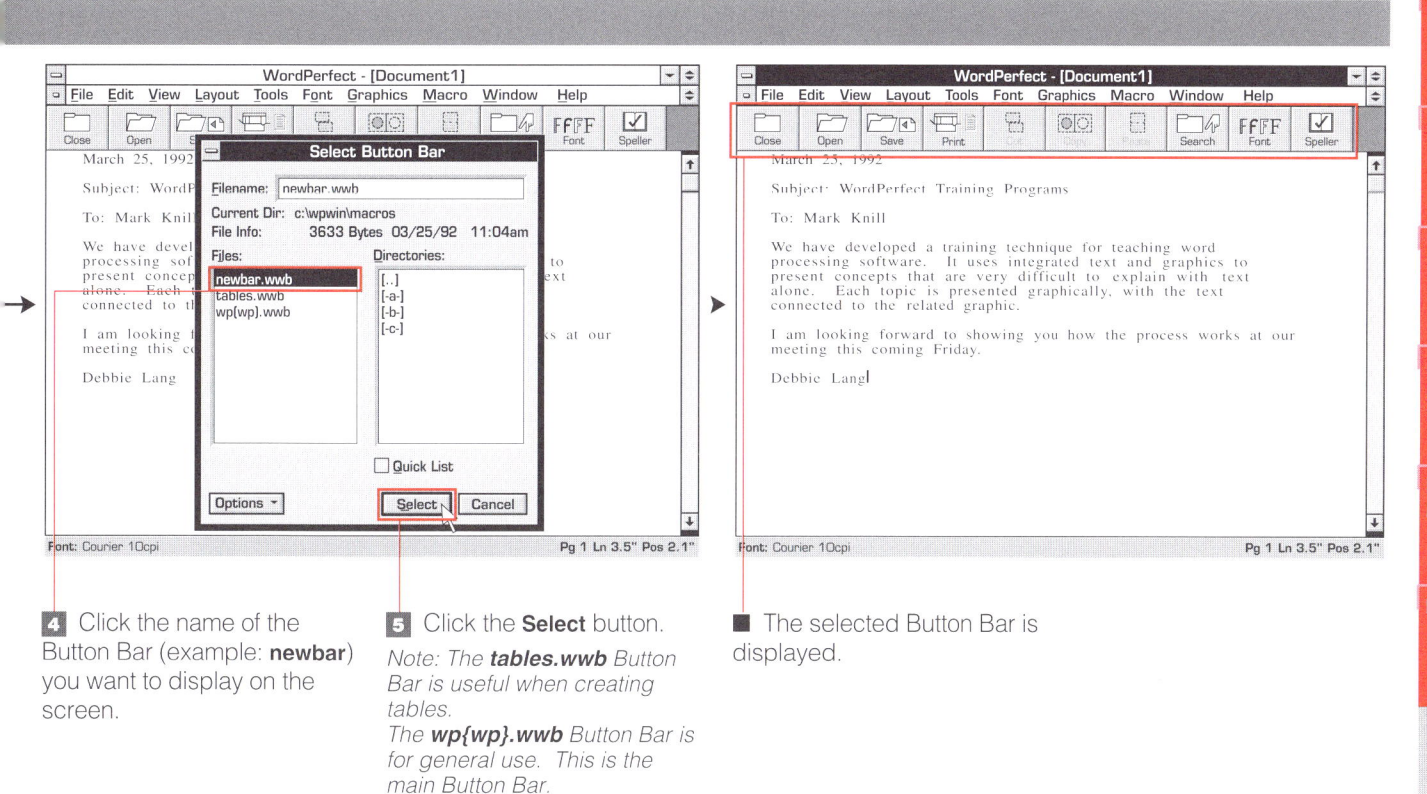

4 Click the name of the Button Bar (example: **newbar**) you want to display on the screen.

5 Click the **Select** button.

Note: The **tables.wwb** Button Bar is useful when creating tables.
The **wp{wp}.wwb** Button Bar is for general use. This is the main Button Bar.

■ The selected Button Bar is displayed.

◀ 15

INSERT AND REPLACE TEXT

INSERT TEXT

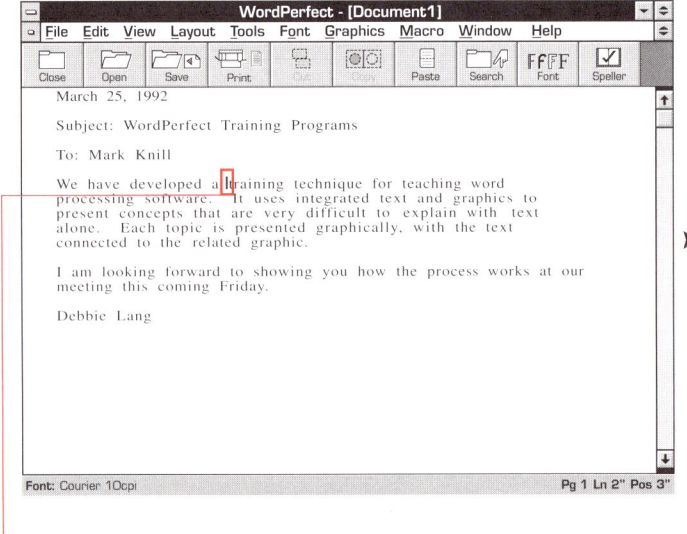

1 Position the insertion point at the location where you want to insert text.

*Note: If the word **Typeover** appears at the bottom left corner of the screen, press **Insert**. This turns off the Typeover mode and allows new characters to be inserted.*

2 Type the text you want to insert (example: **new**).

3 To insert a blank space, press the **Spacebar**.

Note: The words to the right of the inserted text are pushed forward.

INSERT A BLANK LINE

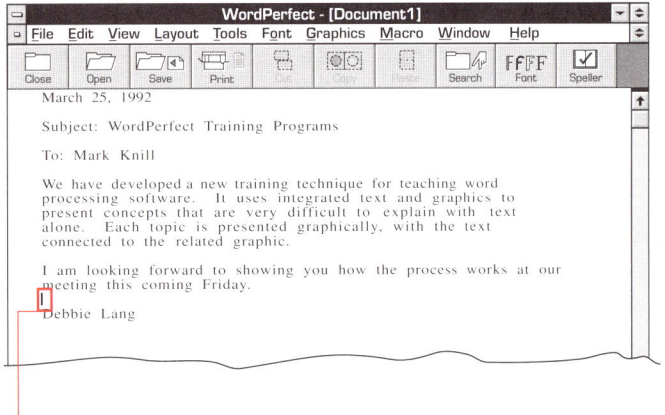

1 Position the insertion point at the location where you want to insert a blank line.

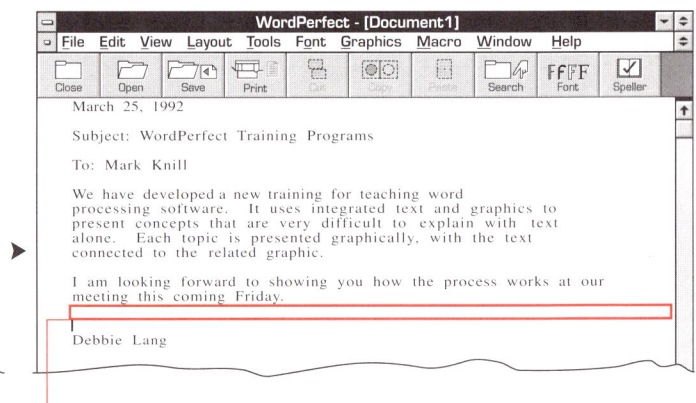

2 Press **Enter** and a blank line is inserted.

16

| INSERT AND REPLACE TEXT | MOVE AND COPY TEXT | DELETE TEXT | UNDO | SPLIT AND JOIN PARAGRAPHS | CHANGE TEXT TO UPPER OR LOWER CASE |

TYPEOVER TEXT

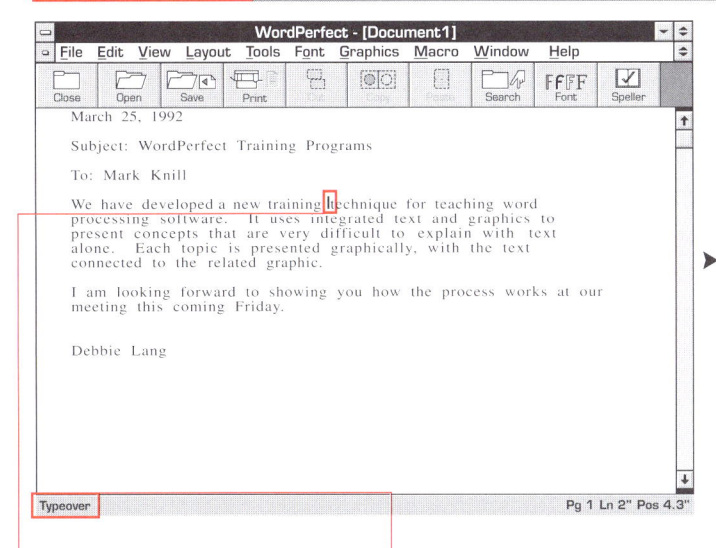

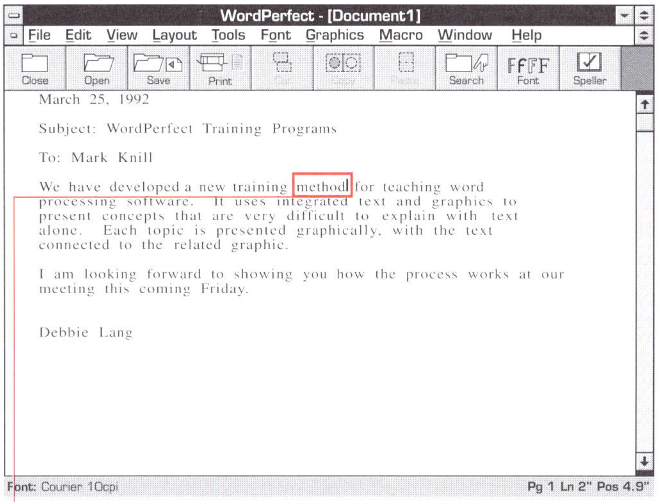

1 Position the insertion point at the exact location where you want to typeover (replace) text.

2 Press **Insert** to turn on the **Typeover** mode and the word **Typeover** appears at the bottom left corner of the screen.

3 Type the text (example: **method**) you want to typeover (replace) existing text.

4 If the text is shorter than the word it replaces, press **Delete** to remove the unwanted characters.

*Note: If the text is longer than the word it replaces, move the word following it over with the **Spacebar** before turning on the **Typeover** mode.*

5 Press **Insert** to turn off the **Typeover** mode, and the word **Typeover** disappears from the bottom left corner of the screen.

REPLACE TEXT

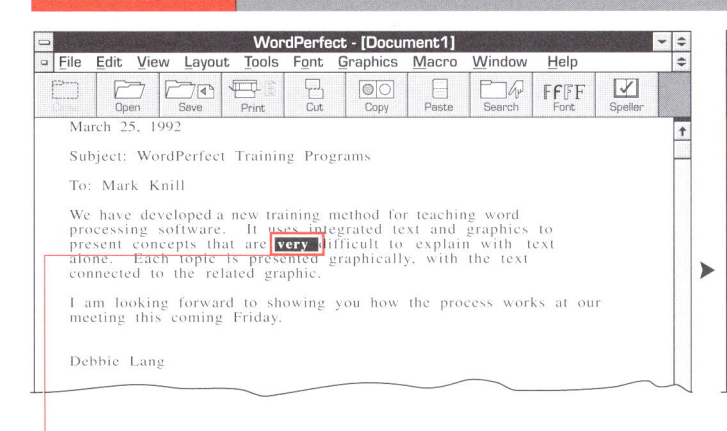

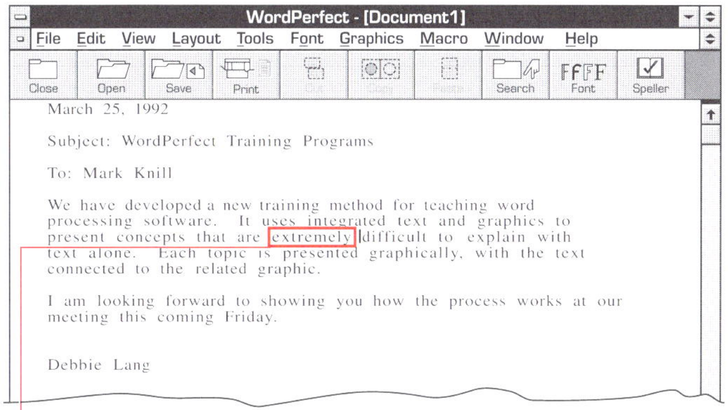

1 Select the text (example: **very**) you want to replace with new text.

Note: To select text, refer to page 6.

2 Type the text (example: **extremely**) you want to replace existing text.

3 To insert a blank space, press the **Spacebar**.

GETTING STARTED

THE BUTTON BAR

EDIT A DOCUMENT

SAVE FILES AND EXIT WORDPERFECT

VIEW DOCUMENTS

CHECK A DOCUMENT

FORMAT A DOCUMENT

TABLES

GRAPHICS

PRINT

MERGE AND SORT FILES

FILE MANAGER

HELP

◀ 17

MOVE AND COPY TEXT

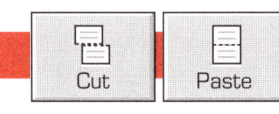

MOVE TEXT

When you move text, WordPerfect removes the text from the document and places it on the clipboard. The text can then be pasted to a new location.

The clipboard is a temporary storage area which retains the text to be moved. The data remains on the clipboard until you cut or copy your next text block.

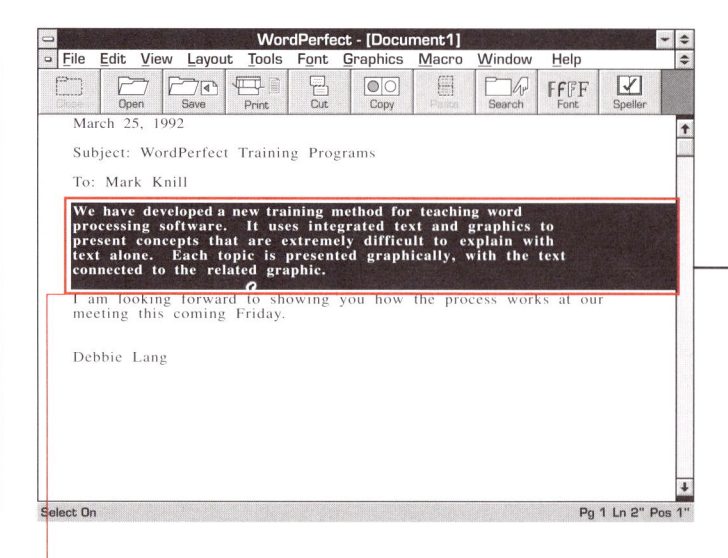

1 Select the text you want to move.

Note: To select text, refer to page 6.

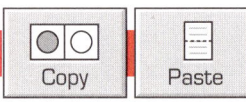

COPY TEXT

When you copy text, WordPerfect copies the text from the document and places it on the clipboard. The text can then be pasted to a new location.

The clipboard is a temporary storage area which retains the text to be copied. The data remains on the clipboard until you cut or copy your next text block.

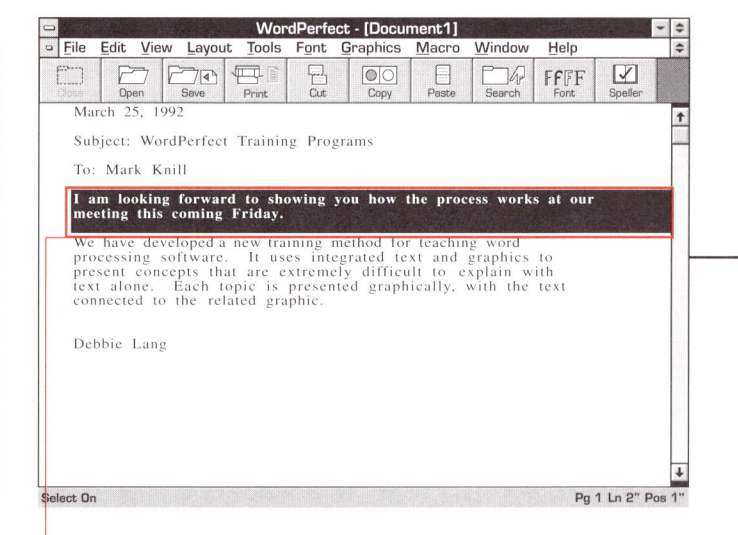

1 Select the text you want to copy.

Note: To select text, refer to page 6.

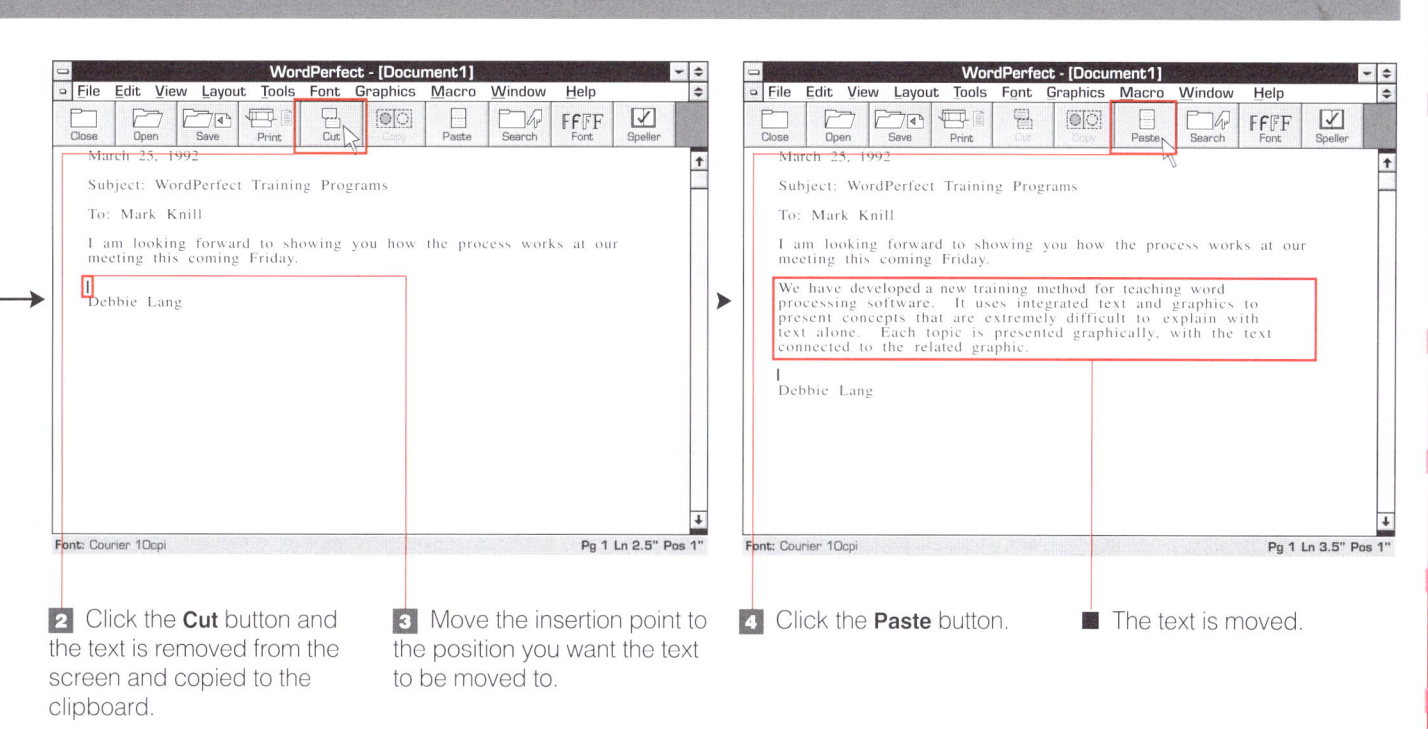

INSERT AND REPLACE TEXT   **MOVE AND COPY TEXT**   DELETE TEXT   UNDO   SPLIT AND JOIN PARAGRAPHS   CHANGE TEXT TO UPPER OR LOWER CASE

2 Click the **Cut** button and the text is removed from the screen and copied to the clipboard.

3 Move the insertion point to the position you want the text to be moved to.

4 Click the **Paste** button.

■ The text is moved.

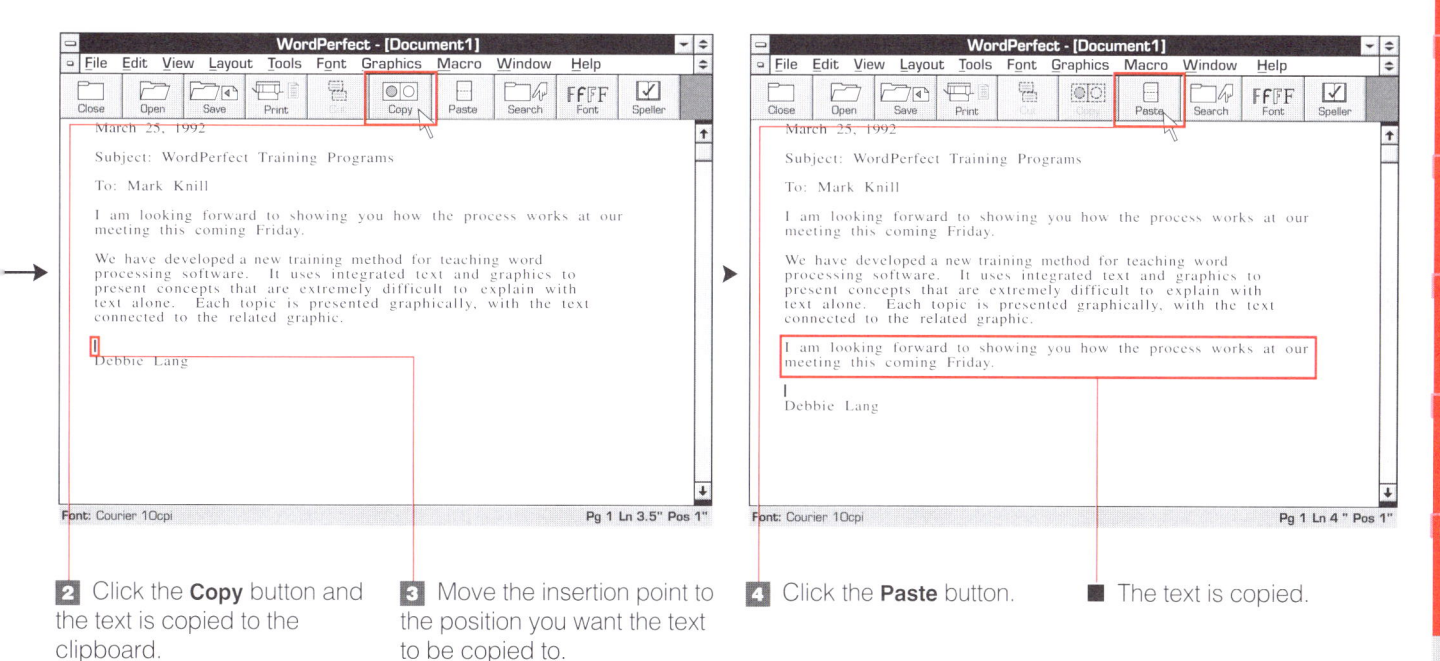

2 Click the **Copy** button and the text is copied to the clipboard.

3 Move the insertion point to the position you want the text to be copied to.

4 Click the **Paste** button.

■ The text is copied.

GETTING STARTED

THE BUTTON BAR

EDIT A DOCUMENT

SAVE FILES AND EXIT WORDPERFECT

VIEW DOCUMENTS

CHECK A DOCUMENT

FORMAT A DOCUMENT

TABLES

GRAPHICS

PRINT

MERGE AND SORT FILES

FILE MANAGER

HELP

◀ 19

DELETE TEXT / UNDO

DELETE TEXT

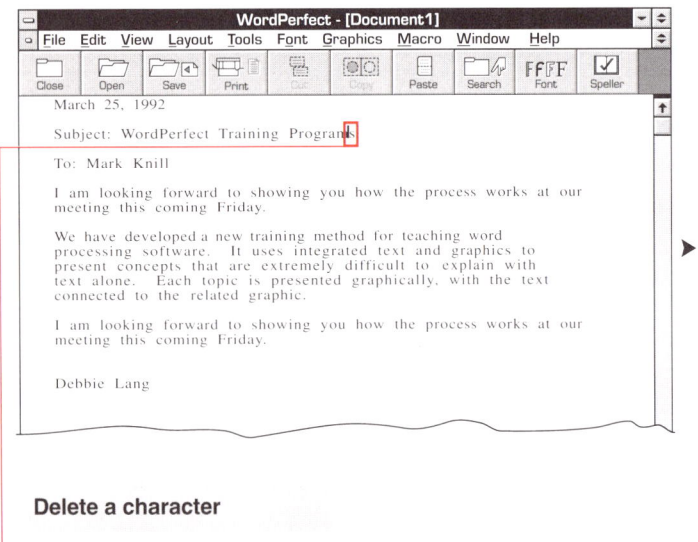

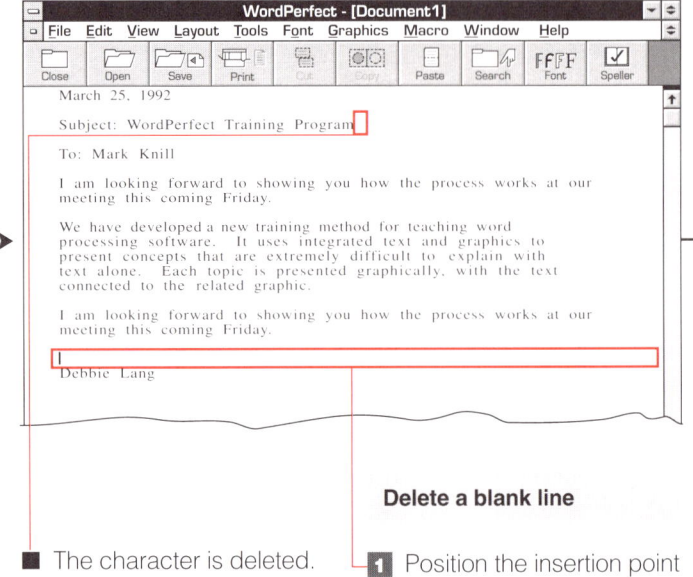

Delete a character

1 Position the insertion point to the left of the character you want to delete (example: **s** in **Programs**). Then press **Delete**.

*Note: A character can also be deleted by positioning the insertion point to the right of the character. Then press **Backspace**.*

■ The character is deleted.

Delete a blank line

1 Position the insertion point on the blank line you want to delete.

2 Press **Delete**.

■ The text is deleted.

UNDO

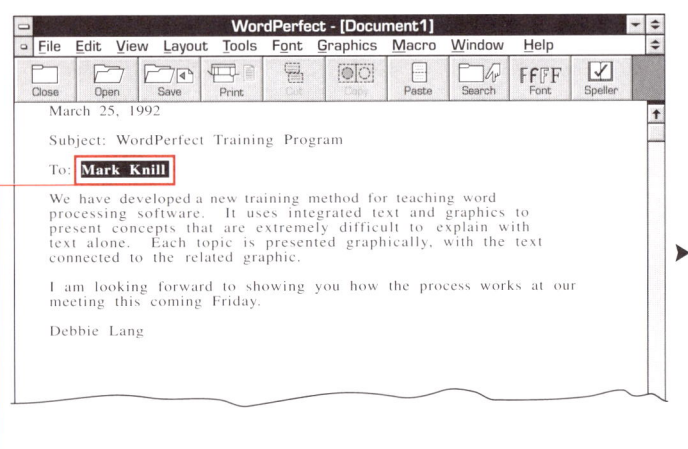

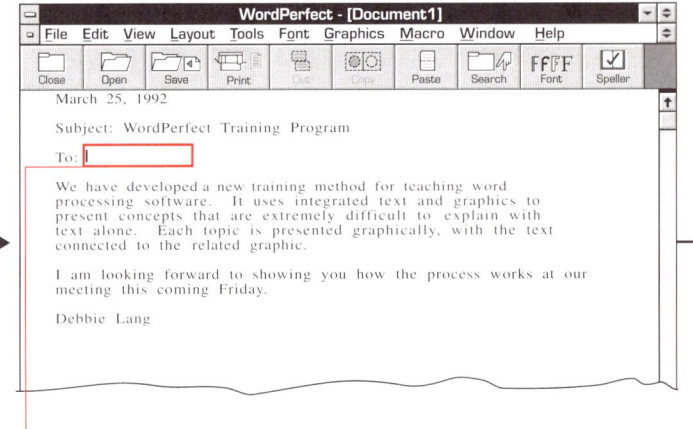

Undo cancels your last action. This only works immediately after the action is performed.

1 Select the text you want to delete.

Note: To select text, refer to page 6.

2 Press **Delete**.

20

INSERT AND REPLACE TEXT | MOVE AND COPY TEXT | **DELETE TEXT** | **UNDO** | SPLIT AND JOIN PARAGRAPHS | CHANGE TEXT TO UPPER OR LOWER CASE

Delete selected text

- The blank line is deleted.

1 Select the text you want to delete.

Note: To select the paragraph, refer to page 7.

2 Press **Delete**.

- The text is deleted.

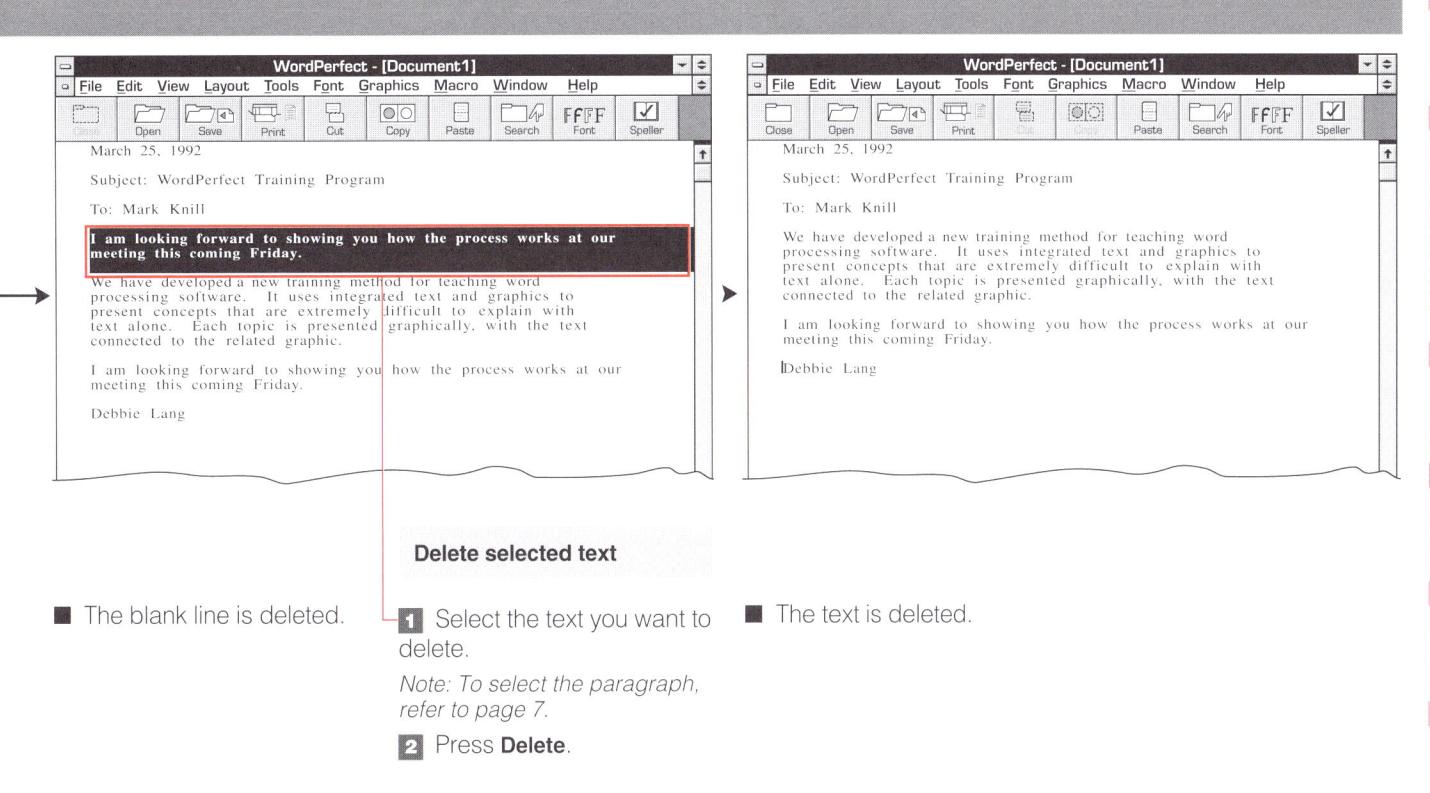

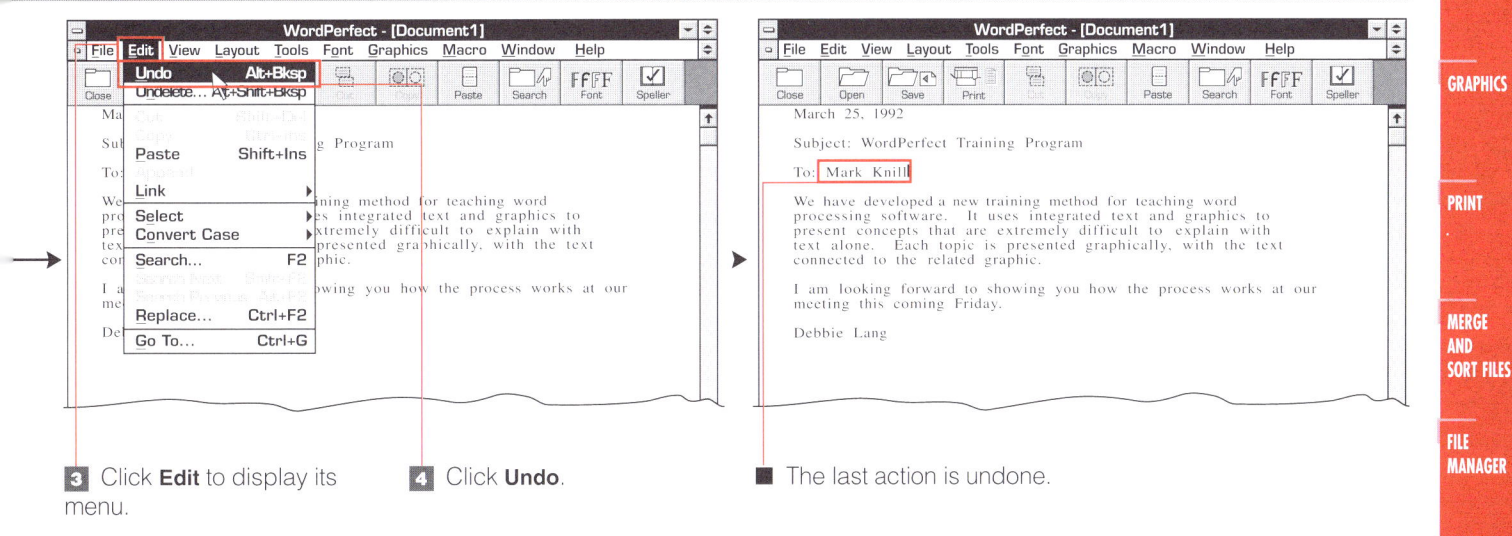

3 Click **Edit** to display its menu.

4 Click **Undo**.

- The last action is undone.

GETTING STARTED

THE BUTTON BAR

EDIT A DOCUMENT

SAVE FILES AND EXIT WORDPERFECT

VIEW DOCUMENTS

CHECK A DOCUMENT

FORMAT A DOCUMENT

TABLES

GRAPHICS

PRINT

MERGE AND SORT FILES

FILE MANAGER

HELP

◀ 21

SPLIT AND JOIN PARAGRAPHS | CHANGE TEXT TO UPPER OR LOWER CASE

SPLIT AND JOIN PARAGRAPHS

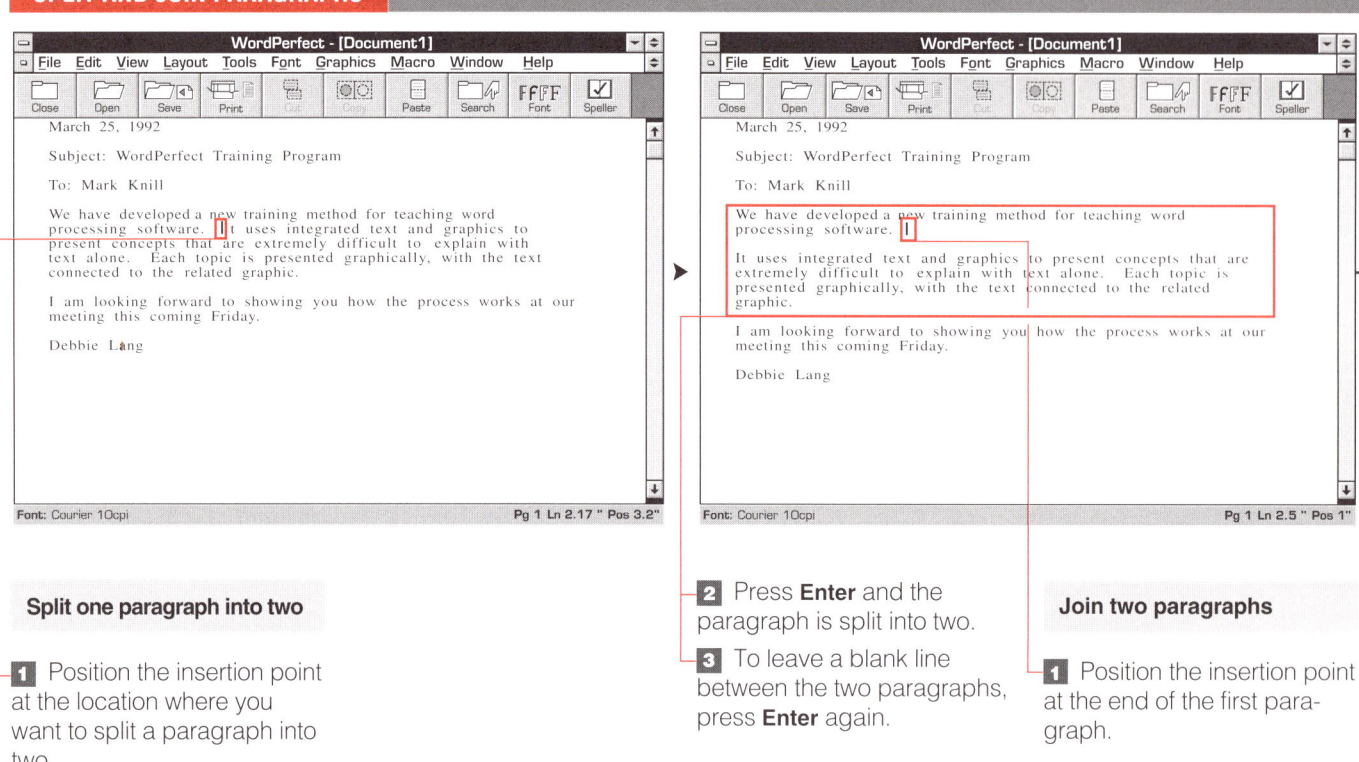

Split one paragraph into two

1 Position the insertion point at the location where you want to split a paragraph into two.

2 Press **Enter** and the paragraph is split into two.

3 To leave a blank line between the two paragraphs, press **Enter** again.

Join two paragraphs

1 Position the insertion point at the end of the first paragraph.

CHANGE TEXT TO UPPER OR LOWER CASE

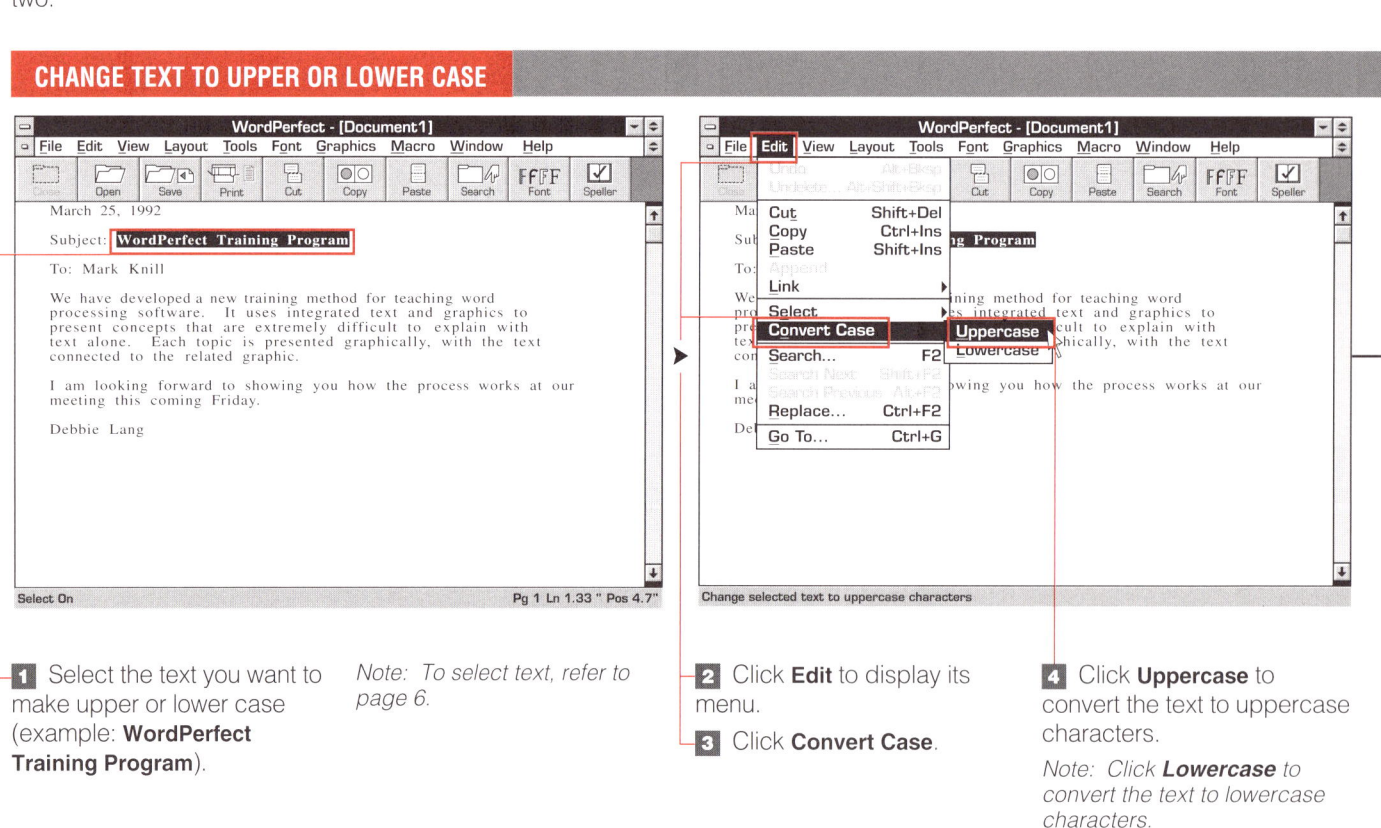

1 Select the text you want to make upper or lower case (example: **WordPerfect Training Program**).

Note: To select text, refer to page 6.

2 Click **Edit** to display its menu.

3 Click **Convert Case**.

4 Click **Uppercase** to convert the text to uppercase characters.

*Note: Click **Lowercase** to convert the text to lowercase characters.*

22

| INSERT AND REPLACE TEXT | MOVE AND COPY TEXT | DELETE TEXT | UNDO | **SPLIT AND JOIN PARAGRAPHS** | **CHANGE TEXT TO UPPER OR LOWER CASE** |

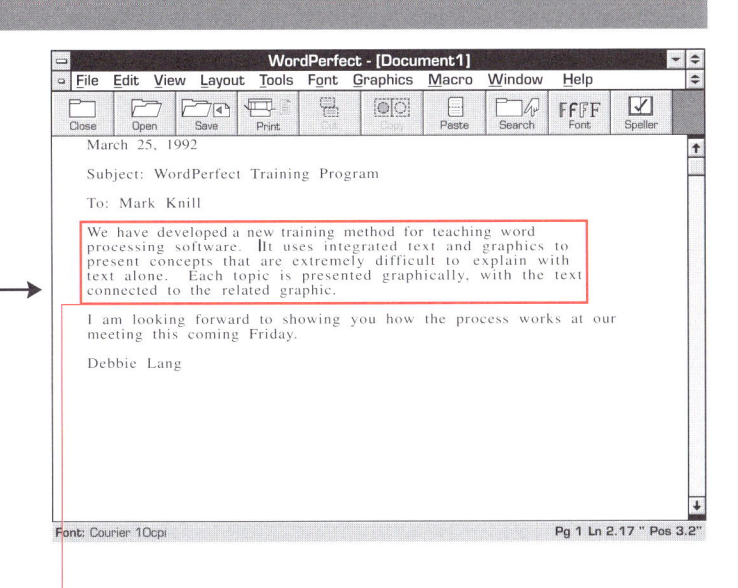

2 Press **Delete** (example: twice) until the paragraphs are joined.

*Note: To insert a blank space, press the **Spacebar**.*

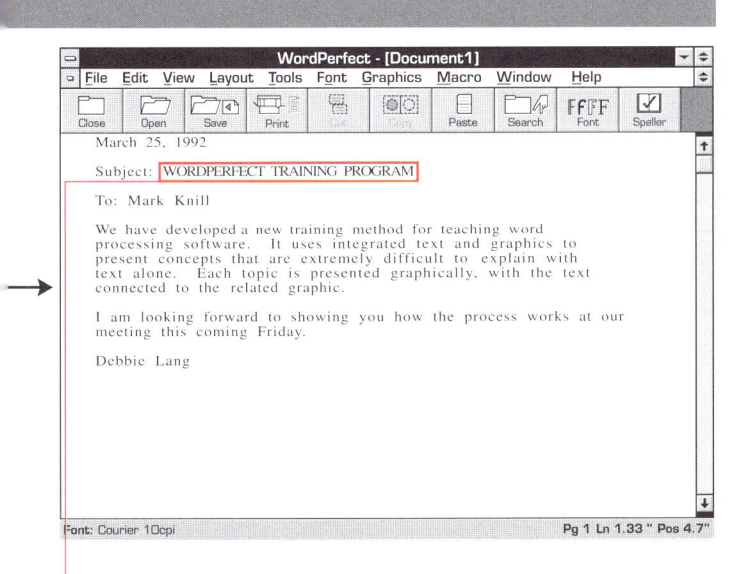

■ The text is converted (example: to uppercase characters).

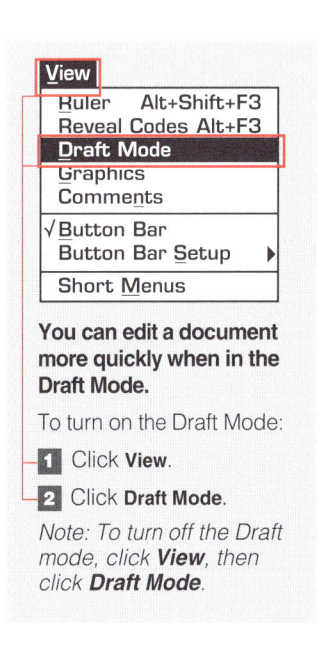

You can edit a document more quickly when in the Draft Mode.

To turn on the Draft Mode:

1 Click **View**.

2 Click **Draft Mode**.

*Note: To turn off the Draft mode, click **View**, then click **Draft Mode**.*

- GETTING STARTED
- THE BUTTON BAR
- EDIT A DOCUMENT
- SAVE FILES AND EXIT WORDPERFECT
- VIEW DOCUMENTS
- CHECK A DOCUMENT
- FORMAT A DOCUMENT
- TABLES
- GRAPHICS
- PRINT
- MERGE AND SORT FILES
- FILE MANAGER
- HELP

◀ 23

FILES AND DIRECTORIES

HOW FILES ARE SPECIFIED

In an efficient and productive office environment, people create, edit, review and organize paper documents (example: letters, worksheets, reports, etc.). These documents are stored in folders, which in turn are placed in cabinets. To retrieve a specific document, you must identify it by location (cabinet and folder) and then name.

Computers work the same way. After creating a document in WordPerfect, it must be named and saved. During the save process, you must tell WordPerfect the drive (cabinet) and directory (folder) the file is to reside in.

In WordPerfect there is a multilevel directory filing system to store and retrieve your documents. The first level of this directory structure is called the root directory. From this directory other subdirectories can be created. A typical multilevel filing system is illustrated on the next page.

Note: The terms "directory" and "subdirectory" are used interchangeably. The "root directory" is the only "directory" that cannot be called a "subdirectory".

FILE SPECIFICATION

A file is specified by describing its drive, path and name (filename and extension).

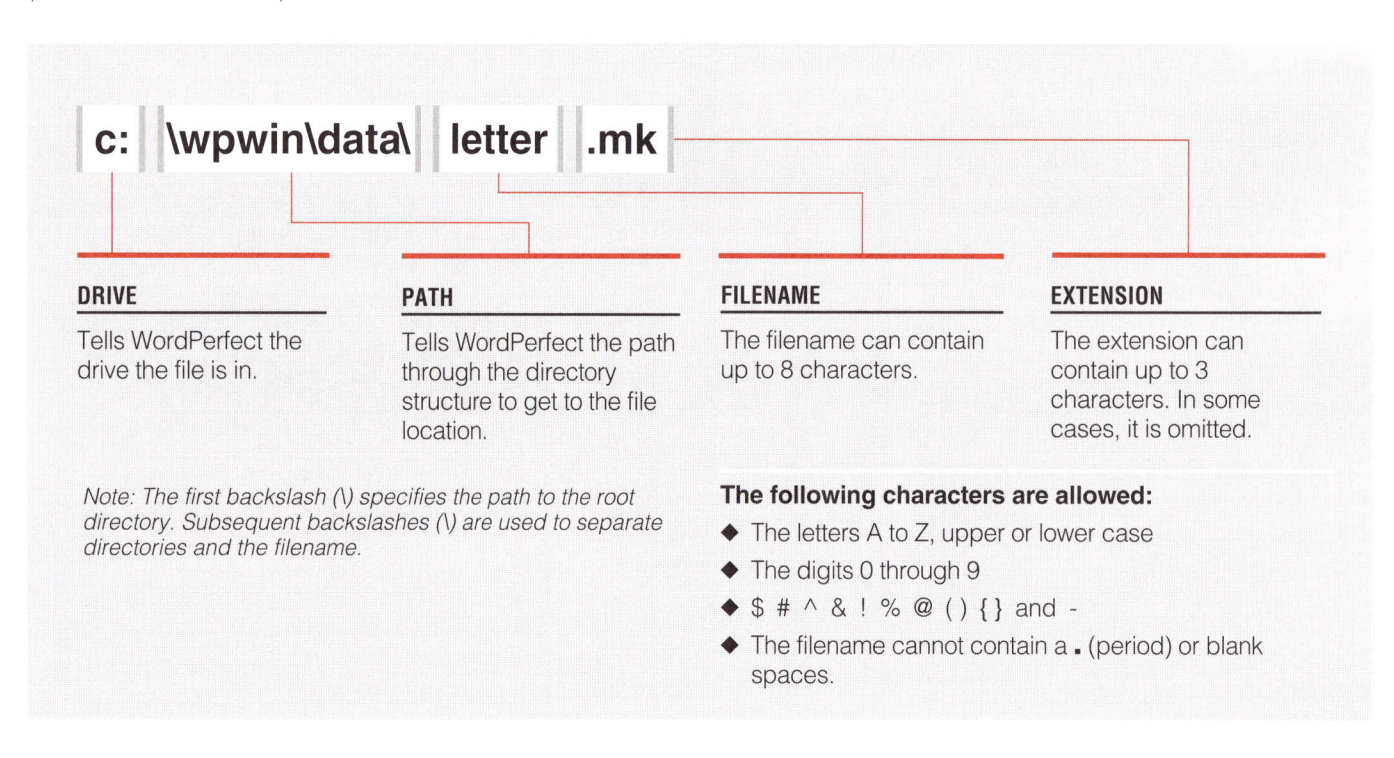

`c:` `\wpwin\data\` `letter` `.mk`

DRIVE
Tells WordPerfect the drive the file is in.

PATH
Tells WordPerfect the path through the directory structure to get to the file location.

FILENAME
The filename can contain up to 8 characters.

EXTENSION
The extension can contain up to 3 characters. In some cases, it is omitted.

Note: The first backslash (\) specifies the path to the root directory. Subsequent backslashes (\) are used to separate directories and the filename.

The following characters are allowed:
◆ The letters A to Z, upper or lower case
◆ The digits 0 through 9
◆ $ # ^ & ! % @ ( ) { } and -
◆ The filename cannot contain a **.** (period) or blank spaces.

| FILES AND DIRECTORIES | LOCATION OF FILES | SAVE FILES | EXIT WORDPERFECT |

USING DIRECTORIES TO ORGANIZE YOUR FILES

Directories can contain files and/or paths to other directories. In this example the root directory has paths to three subdirectories.

Root directory of a hard disk (C:) contains \DOS, \WINDOWS, \WPWIN

- **\DOS** — Contains DOS program files
- **\WINDOWS** — Contains WINDOWS program files
- **\WPWIN** — Contains WPWIN program files and subdirectory \DATA

\DATA — Contains WordPerfect data files

The file specification for this data file is:

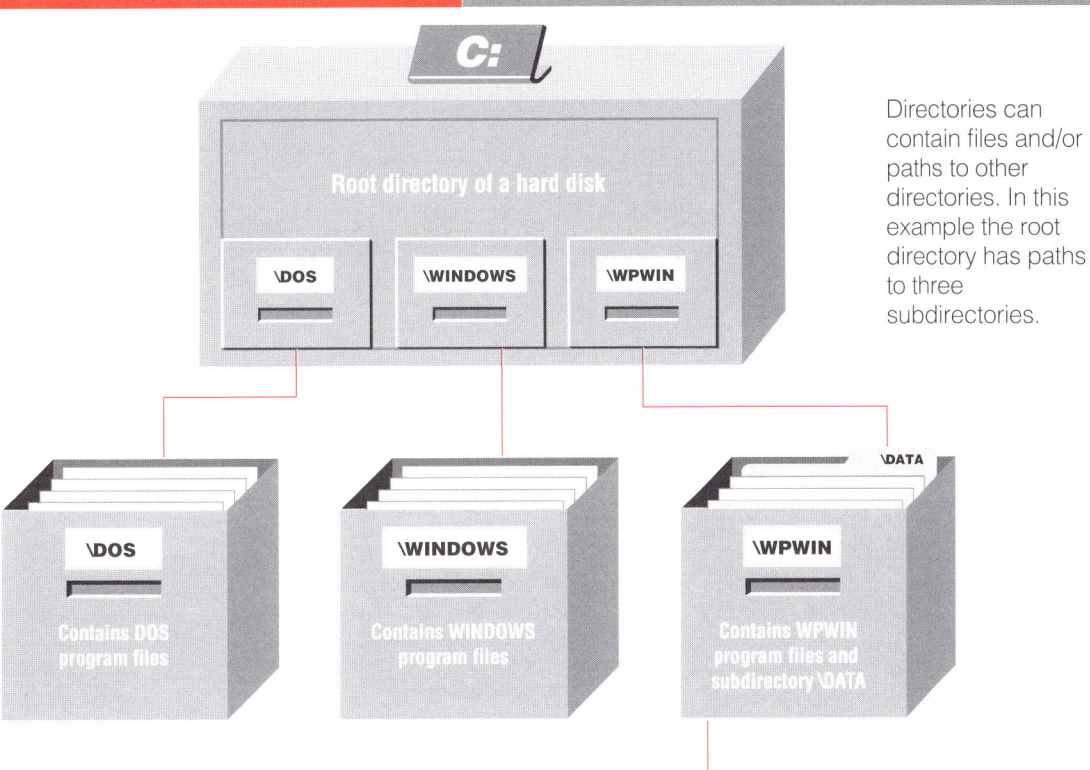

c:\wpwin\data\letter.mk

- GETTING STARTED
- THE BUTTON BAR
- EDIT A DOCUMENT
- **SAVE FILES AND EXIT WORDPERFECT**
- VIEW DOCUMENTS
- CHECK A DOCUMENT
- FORMAT A DOCUMENT
- TABLES
- GRAPHICS
- PRINT
- MERGE AND SORT FILES
- FILE MANAGER
- HELP

◀ 25

LOCATION OF FILES / SAVE FILES

LOCATION OF FILES

All examples in this guide are based on the directory structure illustrated below:

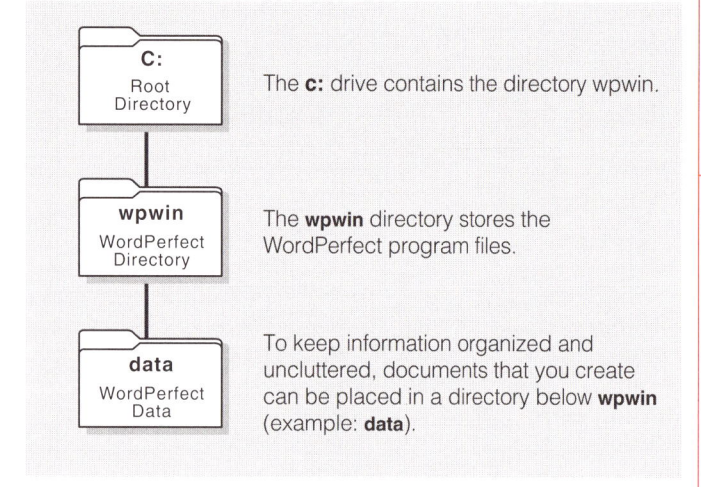

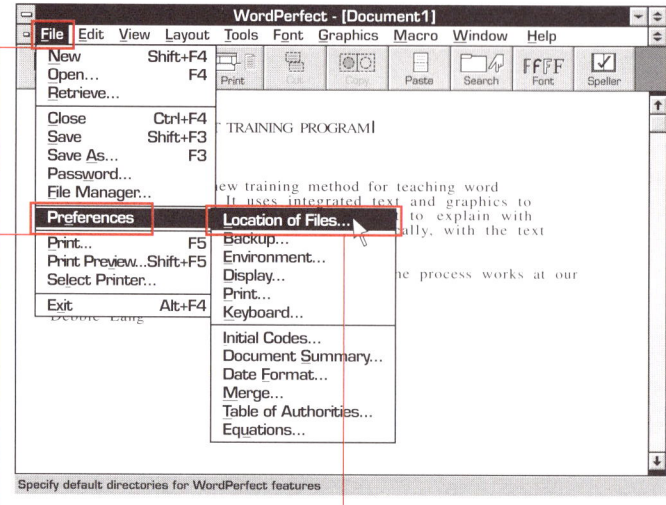

C: Root Directory — The **c:** drive contains the directory wpwin.

wpwin WordPerfect Directory — The **wpwin** directory stores the WordPerfect program files.

data WordPerfect Data — To keep information organized and uncluttered, documents that you create can be placed in a directory below **wpwin** (example: **data**).

WordPerfect allows you to specify a location (directory) to store your files. If this directory does not exist, the program lets you create it.

1 Click **File**. Then click **Preferences**.

2 Click **Location of Files**, and the **Location of Files** dialog box appears.

SAVE A NEW FILE

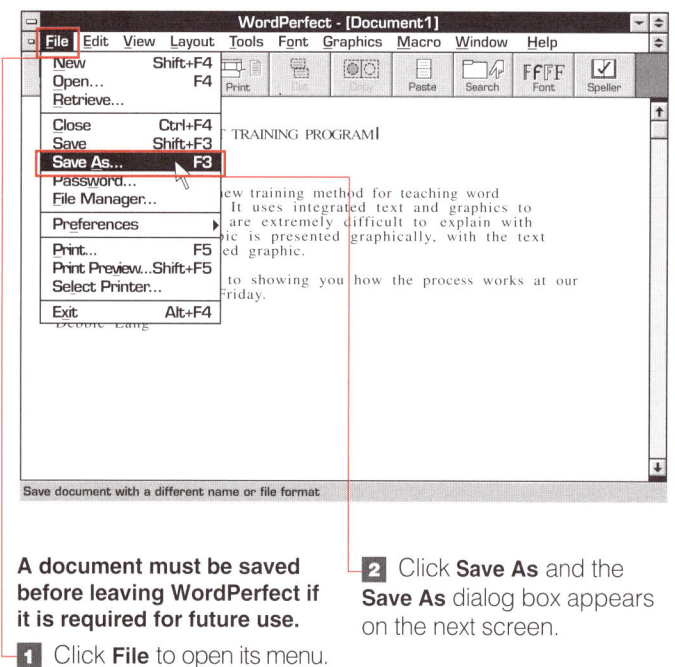

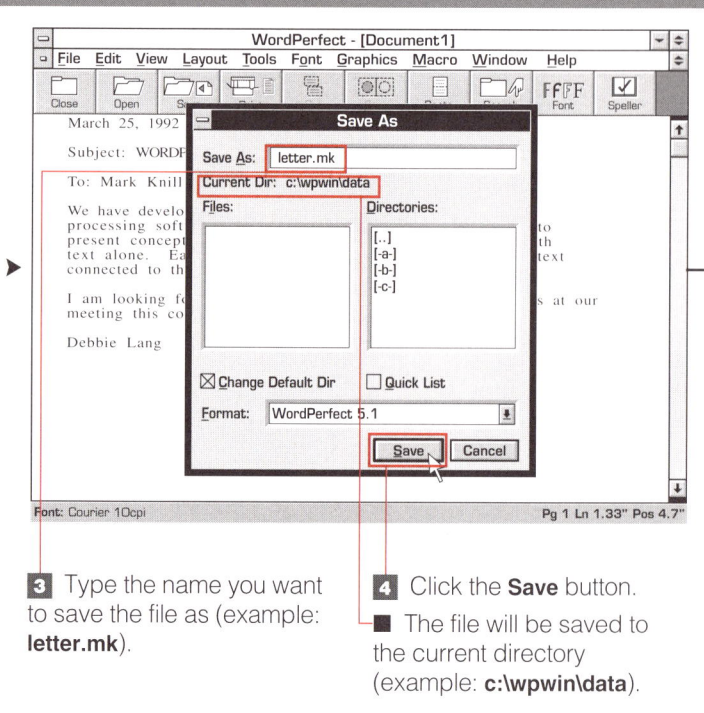

A document must be saved before leaving WordPerfect if it is required for future use.

1 Click **File** to open its menu.

2 Click **Save As** and the **Save As** dialog box appears on the next screen.

3 Type the name you want to save the file as (example: **letter.mk**).

4 Click the **Save** button.

■ The file will be saved to the current directory (example: **c:\wpwin\data**).

26

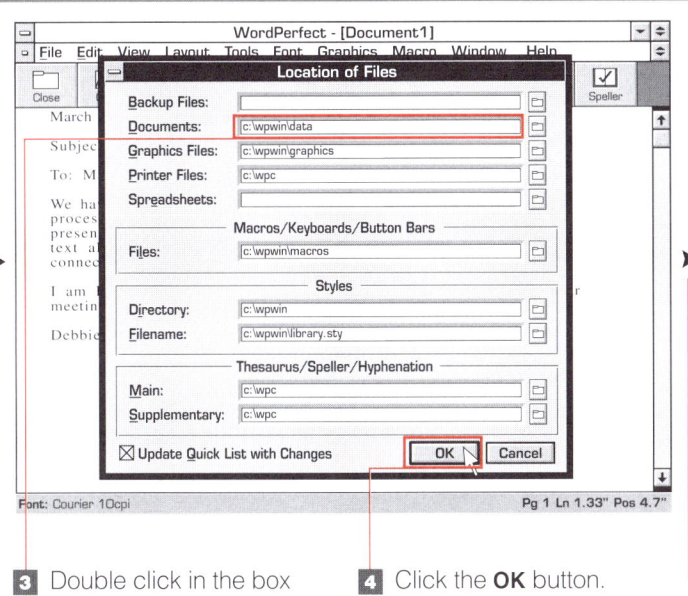

FILES AND DIRECTORIES | **LOCATION OF FILES** | **SAVE FILES** | EXIT WORDPERFECT

3 Double click in the box beside **Documents:**. Then type a new directory location (example: **c:\wpwin\data**).

4 Click the **OK** button.

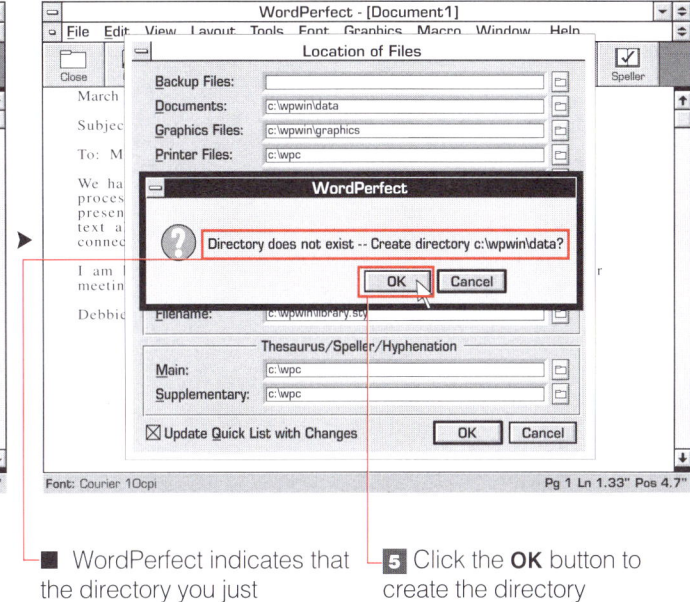

■ WordPerfect indicates that the directory you just specified does not exist.

5 Click the **OK** button to create the directory (example: **c:\wpwin\data**) and return to the document.

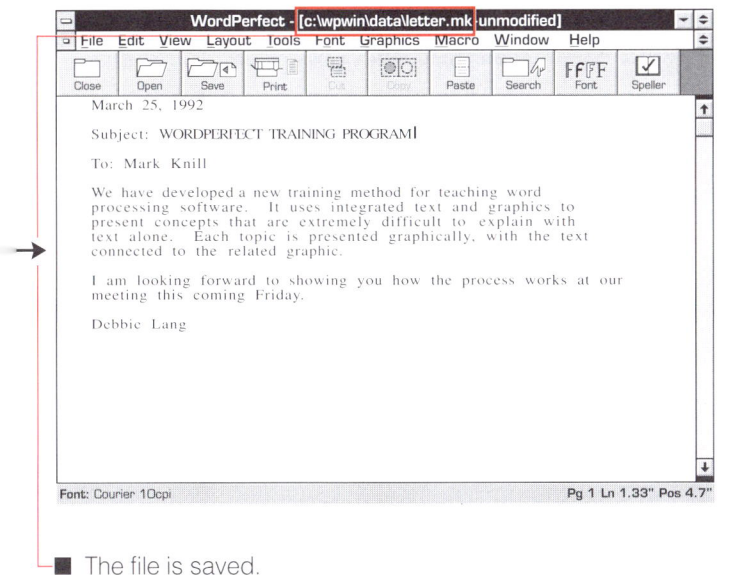

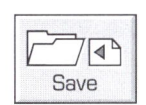

SAVE A DOCUMENT USING THIS BUTTON

Click the **Save** button to quickly save your document to the current directory, using the same name.

CAUTION

The document will replace the previously saved document.

Note: You should save regularly to prevent losing work due to power failure or hardware malfunctions.

■ The file is saved.

GETTING STARTED

THE BUTTON BAR

EDIT A DOCUMENT

SAVE FILES AND EXIT WORDPERFECT

VIEW DOCUMENTS

CHECK A DOCUMENT

FORMAT A DOCUMENT

TABLES

GRAPHICS

PRINT

MERGE AND SORT FILES

FILE MANAGER

HELP

◀ 27

SAVE FILES / EXIT WORDPERFECT

SAVE A DOCUMENT TO A FLOPPY DISK

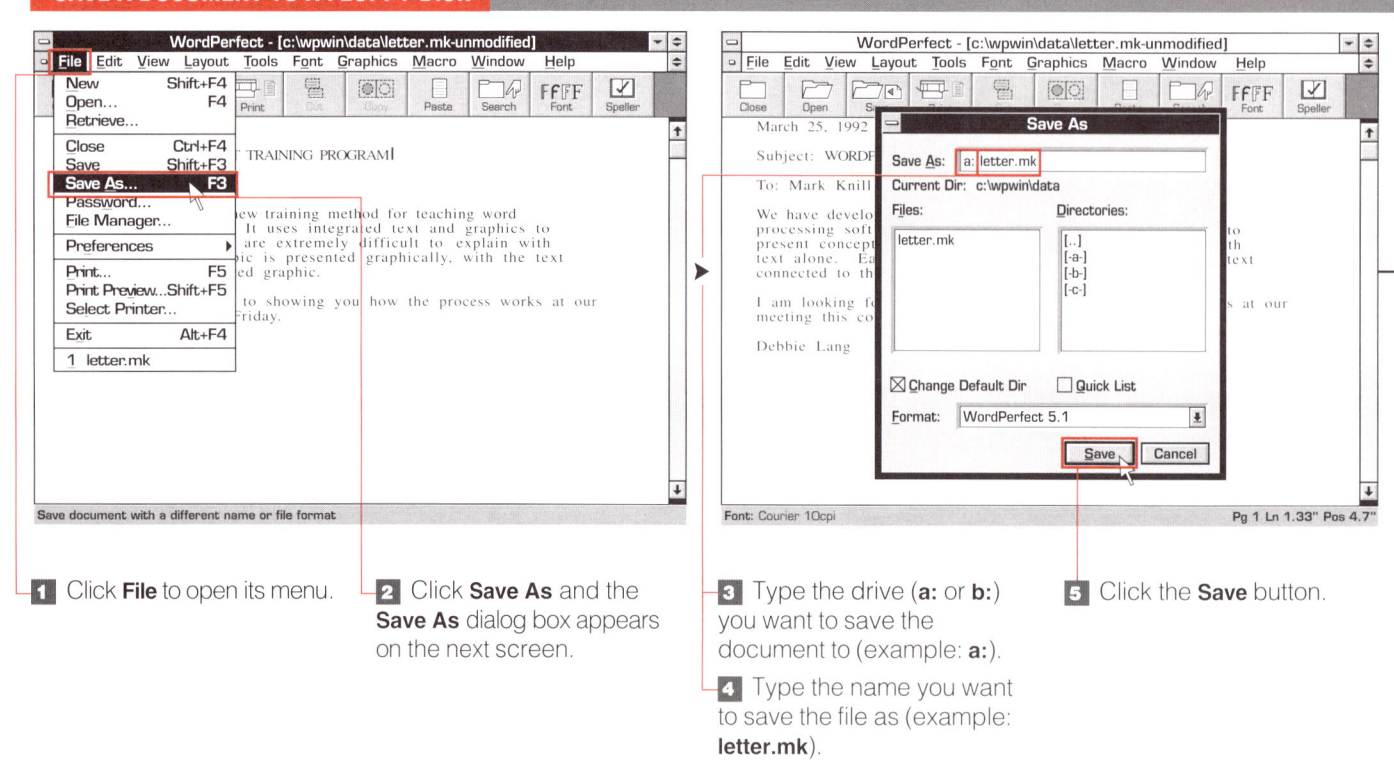

1 Click **File** to open its menu.

2 Click **Save As** and the **Save As** dialog box appears on the next screen.

3 Type the drive (**a:** or **b:**) you want to save the document to (example: **a:**).

4 Type the name you want to save the file as (example: **letter.mk**).

5 Click the **Save** button.

EXIT WORDPERFECT

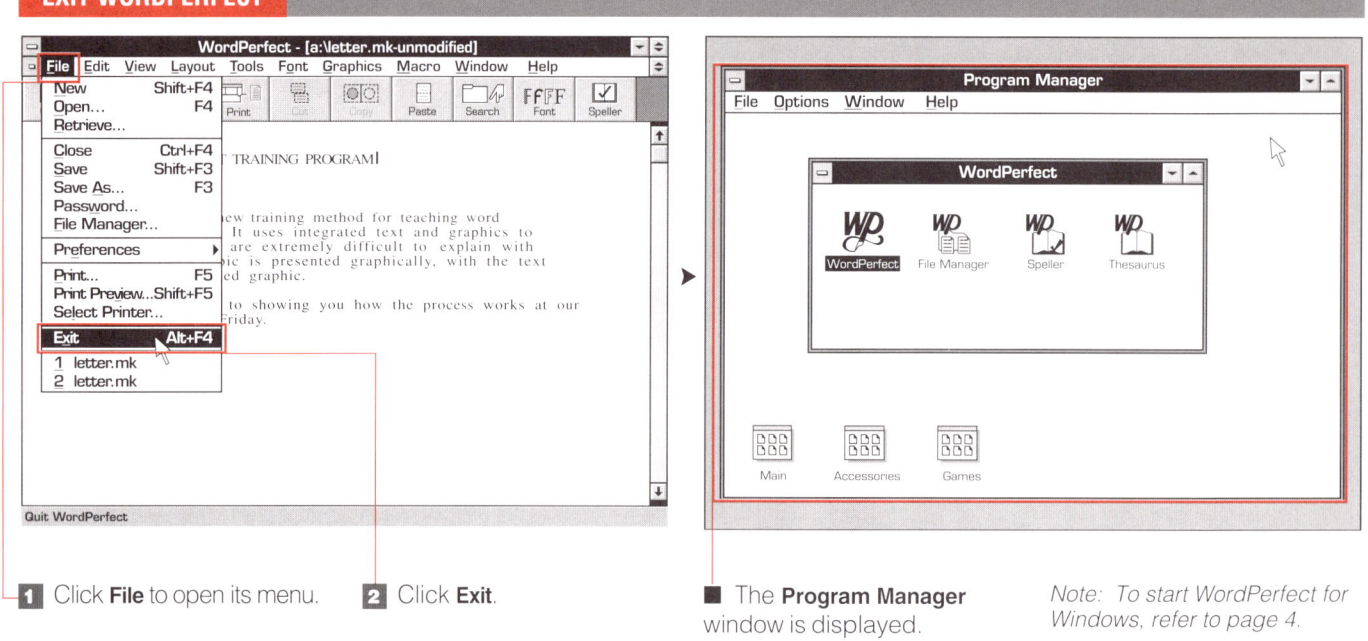

1 Click **File** to open its menu.

2 Click **Exit**.

■ The **Program Manager** window is displayed.

Note: To start WordPerfect for Windows, refer to page 4.

28

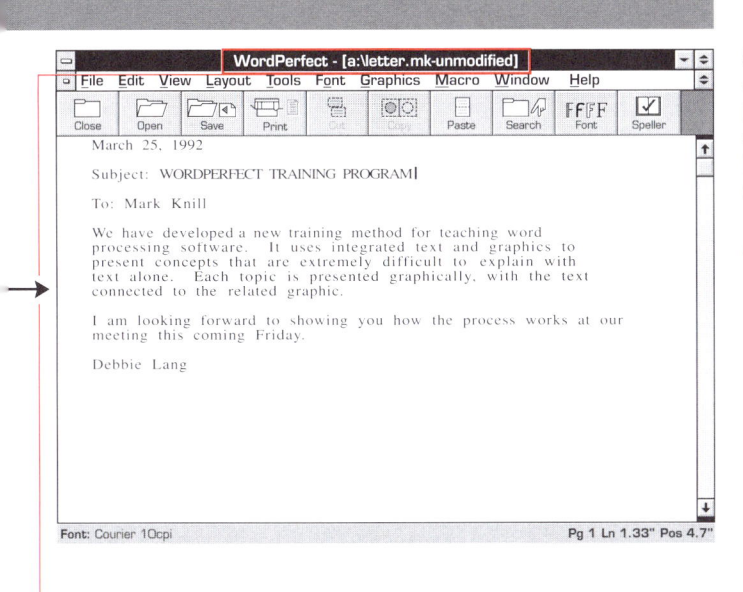

FILES AND DIRECTORIES | LOCATION OF FILES | **SAVE FILES** | **EXIT WORDPERFECT**

Saving to a floppy disk or other backup medium protects your data in case of a catastrophic failure of your hard disk or accidental erasure of important files.

Backup your work regularly (daily or weekly).

■ The document is saved to a floppy disk.

If this dialog box appears when trying to exit WordPerfect, you have not saved a modified document.

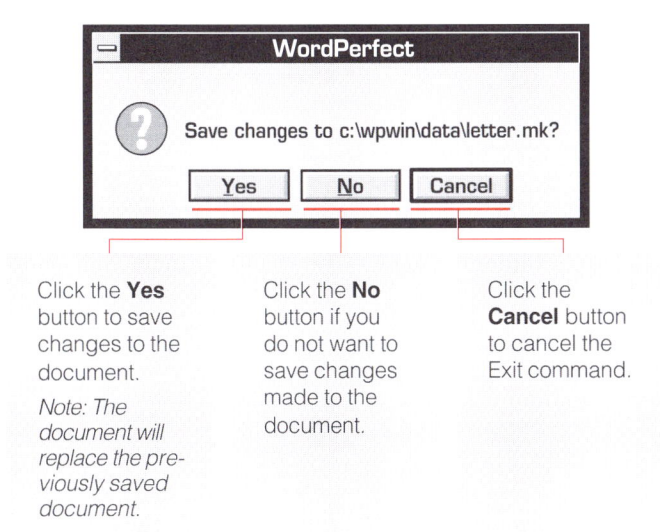

Click the **Yes** button to save changes to the document.

Note: The document will replace the previously saved document.

Click the **No** button if you do not want to save changes made to the document.

Click the **Cancel** button to cancel the Exit command.

GETTING STARTED

THE BUTTON BAR

EDIT A DOCUMENT

SAVE FILES AND EXIT WORDPERFECT

VIEW DOCUMENTS

CHECK A DOCUMENT

FORMAT A DOCUMENT

TABLES

GRAPHICS

PRINT

MERGE AND SORT FILES

FILE MANAGER

HELP

◀ 29

OPEN A DOCUMENT / SWITCH BETWEEN DOCUMENTS

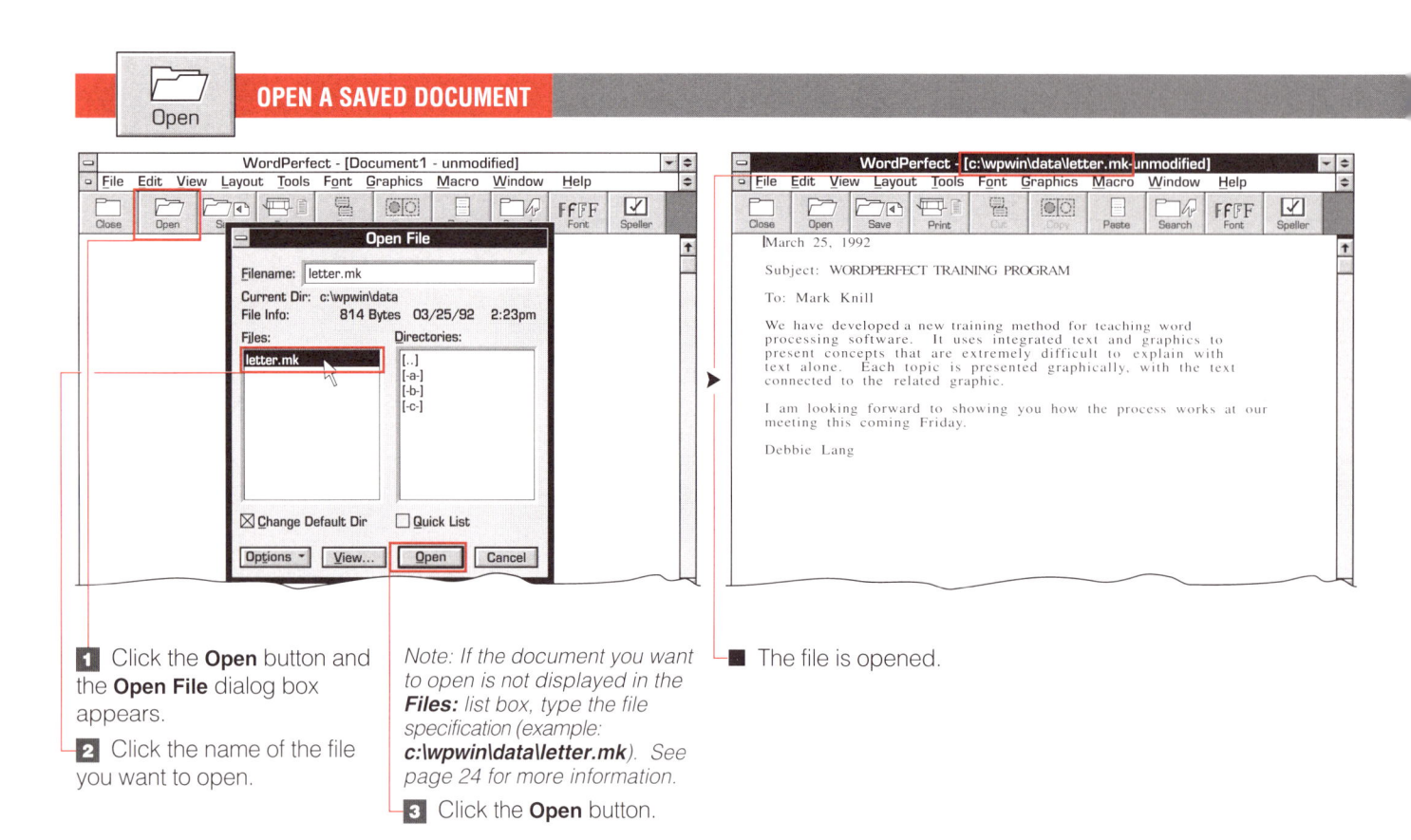

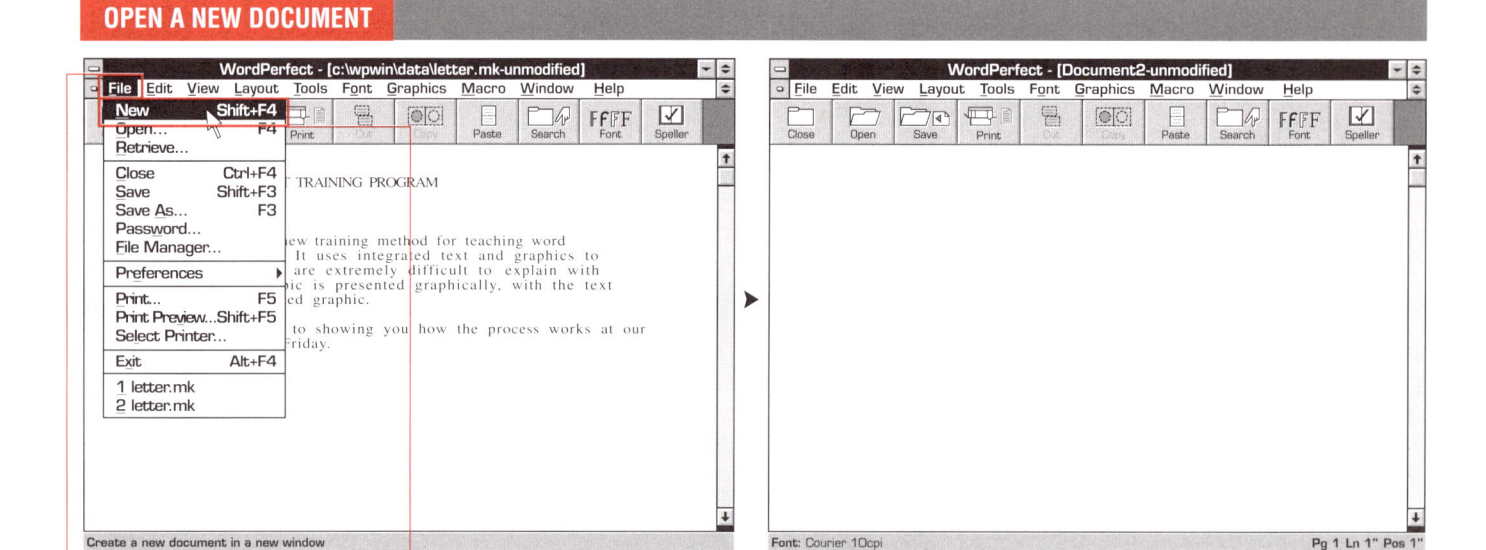

OPEN A SAVED DOCUMENT

1 Click the **Open** button and the **Open File** dialog box appears.

2 Click the name of the file you want to open.

*Note: If the document you want to open is not displayed in the **Files:** list box, type the file specification (example: **c:\wpwin\data\letter.mk**). See page 24 for more information.*

3 Click the **Open** button.

■ The file is opened.

OPEN A NEW DOCUMENT

1 Click **File** to open its menu.

2 Click **New**.

■ A new document appears.

30

| OPEN A DOCUMENT | SWITCH BETWEEN DOCUMENTS | CASCADE OR TILE DOCUMENTS | CLOSE A DOCUMENT | MAXIMIZE A DOCUMENT |

WordPerfect remembers the last four documents you opened. To open one of these documents:

1 Click **File** to display its menu.

2 Click the name of the file you want to open (example: **letter.mk**)

Note: In this example, **1 letter.mk** represents the document saved to drive **a:**.

2 letter.mk represents the document saved to the **c:\wpwin\data** directory.

SWITCH BETWEEN DOCUMENTS

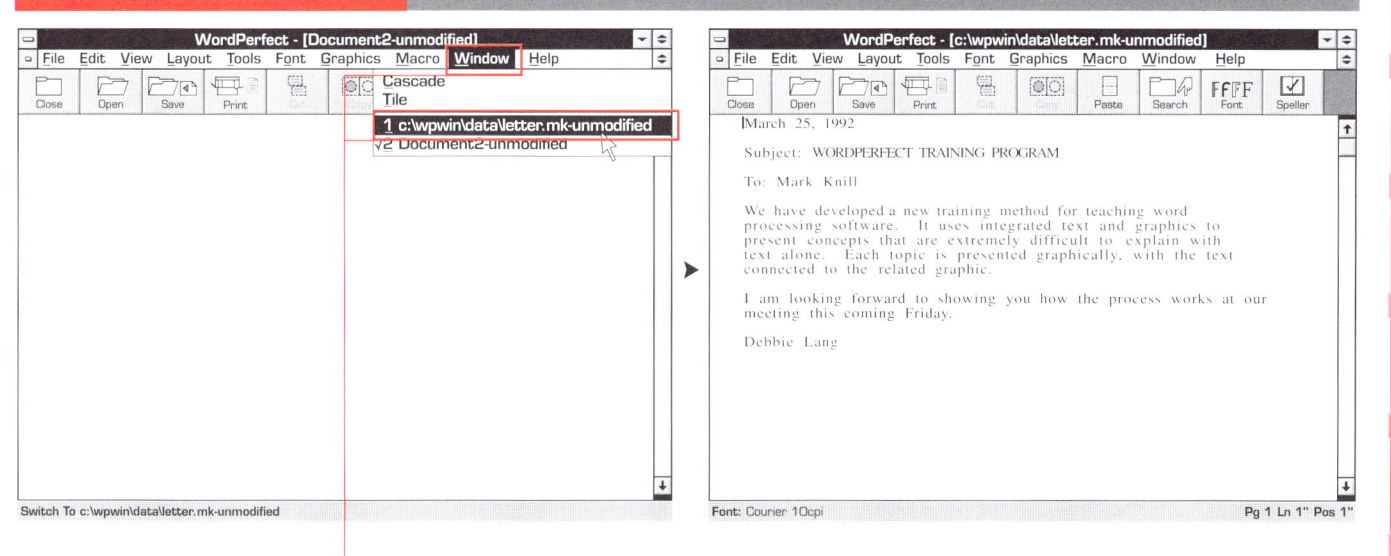

Currently open documents can be viewed by choosing their name from the Window menu. WordPerfect allows you to have as many as nine documents open at one time.

1 Click **Window** to open its menu.

2 Click the name of the document you want to view (example: **c:\wpwin\data\letter.mk**).

■ The document is displayed.

GETTING STARTED

THE BUTTON BAR

EDIT A DOCUMENT

SAVE FILES AND EXIT WORDPERFECT

VIEW DOCUMENTS

CHECK A DOCUMENT

FORMAT A DOCUMENT

TABLES

GRAPHICS

PRINT

MERGE AND SORT FILES

FILE MANAGER

HELP

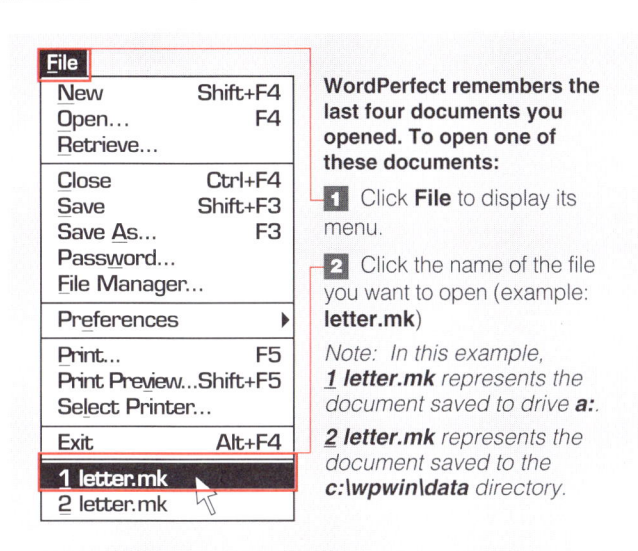

◀ 31

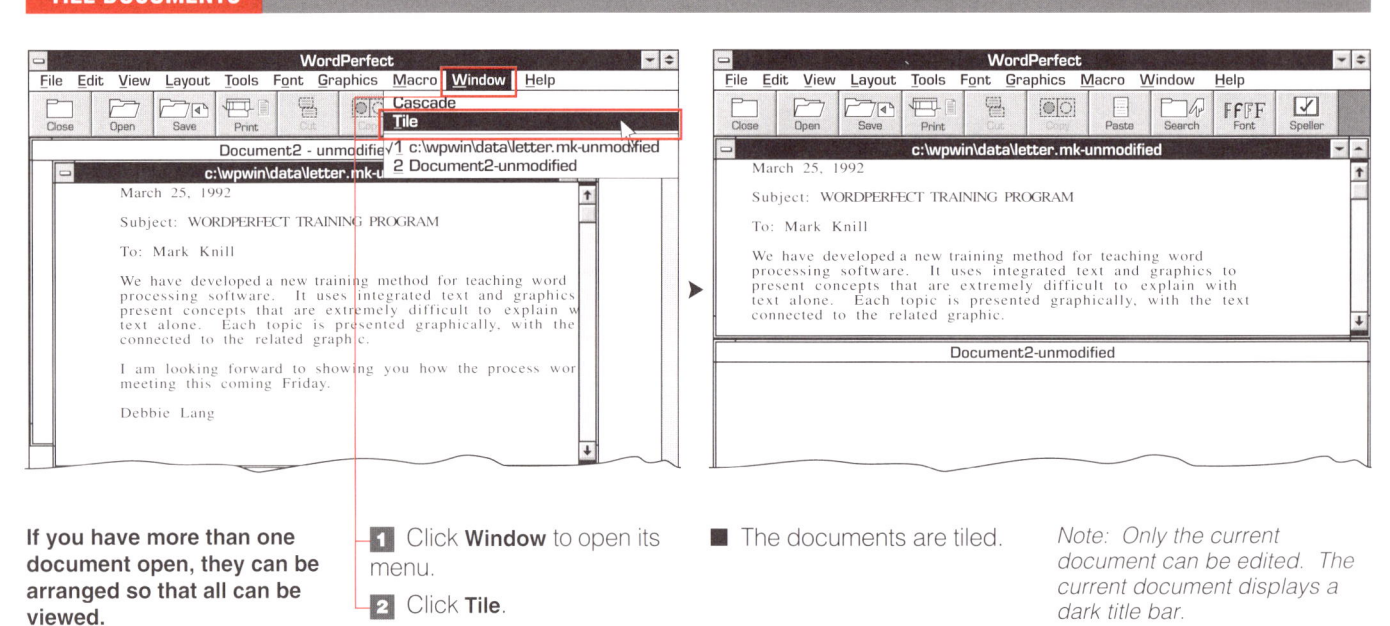

CASCADE OR TILE DOCUMENTS / CLOSE A DOCUMENT / MAXIMIZE A DOCUMENT

CASCADE DOCUMENTS

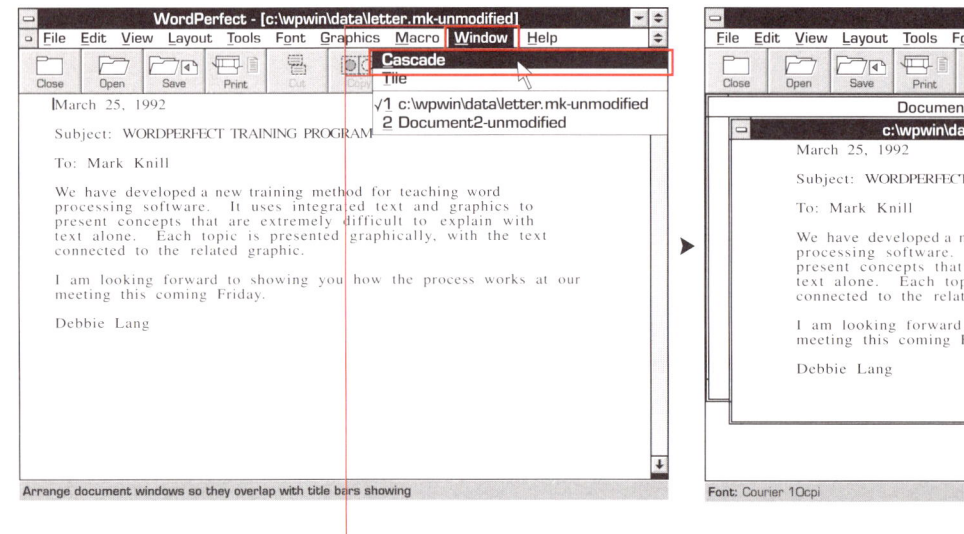

If you have more than one document open, the documents can be arranged to overlap each other.

1 Click **Window** to open its menu.

2 Click **Cascade**.

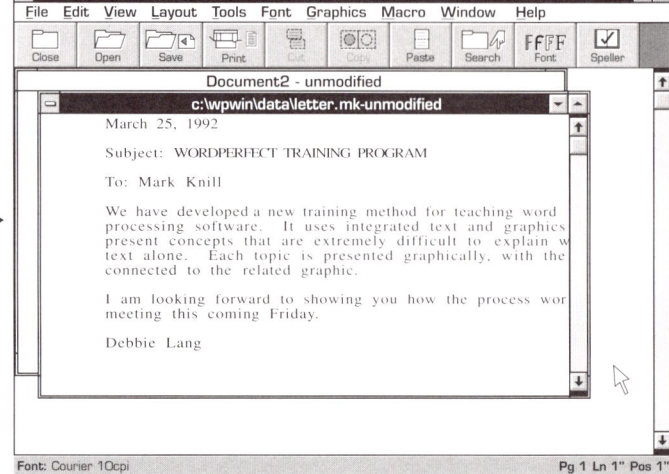

■ The documents are cascaded.

Note: Only the current document can be edited. The current document displays a dark title bar.

TILE DOCUMENTS

If you have more than one document open, they can be arranged so that all can be viewed.

1 Click **Window** to open its menu.

2 Click **Tile**.

■ The documents are tiled.

Note: Only the current document can be edited. The current document displays a dark title bar.

OPEN A DOCUMENT | SWITCH BETWEEN DOCUMENTS | **CASCADE OR TILE DOCUMENTS** | **CLOSE A DOCUMENT** | **MAXIMIZE A DOCUMENT**

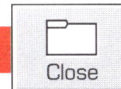

CLOSE A DOCUMENT

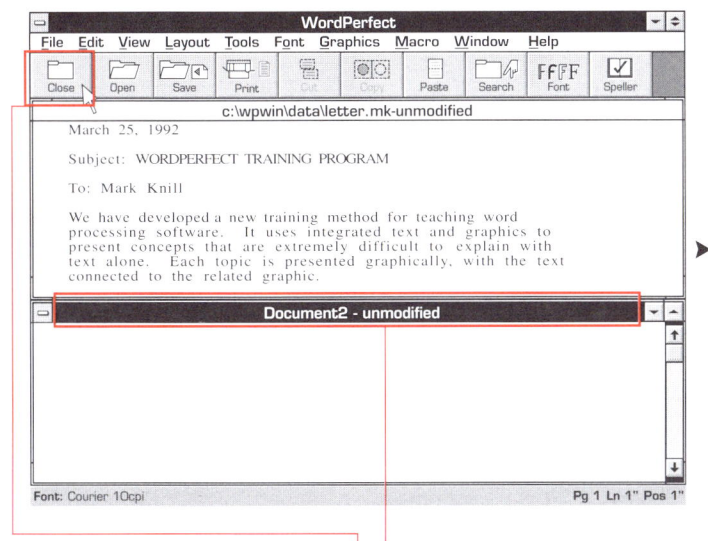

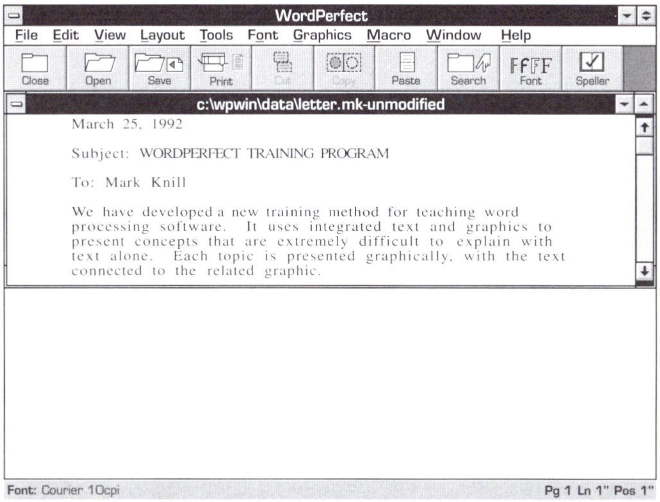

To simplify your workspace, you can close documents currently not in use.

1 Click the title bar of the document you want to close.

Note: WordPerfect closes the current document. The current document displays a dark title bar.

2 Click the **Close** button.

■ The document is closed.

MAXIMIZE A DOCUMENT

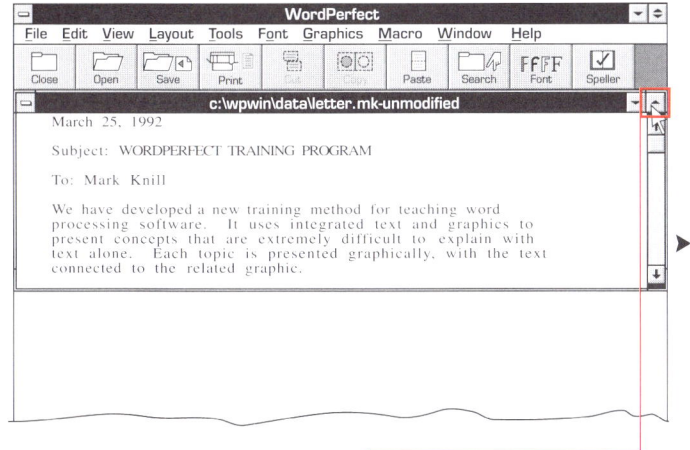

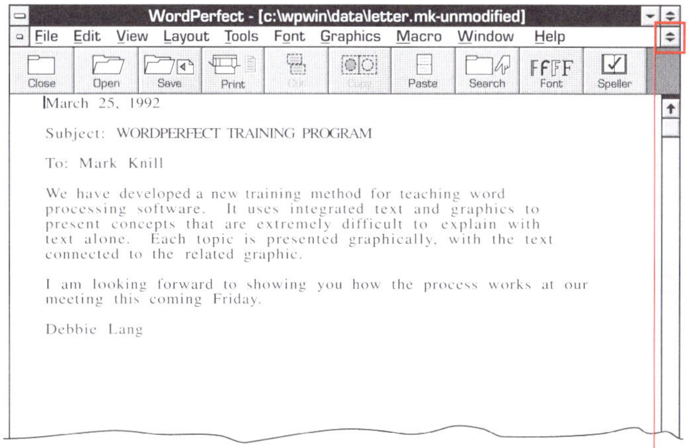

A document can be enlarged to create a larger working area.

1 Click the **Maximize** button of the document you want to enlarge.

■ The document is maximized.

■ To restore the document to its previous size, click the **Restore** button.

GETTING STARTED

THE BUTTON BAR

EDIT A DOCUMENT

SAVE FILES AND EXIT WORDPERFECT

VIEW DOCUMENTS

CHECK A DOCUMENT

FORMAT A DOCUMENT

TABLES

GRAPHICS

PRINT

MERGE AND SORT FILES

FILE MANAGER

HELP

◀ 33

SPELL CHECK A DOCUMENT

SPELL CHECK A DOCUMENT

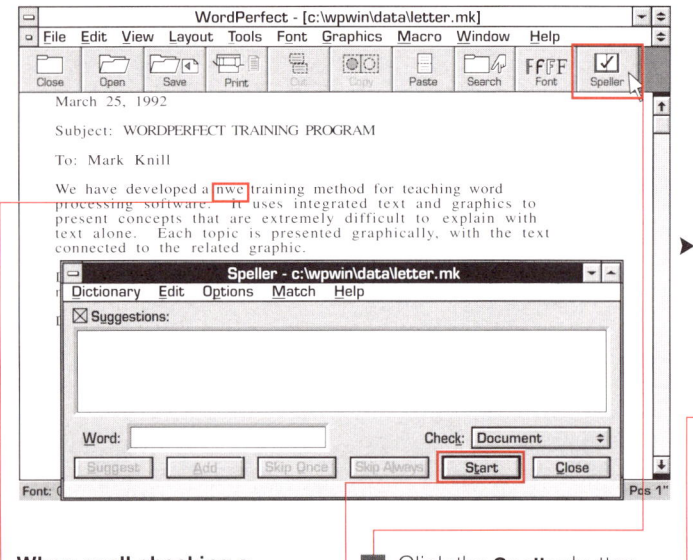

When spell checking a document, WordPerfect compares each word in your document with a list of words in the WordPerfect dictionary. If no match is found, the word is considered to be misspelled.

■ For the following example, the spelling of 'new' has been changed to 'nwe'.

1 Position the insertion point anywhere in the document you want to spell check

or

Select the text you want to spell check.

Note: To select text, refer to page 6.

2 Click the **Speller** button and the **Speller** dialog box appears.

3 To begin the spell check, click **Start**.

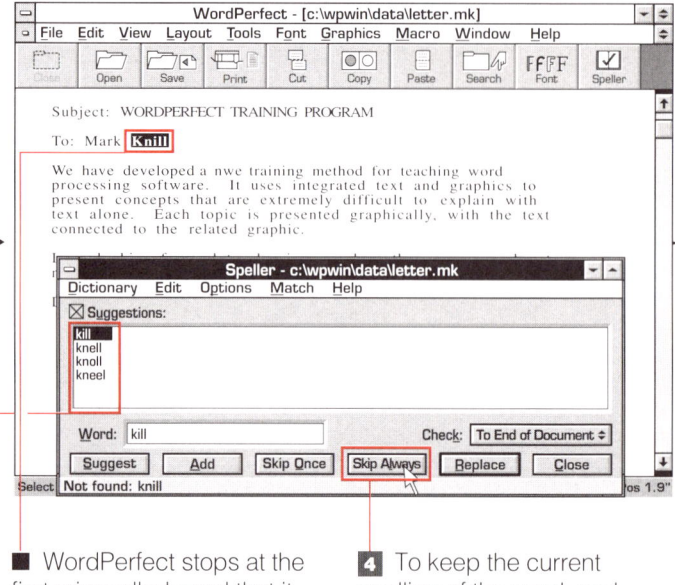

■ WordPerfect stops at the first misspelled word that it finds.

■ Suggestions for the correct spelling are displayed.

Note: In the above example, WordPerfect does not recognize the last name 'Knill'. Therefore, it is considered to be a misspelled word.

4 To keep the current spelling of the word, and ignore all other occurrences of the word in the document, click **Skip Always**

or

To keep the current spelling of the word, but continue to spell check all other occurrences of the word in the document, click **Skip Once**.

Note: To change the spelling of a misspelled word, go to step **5**.

34

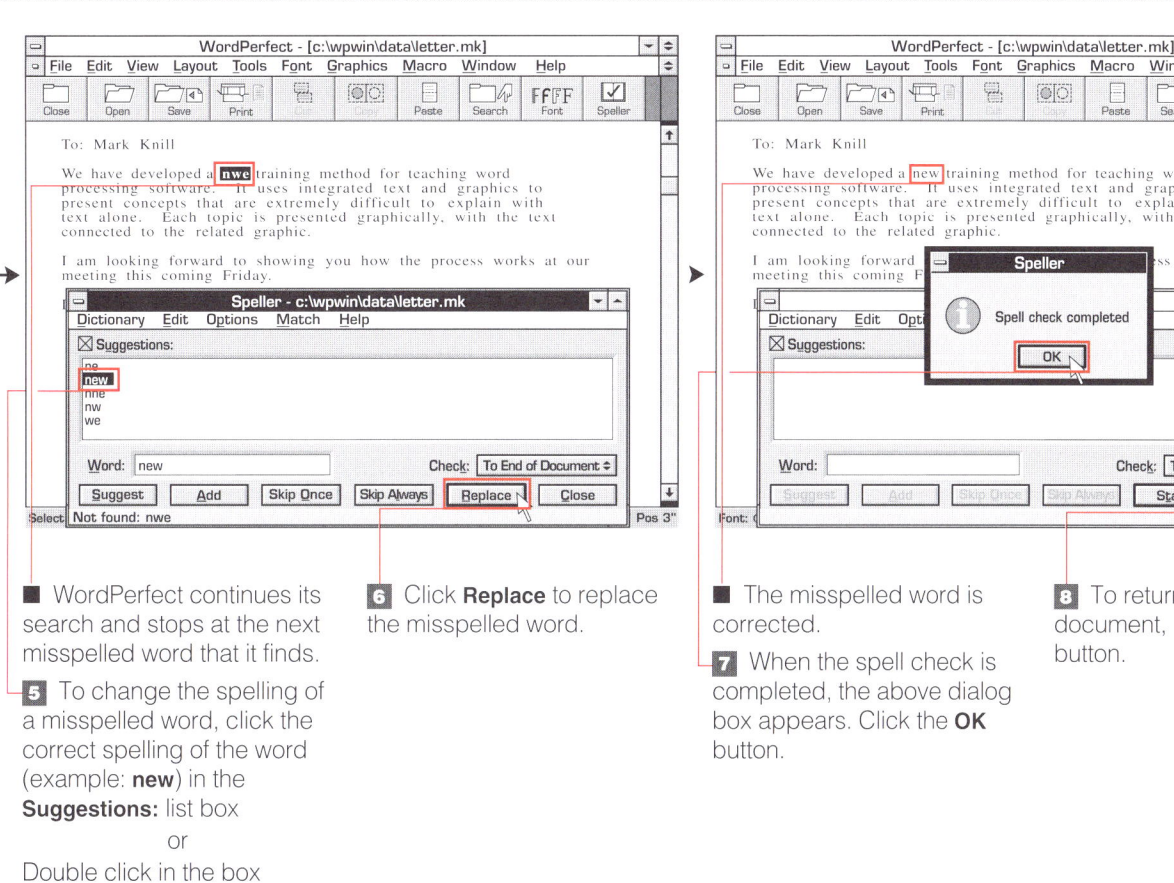

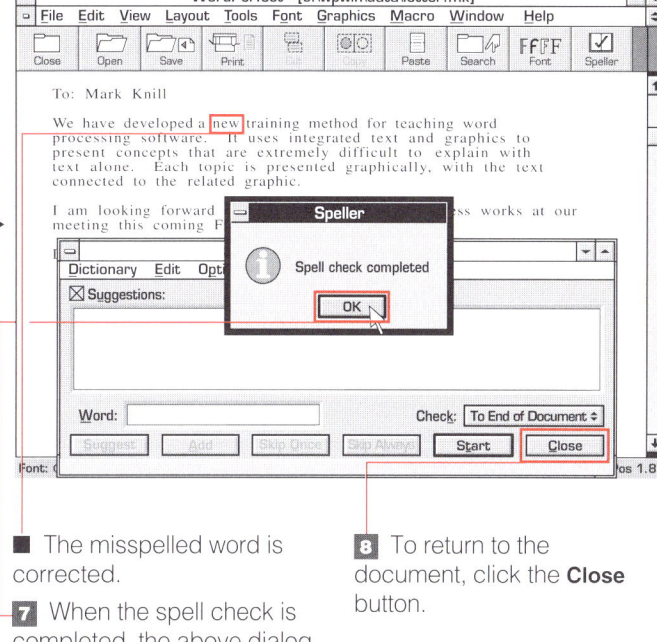

SPELL CHECK A DOCUMENT | THESAURUS | WORD COUNT | SEARCH | SEARCH AND REPLACE

■ WordPerfect continues its search and stops at the next misspelled word that it finds.

5 To change the spelling of a misspelled word, click the correct spelling of the word (example: **new**) in the **Suggestions:** list box
or
Double click in the box beside **Word:**, then type the correct spelling of the word.

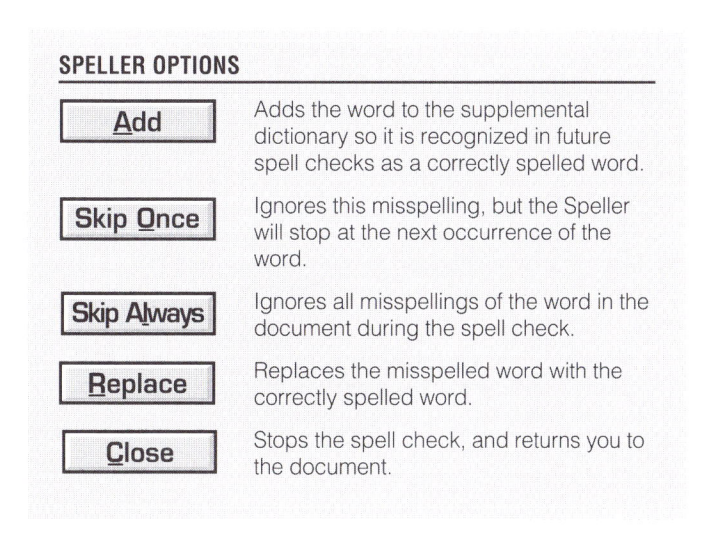

6 Click **Replace** to replace the misspelled word.

■ The misspelled word is corrected.

7 When the spell check is completed, the above dialog box appears. Click the **OK** button.

8 To return to the document, click the **Close** button.

SPELLER OPTIONS

Button	Description
Add	Adds the word to the supplemental dictionary so it is recognized in future spell checks as a correctly spelled word.
Skip Once	Ignores this misspelling, but the Speller will stop at the next occurrence of the word.
Skip Always	Ignores all misspellings of the word in the document during the spell check.
Replace	Replaces the misspelled word with the correctly spelled word.
Close	Stops the spell check, and returns you to the document.

GETTING STARTED

THE BUTTON BAR

EDIT A DOCUMENT

SAVE FILES AND EXIT WORDPERFECT

VIEW DOCUMENTS

CHECK A DOCUMENT

FORMAT A DOCUMENT

TABLES

GRAPHICS

PRINT

MERGE AND SORT FILES

FILE MANAGER

HELP

◄ 35

THESAURUS / WORD COUNT

THESAURUS

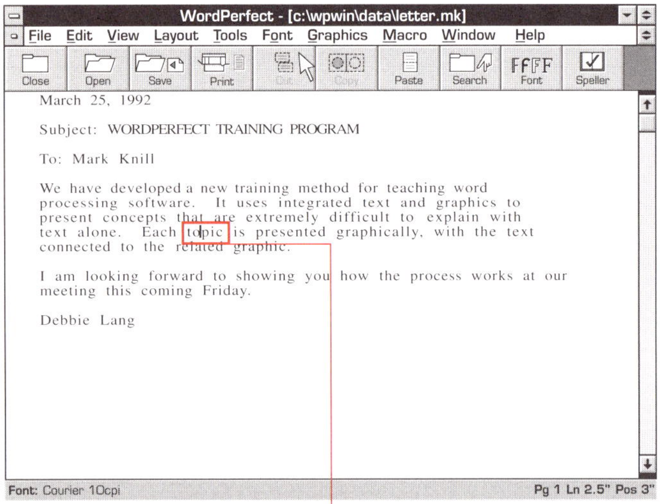

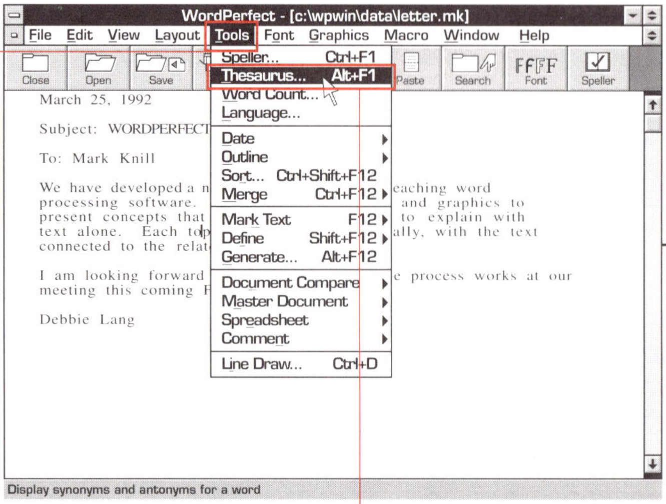

The Thesaurus searches for words with the same meaning (synonyms) and words with the opposite meaning (antonyms).

1 Position the insertion point on the word (example: **topic**) you want a synonym or antonym for.

2 Click **Tools** to open its menu.

3 Click **Thesaurus**.

WORD COUNT

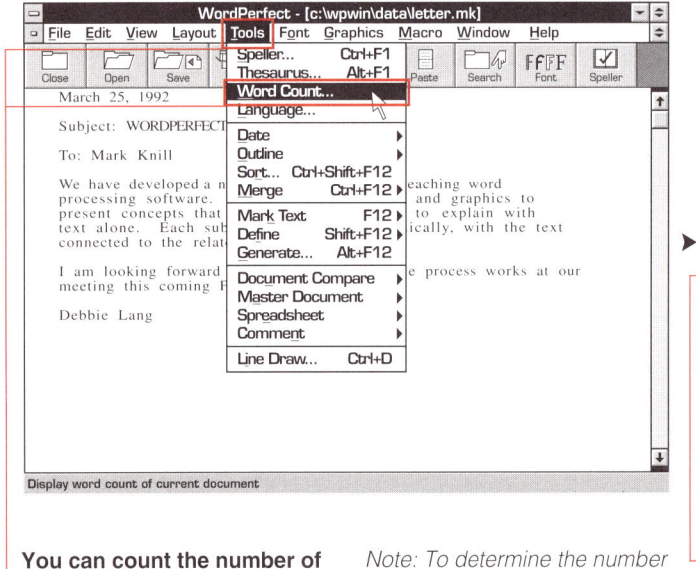

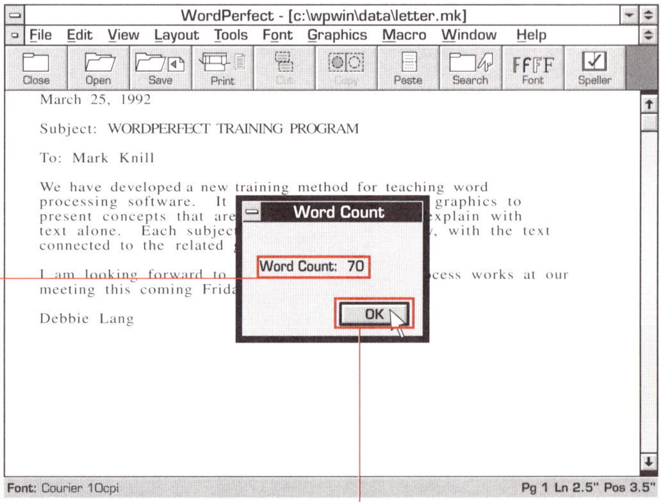

You can count the number of words in a document.

1 Click **Tools** to open its menu.

2 Click **Word Count**.

Note: To determine the number of words in a section of text, select the text, before executing step **1**.

■ The **Word Count** dialog box appears, displaying the number of words in your document.

3 To return to the document, click the **OK** button.

36

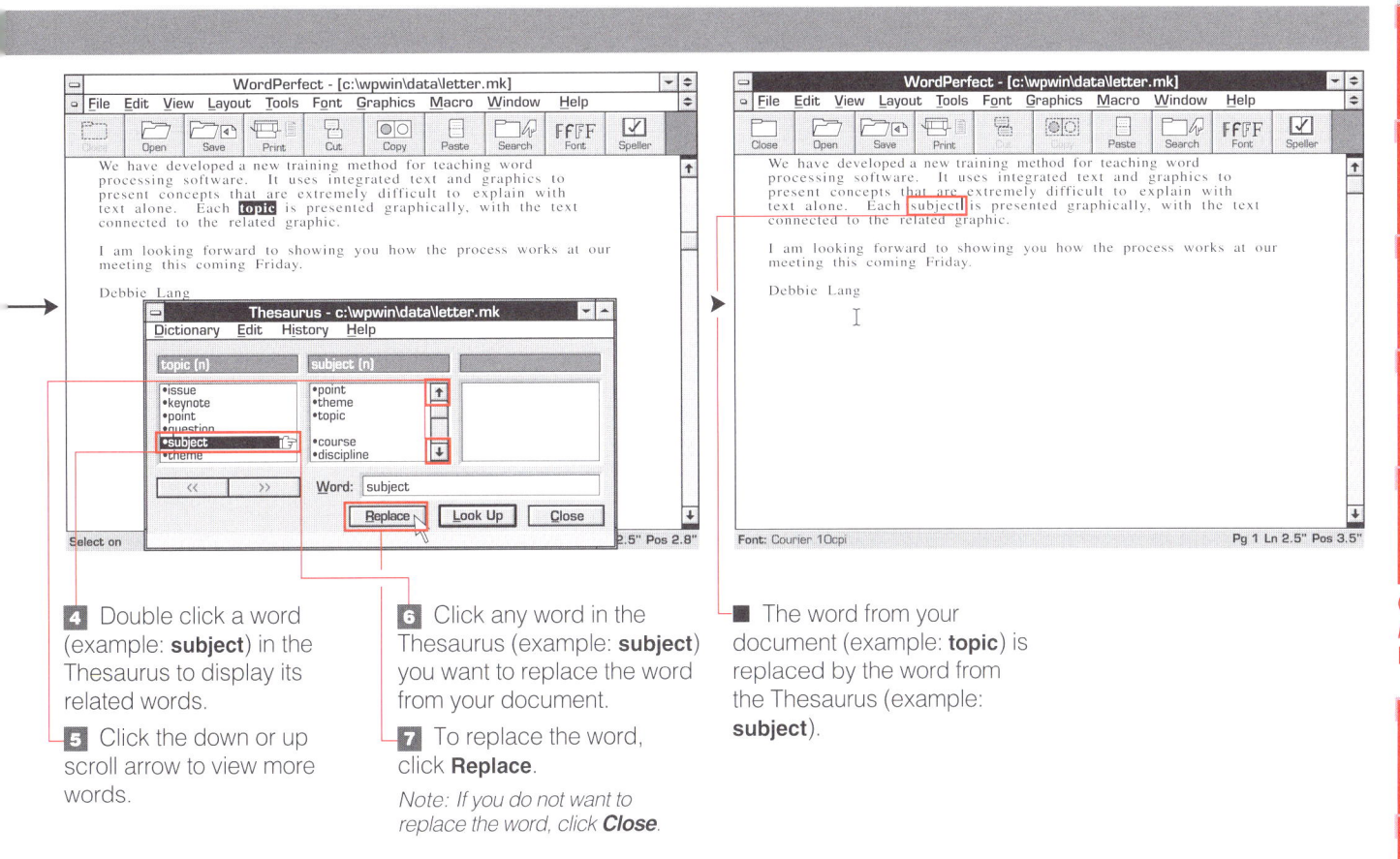

SPELL CHECK A DOCUMENT	**THESAURUS**	WORD COUNT	SEARCH	SEARCH AND REPLACE

4 Double click a word (example: **subject**) in the Thesaurus to display its related words.

5 Click the down or up scroll arrow to view more words.

6 Click any word in the Thesaurus (example: **subject**) you want to replace the word from your document.

7 To replace the word, click **Replace**.

*Note: If you do not want to replace the word, click **Close**.*

■ The word from your document (example: **topic**) is replaced by the word from the Thesaurus (example: **subject**).

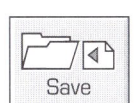

REMEMBER TO SAVE YOUR DOCUMENT USING THIS BUTTON

Click the **Save** button to quickly save your document to the current directory, using the same name.

Note: You should save regularly to prevent losing work due to power failure or hardware malfunctions.

GETTING STARTED

THE BUTTON BAR

EDIT A DOCUMENT

SAVE FILES AND EXIT WORDPERFECT

VIEW DOCUMENTS

CHECK A DOCUMENT

FORMAT A DOCUMENT

TABLES

GRAPHICS

PRINT

MERGE AND SORT FILES

FILE MANAGER

HELP

◀ 37

SEARCH / SEARCH AND REPLACE

SEARCH

SEARCH GUIDELINES

■ A search word containing lowercase characters will find matching lowercase and uppercase words. For example, **subject** matches **subject**, **Subject** or **SUBJECT**.

■ A search word containing uppercase characters will only find matching uppercase words. For example, **SUBJECT** only matches **SUBJECT**.

■ WordPerfect will find the word even if it is part of a larger word. For example, **place** matches common**place**, **place**ment, **place**s, etc.

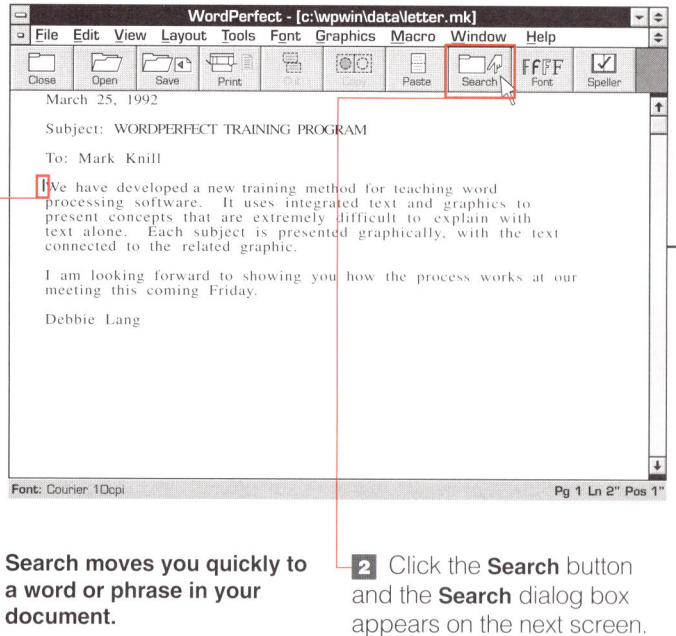

Search moves you quickly to a word or phrase in your document.

1 Position the insertion point where you want the search to begin.

2 Click the **Search** button and the **Search** dialog box appears on the next screen.

SEARCH AND REPLACE

You can search and replace text in your document.

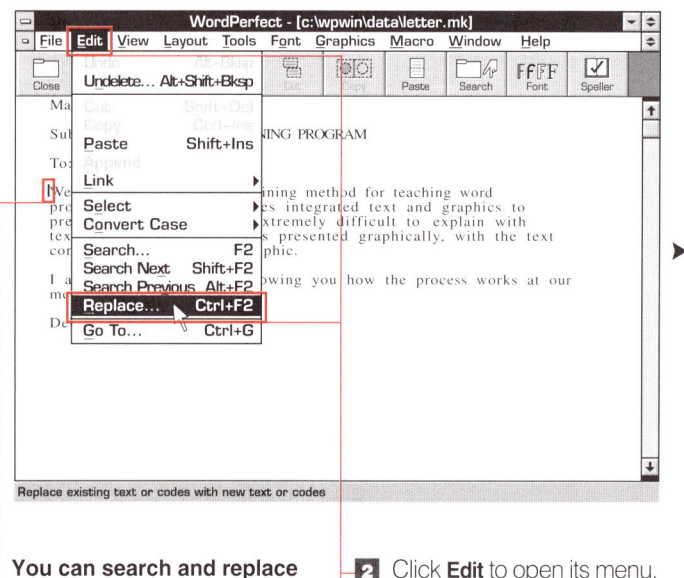

1 Position the insertion point where you want the search and replace function to begin.

2 Click **Edit** to open its menu.

3 Click **Replace**.

4 Type the text you want to search for (example: **subject**).

5 Double click in the box beside **Replace With:**. Then type the text to replace the searched term (example: **topic**).

38

SPELL CHECK A DOCUMENT THESAURUS WORD COUNT **SEARCH** **SEARCH AND REPLACE**

3 Type the text you want to search for (example: **subject**).

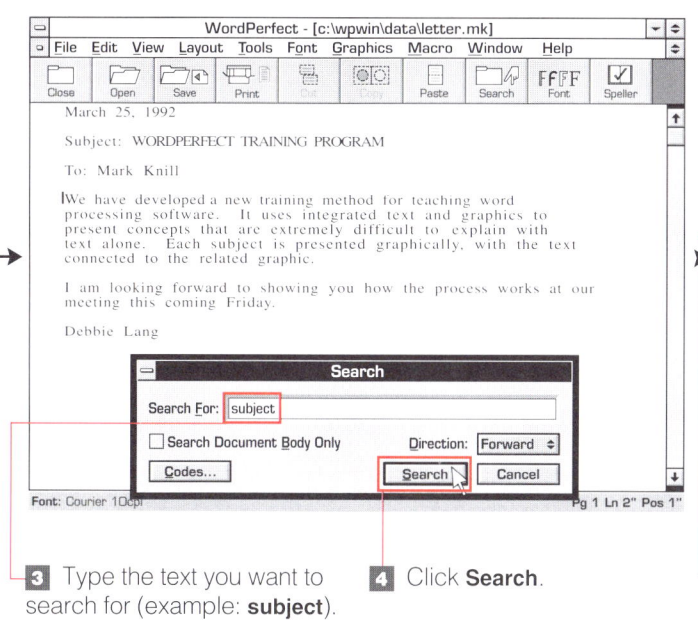

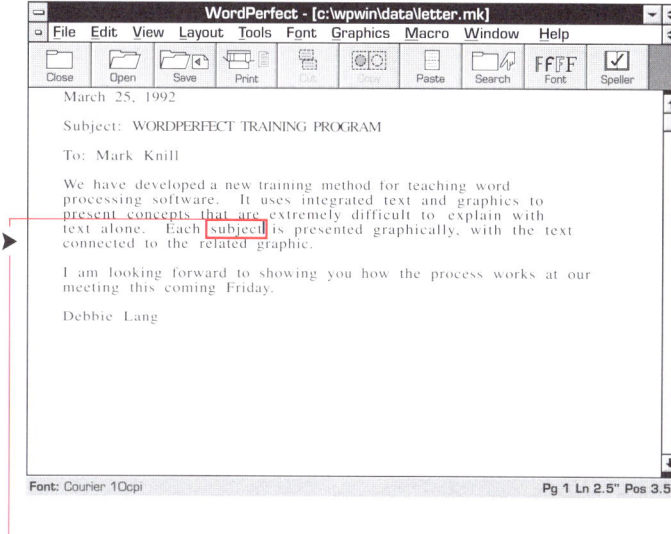

4 Click **Search**.

■ The insertion point moves to the first occurrence of the search text.

Note: To search for the next occurrence of the search text, click **Edit**. *Then click* **Search Next**.

To search for the previous occurrence of the search text, click **Edit**. *Then click* **Search Previous**.

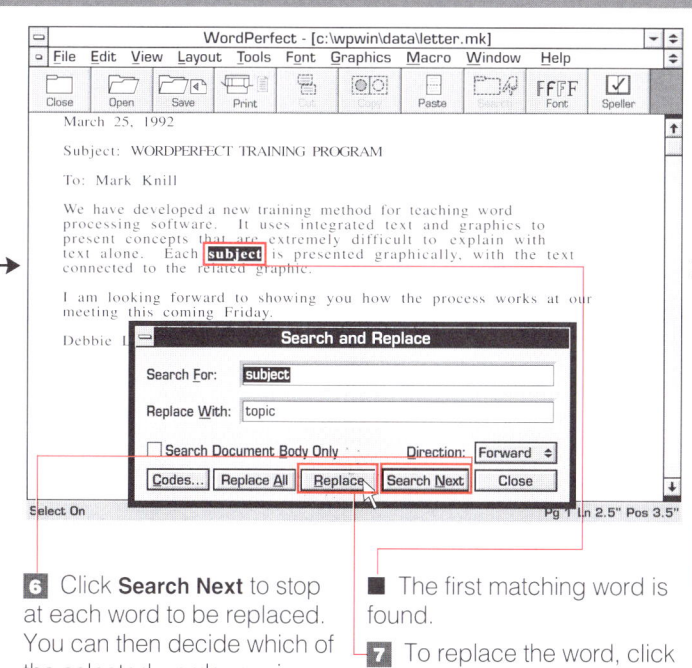

6 Click **Search Next** to stop at each word to be replaced. You can then decide which of the selected words require replacement.

Note: Click **Replace All** *to replace all of the words at the same time.*

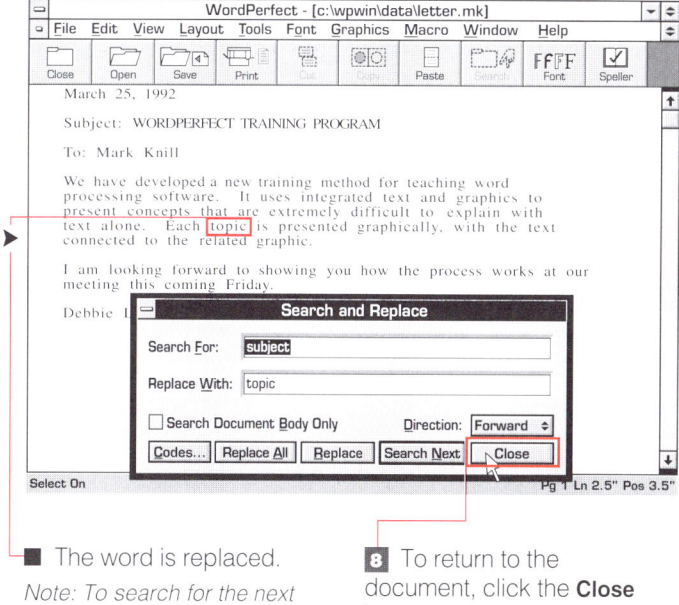

■ The first matching word is found.

7 To replace the word, click **Replace**.

Note: If you do not want to replace the word, click **Search Next**.

■ The word is replaced.

Note: To search for the next occurrence of the word, click **Search Next**.

8 To return to the document, click the **Close** button.

GETTING STARTED

THE BUTTON BAR

EDIT A DOCUMENT

SAVE FILES AND EXIT WORDPERFECT

VIEW DOCUMENTS

CHECK A DOCUMENT

FORMAT A DOCUMENT

TABLES

GRAPHICS

PRINT

MERGE AND SORT FILES

FILE MANAGER

HELP

◀ 39

VIEW THE RULER / ALIGN TEXT / CHANGE LINE SPACING

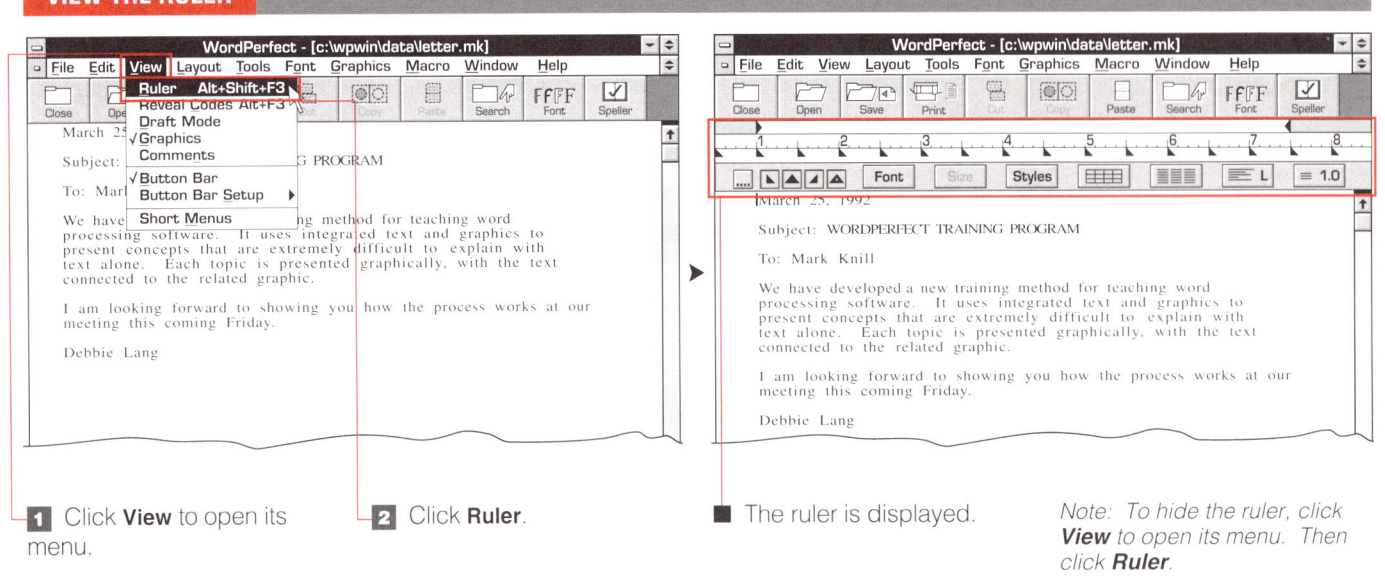

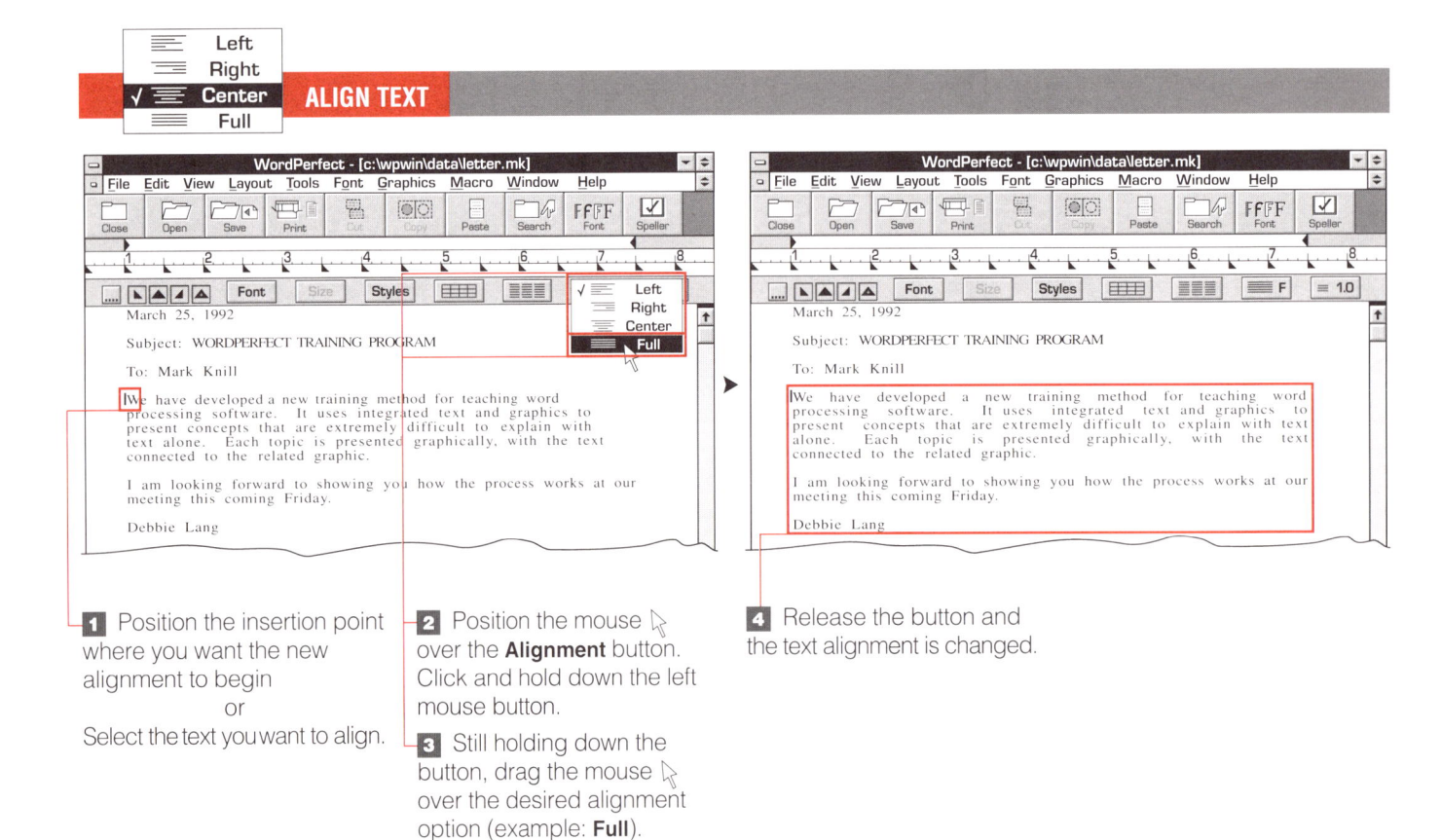

VIEW THE RULER

1 Click **View** to open its menu.

2 Click **Ruler**.

■ The ruler is displayed.

*Note: To hide the ruler, click **View** to open its menu. Then click **Ruler**.*

ALIGN TEXT

1 Position the insertion point where you want the new alignment to begin
or
Select the text you want to align.

2 Position the mouse over the **Alignment** button. Click and hold down the left mouse button.

3 Still holding down the button, drag the mouse over the desired alignment option (example: **Full**).

4 Release the button and the text alignment is changed.

40 ▶

CHANGE LINE SPACING

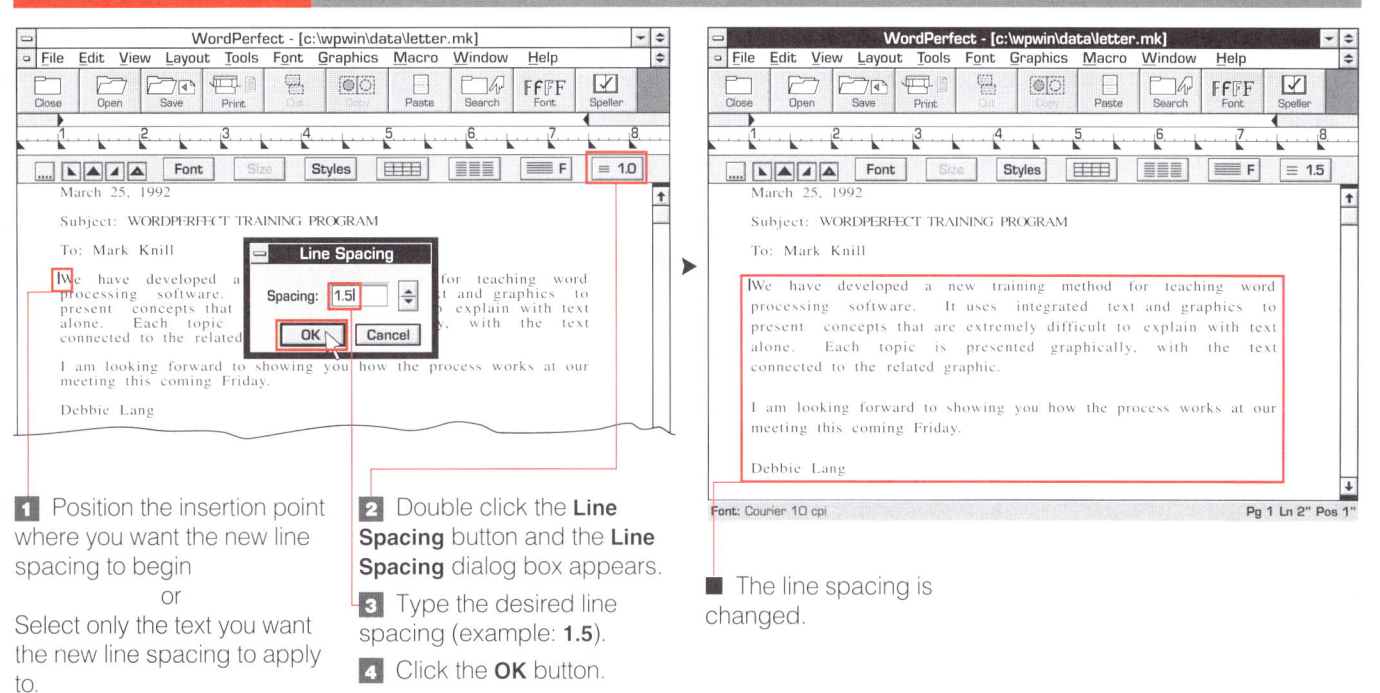

1 Position the insertion point where you want the new line spacing to begin
or
Select only the text you want the new line spacing to apply to.

2 Double click the **Line Spacing** button and the **Line Spacing** dialog box appears.

3 Type the desired line spacing (example: **1.5**).

4 Click the **OK** button.

■ The line spacing is changed.

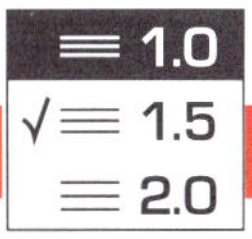

CHANGE LINE SPACING (A Faster Method)

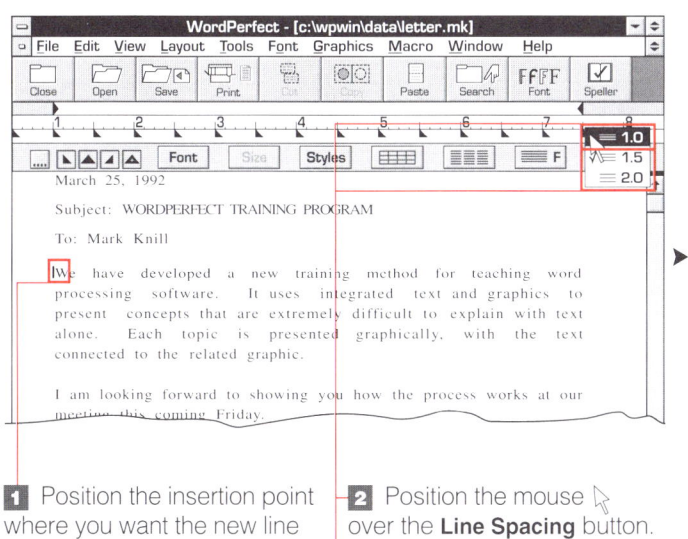

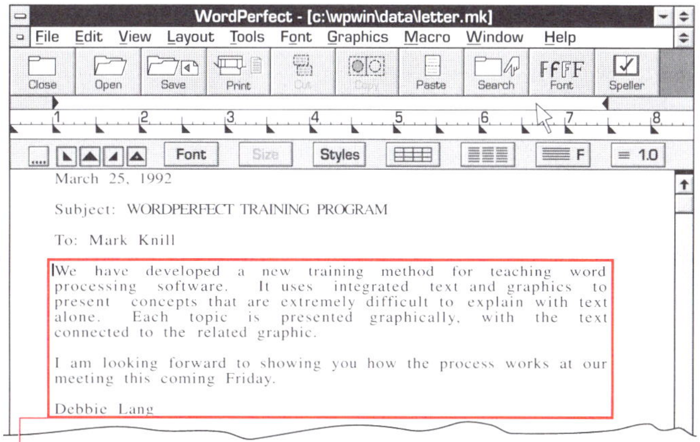

1 Position the insertion point where you want the new line spacing to begin
or
Select only the text you want the new line spacing to apply to.

2 Position the mouse over the **Line Spacing** button. Click and hold down the left mouse button.

3 Still holding down the button, drag the mouse over the desired line spacing (example: **1.0**).

4 Release the button and the line spacing is changed.

41

INDENT A PARAGRAPH

INDENT A PARAGRAPH FROM THE LEFT MARGIN

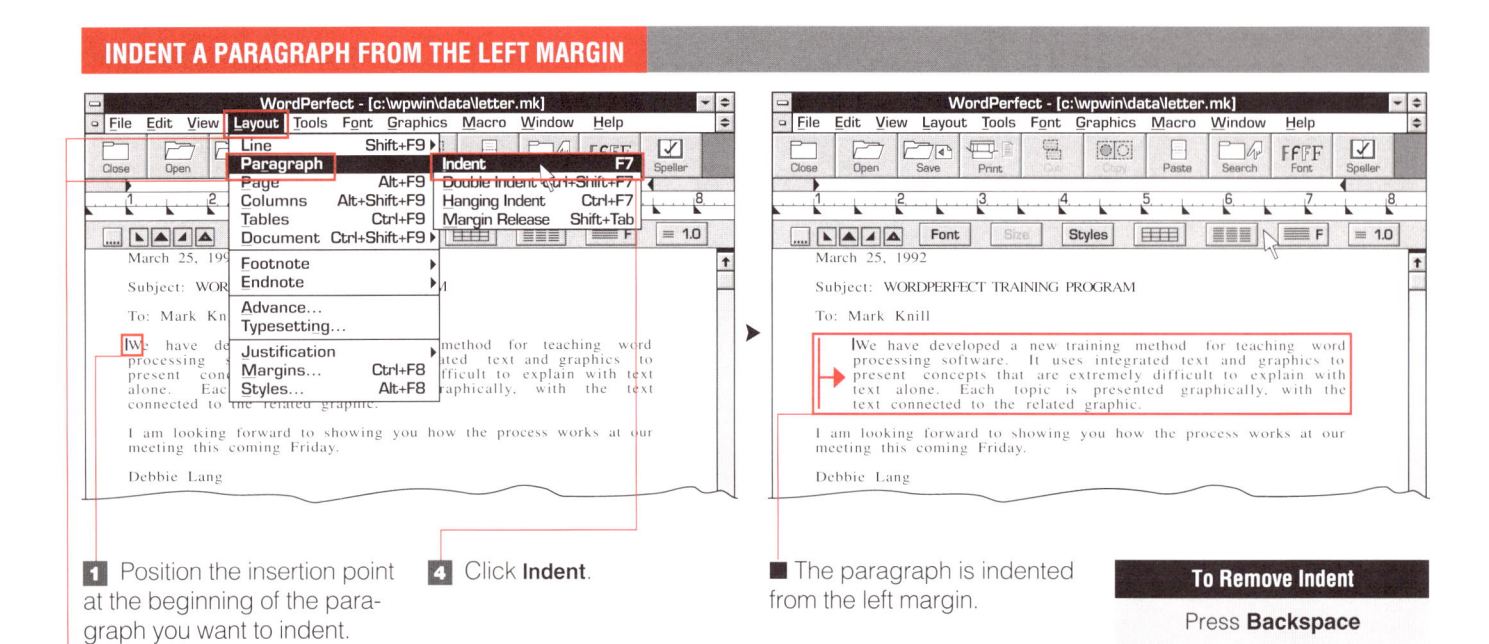

1 Position the insertion point at the beginning of the paragraph you want to indent.

2 Click **Layout**.

3 Click **Paragraph**.

4 Click **Indent**.

■ The paragraph is indented from the left margin.

To Remove Indent

Press **Backspace**

INDENT A PARAGRAPH FROM BOTH MARGINS

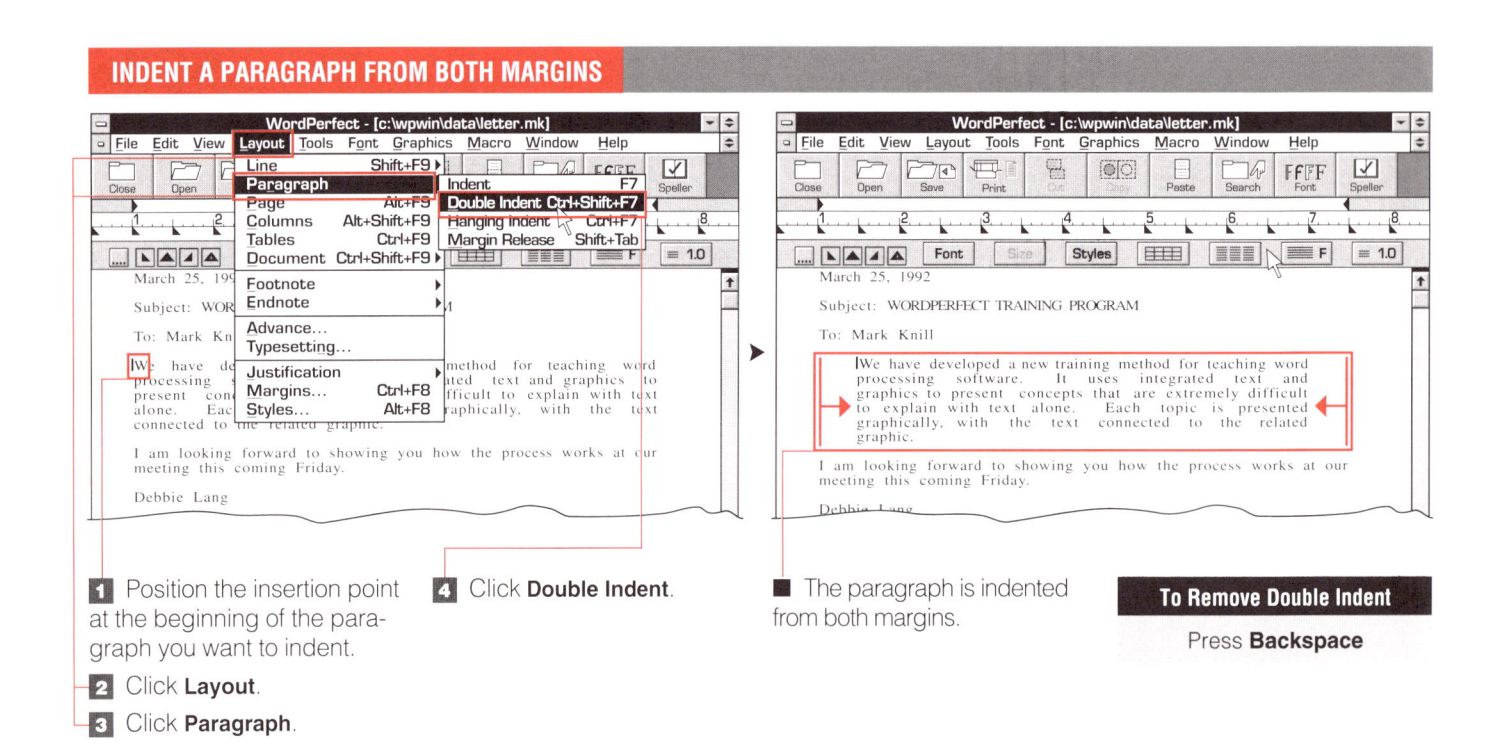

1 Position the insertion point at the beginning of the paragraph you want to indent.

2 Click **Layout**.

3 Click **Paragraph**.

4 Click **Double Indent**.

■ The paragraph is indented from both margins.

To Remove Double Indent

Press **Backspace**

42

| VIEW THE RULER | ALIGN TEXT | CHANGE LINE SPACING | **INDENT A PARAGRAPH** | CHANGE MARGINS | SETTING TABS | CHANGE FONTS | PAGE BREAKS | CENTER TEXT ON A PAGE | AUTOMATIC PAGE NUMBERING | HEADERS AND FOOTERS | FOOTNOTES AND ENDNOTES |

GETTING STARTED
THE BUTTON BAR
EDIT A DOCUMENT
SAVE FILES AND EXIT WORDPERFECT
VIEW DOCUMENTS
CHECK A DOCUMENT
FORMAT A DOCUMENT
TABLES
GRAPHICS
PRINT
MERGE AND SORT FILES
FILE MANAGER
HELP

INDENT ALL LINES OF A PARAGRAPH EXCEPT THE FIRST LINE

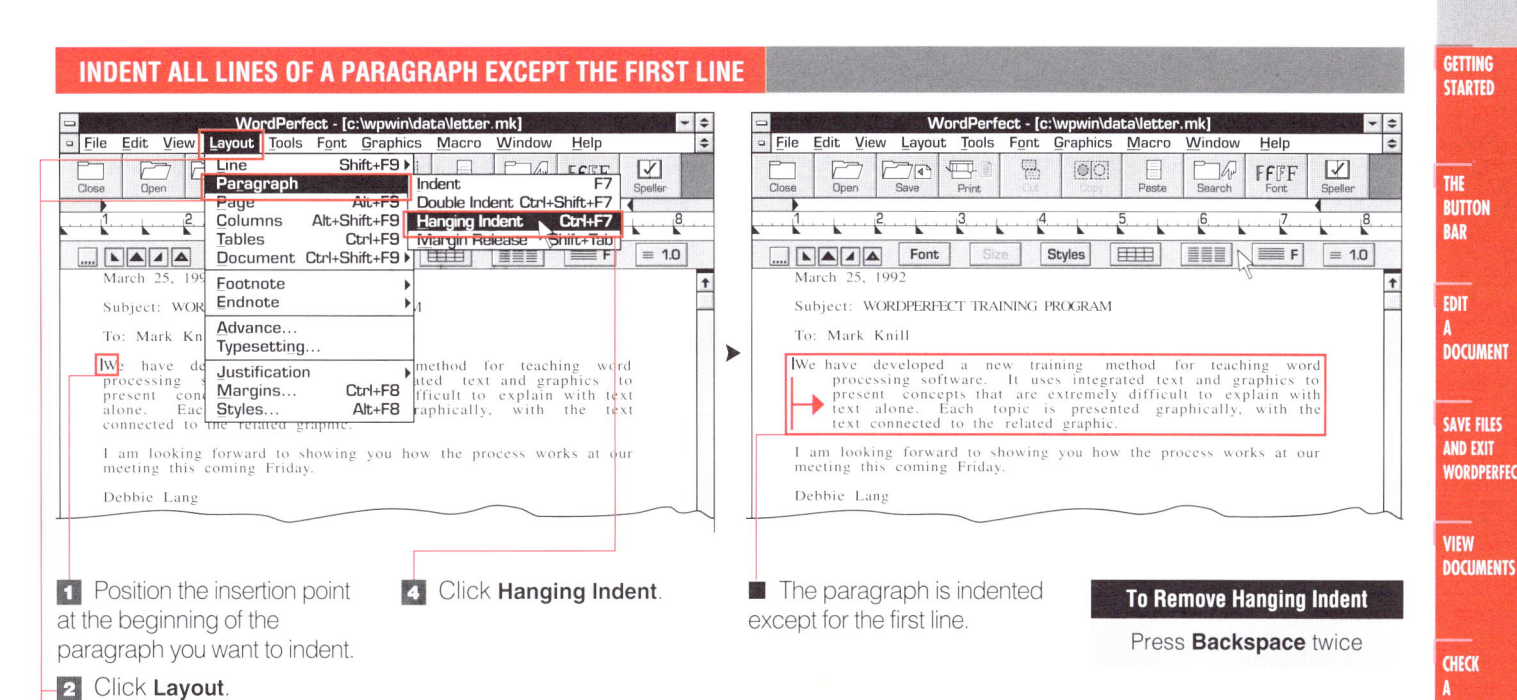

1 Position the insertion point at the beginning of the paragraph you want to indent.

2 Click **Layout**.

3 Click **Paragraph**.

4 Click **Hanging Indent**.

■ The paragraph is indented except for the first line.

To Remove Hanging Indent

Press **Backspace** twice

MOVE THE FIRST LINE OF A PARAGRAPH ONE TAB STOP TO THE LEFT

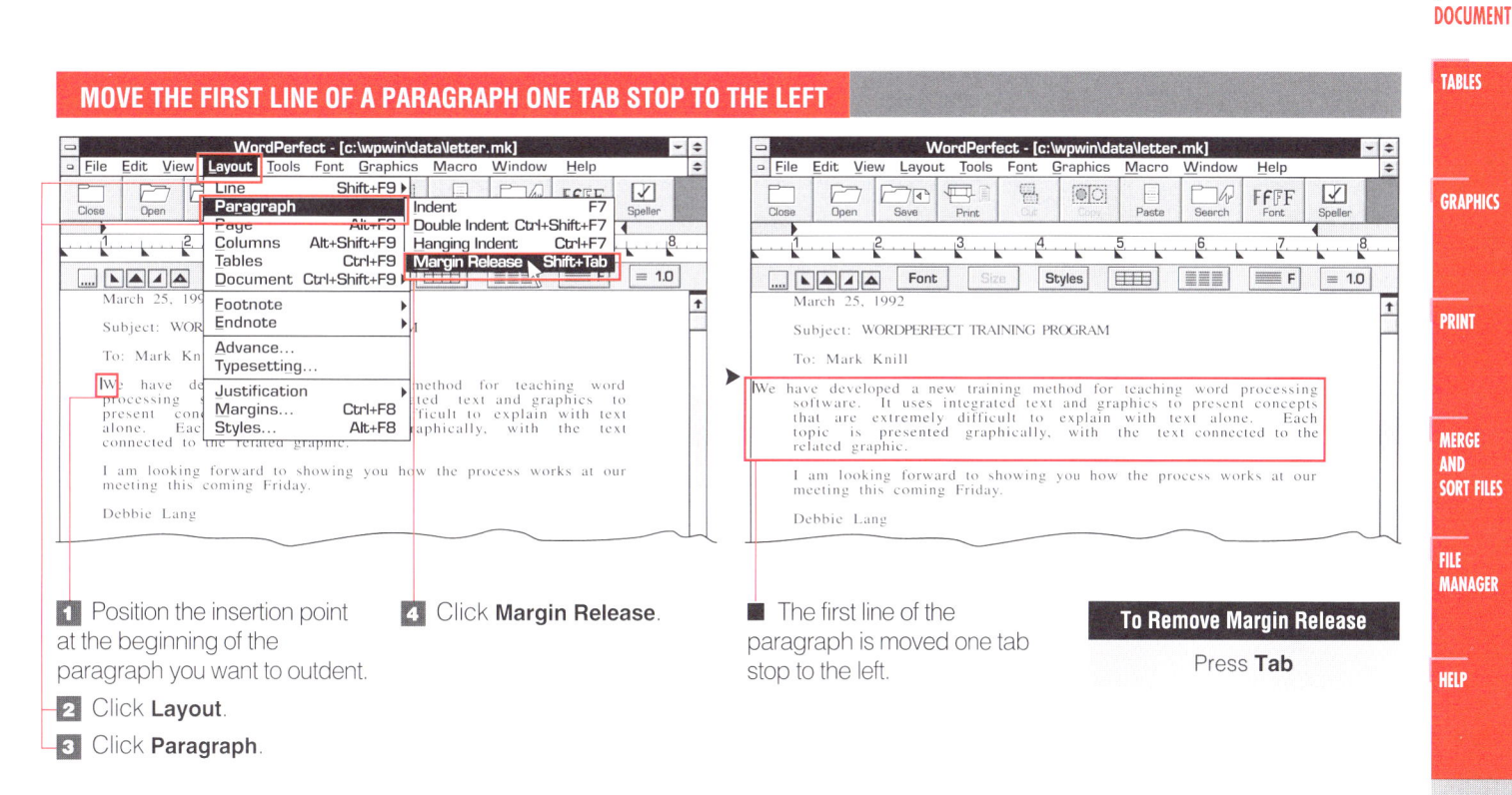

1 Position the insertion point at the beginning of the paragraph you want to outdent.

2 Click **Layout**.

3 Click **Paragraph**.

4 Click **Margin Release**.

■ The first line of the paragraph is moved one tab stop to the left.

To Remove Margin Release

Press **Tab**

◀ 43

CHANGE MARGINS

CHANGE THE LEFT MARGIN

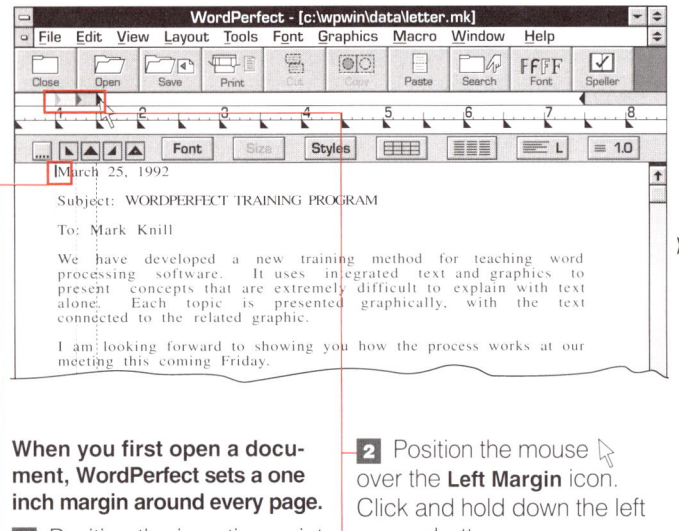

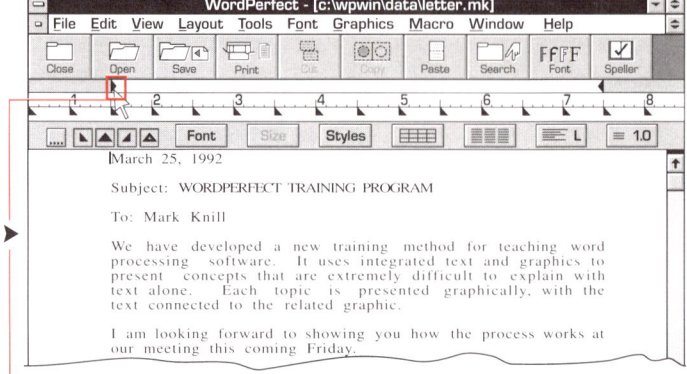

When you first open a document, WordPerfect sets a one inch margin around every page.

1 Position the insertion point where you want the new margin to begin.

2 Position the mouse over the **Left Margin** icon. Click and hold down the left mouse button.

3 Still holding down the button, drag the margin to a new position.

Note: The dotted line displays the current margin setting.

4 Release the button and the margin is changed.

CHANGE THE TOP AND BOTTOM MARGINS

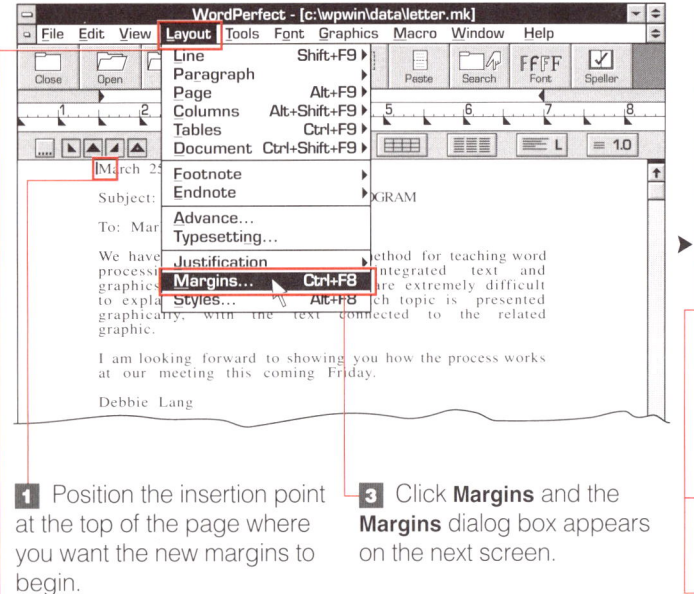

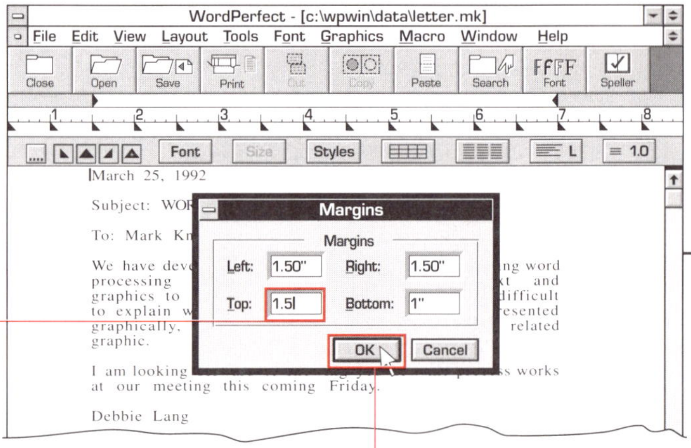

1 Position the insertion point at the top of the page where you want the new margins to begin.

2 Click **Layout** to open its menu.

3 Click **Margins** and the **Margins** dialog box appears on the next screen.

4 Double click in the box beside the margin you want to change (example: **Top**).

5 Type the new margin in inches (example: **1.5**).

6 Click the **OK** button.

Note: The left, right, top and bottom margins can be changed in this way.

| VIEW THE RULER | ALIGN TEXT | CHANGE LINE SPACING | INDENT A PARAGRAPH | **CHANGE MARGINS** | SETTING TABS | CHANGE FONTS | PAGE BREAKS | CENTER TEXT ON A PAGE | AUTOMATIC PAGE NUMBERING | HEADERS AND FOOTERS | FOOTNOTES AND ENDNOTES |

CHANGE THE RIGHT MARGIN

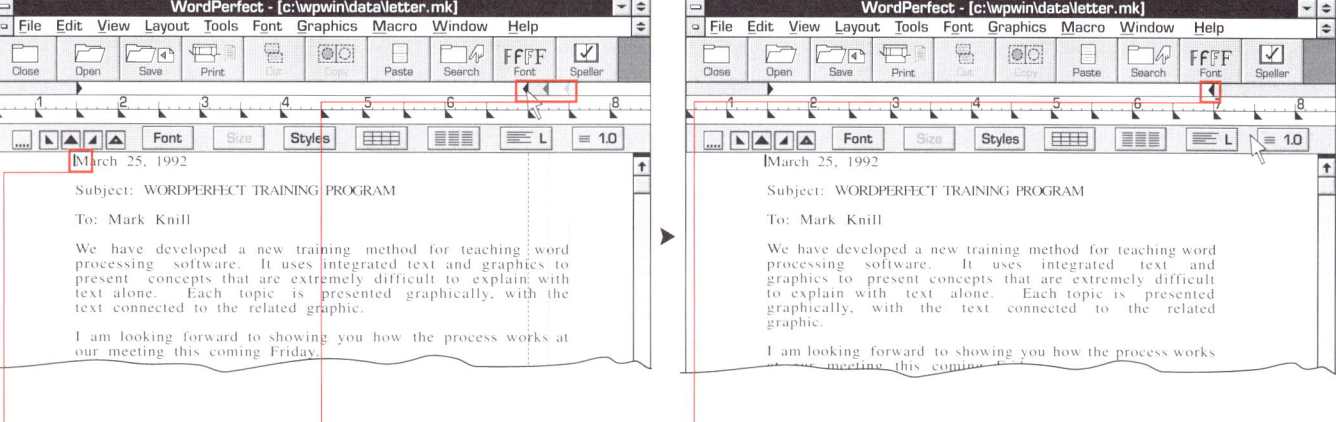

1 Position the insertion point where you want the new margin to begin.

2 Position the mouse over the **Right Margin** icon. Click and hold down the left mouse button.

3 Still holding down the button, drag the margin to a new position.

Note: The dotted line displays the current margin setting.

4 Release the button and the margin is changed.

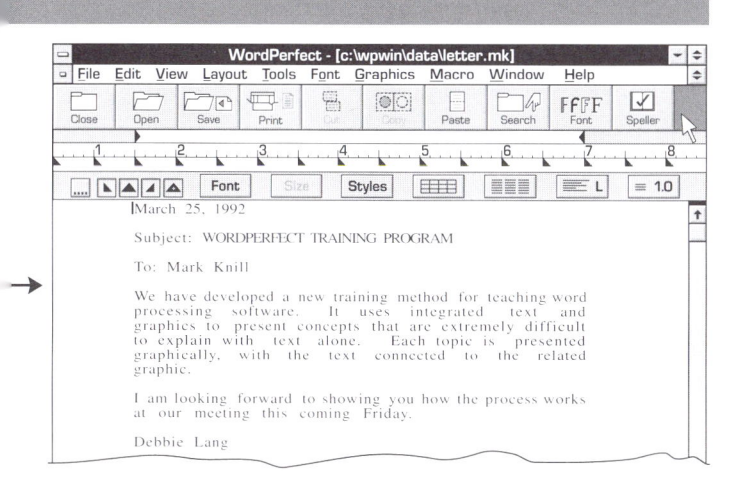

■ The margin is changed.

Note: The top and bottom margins are not displayed on the screen.

To view the new margin before printing the document, refer to page 68.

GETTING STARTED

THE BUTTON BAR

EDIT A DOCUMENT

SAVE FILES AND EXIT WORDPERFECT

VIEW DOCUMENTS

CHECK A DOCUMENT

FORMAT A DOCUMENT

TABLES

GRAPHICS

PRINT

MERGE AND SORT FILES

FILE MANAGER

HELP

◀ 45

SETTING TABS

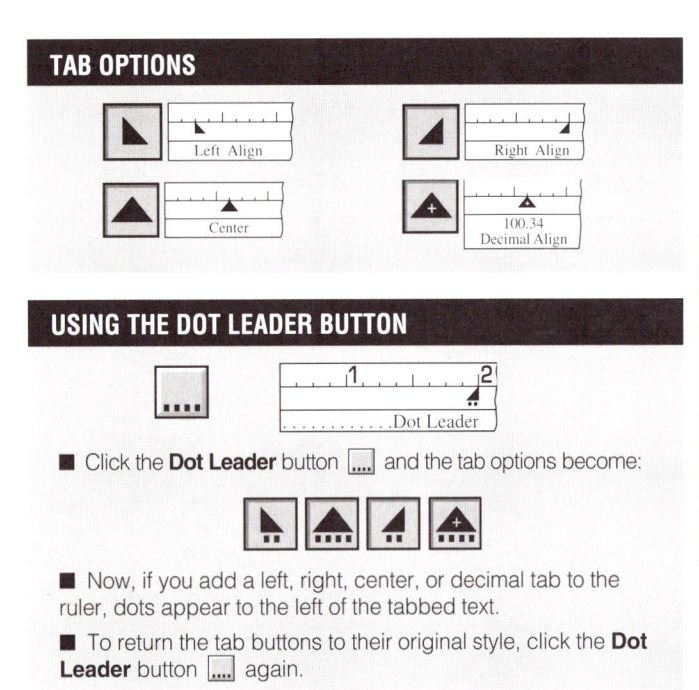

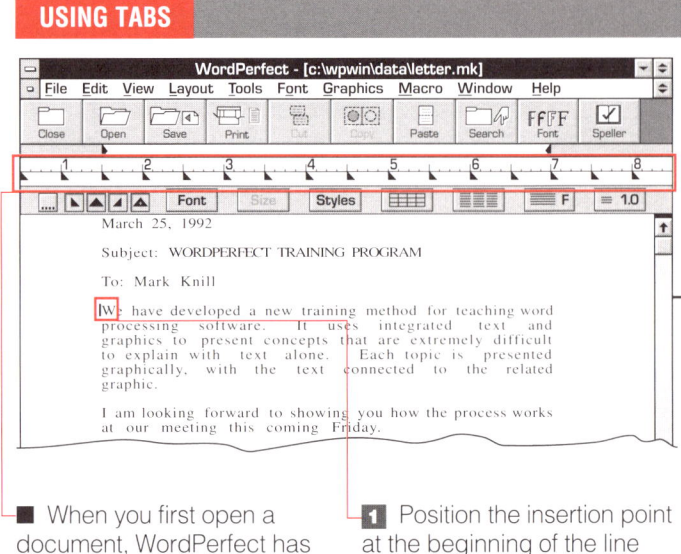

TAB OPTIONS

Left Align

Right Align

Center

100.34
Decimal Align

USING THE DOT LEADER BUTTON

................Dot Leader

■ Click the **Dot Leader** button [....] and the tab options become:

■ Now, if you add a left, right, center, or decimal tab to the ruler, dots appear to the left of the tabbed text.

■ To return the tab buttons to their original style, click the **Dot Leader** button [....] again.

USING TABS

■ When you first open a document, WordPerfect has a tab set at every half inch.

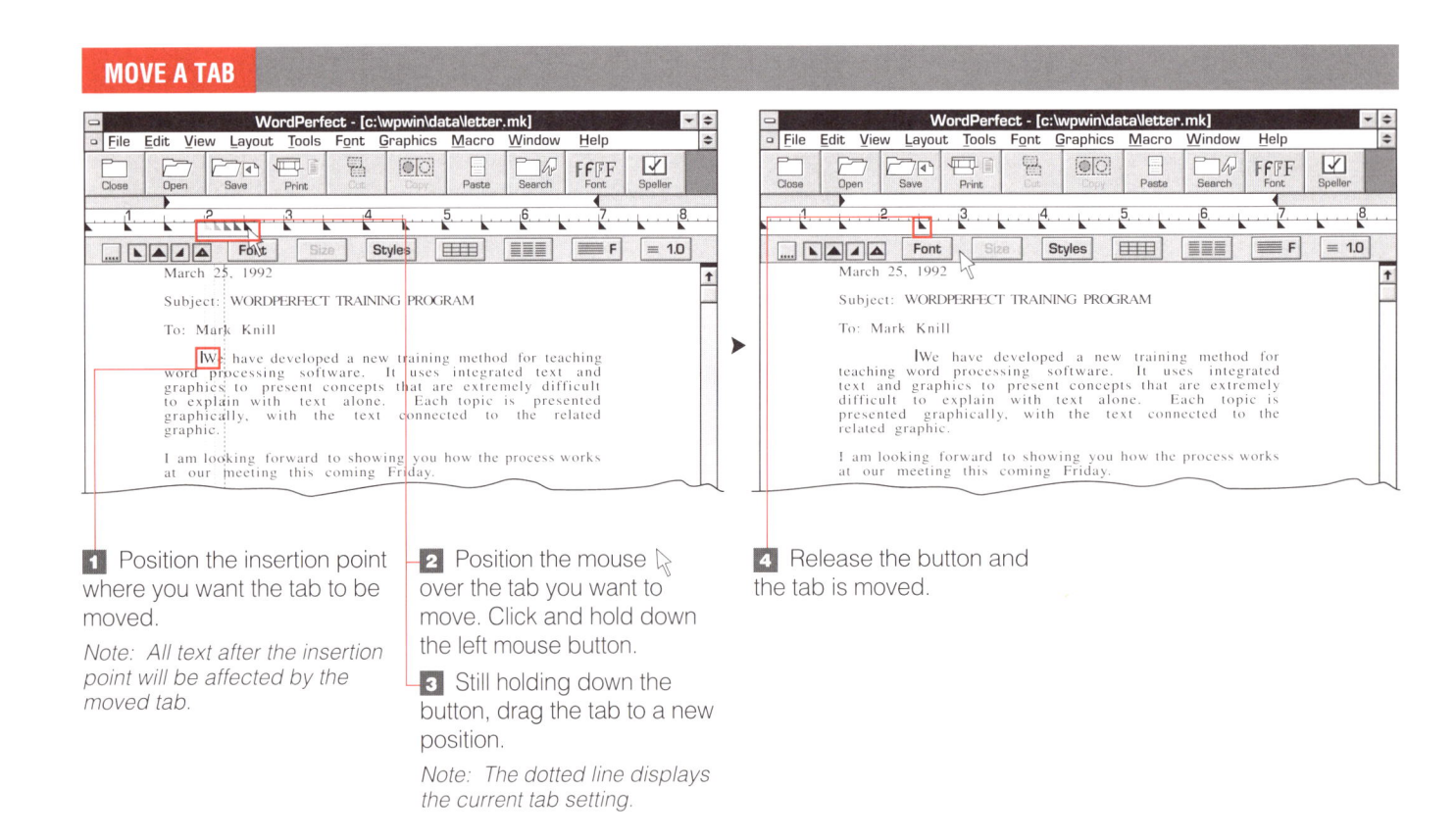

1 Position the insertion point at the beginning of the line you want to tab over.

MOVE A TAB

1 Position the insertion point where you want the tab to be moved.

Note: All text after the insertion point will be affected by the moved tab.

2 Position the mouse over the tab you want to move. Click and hold down the left mouse button.

3 Still holding down the button, drag the tab to a new position.

Note: The dotted line displays the current tab setting.

4 Release the button and the tab is moved.

46

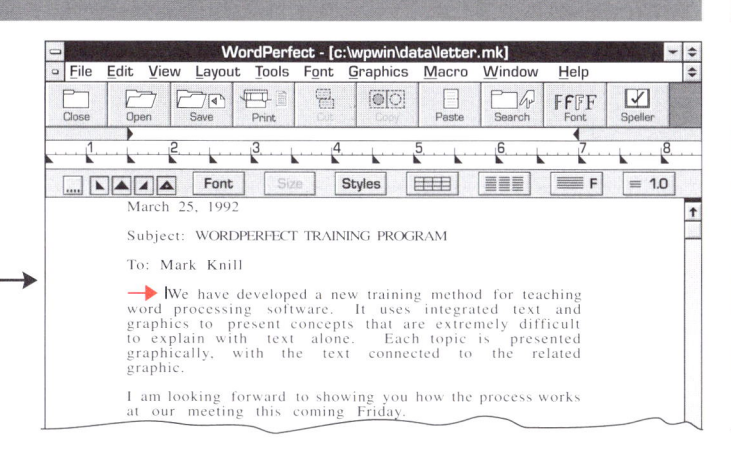

| VIEW THE RULER | ALIGN TEXT | CHANGE LINE SPACING | INDENT A PARAGRAPH | CHANGE MARGINS | **SETTING TABS** | CHANGE FONTS | PAGE BREAKS | CENTER TEXT ON A PAGE | AUTOMATIC PAGE NUMBERING | HEADERS AND FOOTERS | FOOTNOTES AND ENDNOTES |

REMOVE A TAB

2 Press **Tab** and the text is moved to the first tab stop.

*Note: Press **Backspace** to return to the left margin.*

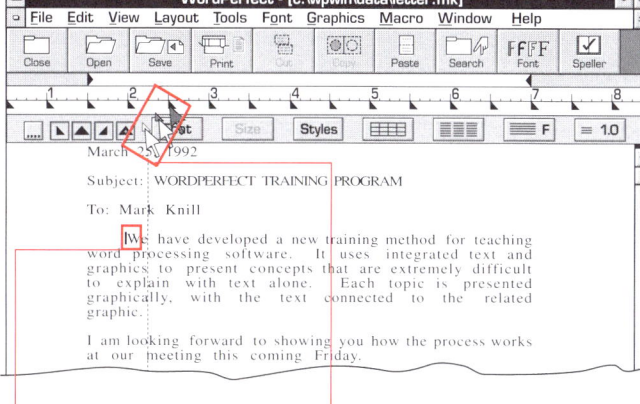

1 Position the insertion point where you want the tab to be removed.

Note: All text after the insertion point will be affected by the removed tab.

2 Position the mouse over the tab you want to remove from the ruler.

3 Click and hold down the left mouse button as you drag the tab off the ruler.

4 Release the button and the tab is removed.

ADD A TAB

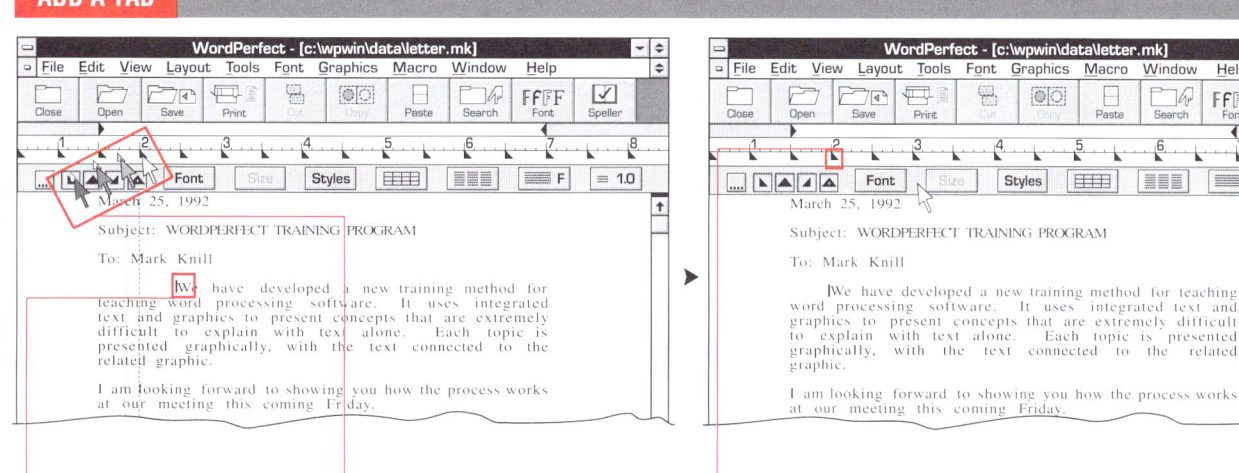

1 Position the insertion point where you want the new tab to begin.

Note: All text after the insertion point will be affected by the new tab.

2 Position the mouse over the desired tab icon. Click and hold down the left mouse button.

3 Still holding down the button, drag the tab to the desired position.

Note: The dotted line displays where the new tab will be placed.

4 Release the button and the tab is added to the ruler.

*Note: To hide the ruler, click **View**, then click **Ruler**.*

GETTING STARTED

THE BUTTON BAR

EDIT A DOCUMENT

SAVE FILES AND EXIT WORDPERFECT

VIEW DOCUMENTS

CHECK A DOCUMENT

FORMAT A DOCUMENT

TABLES

GRAPHICS

PRINT

MERGE AND SORT FILES

FILE MANAGER

HELP

◀ 47

CHANGE FONTS

CHANGE FONTS

A font specifies the design and size of displayed characters.

1 Select the text you want to change to a new font
or
Position the insertion point where you are about to type new text.

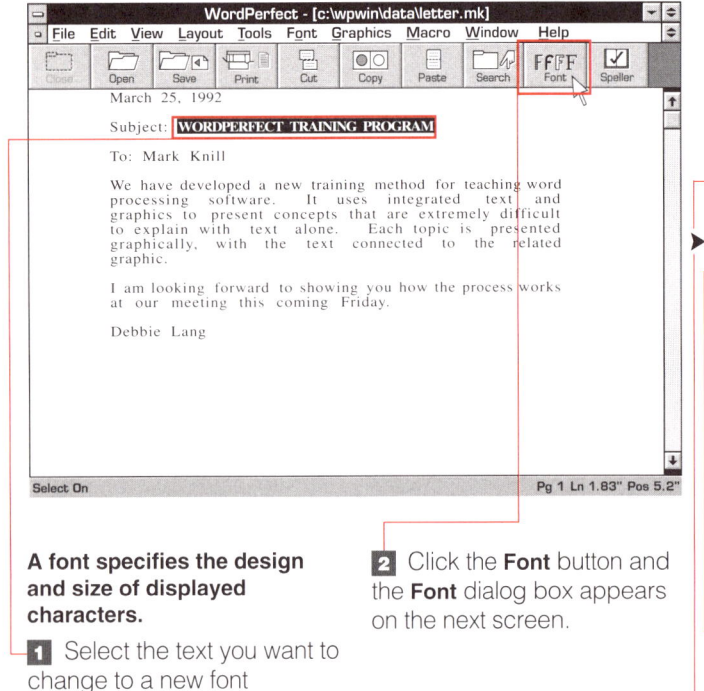

2 Click the **Font** button and the **Font** dialog box appears on the next screen.

■ The **Font:** box displays the font options.

3 Click the up or down scroll arrows to move through the font options.

4 Click the desired font name (example: **CG Times**).

5 If the font you selected is scalable, a list of available point sizes appear in the **Point Size:** list box. Click the desired point size (36 points is 1/2 of an inch).

■ A sample of the selected font and point size appears.

Note: The fonts listed in the **Font:** *list box depend on the printer and the printer driver selected. For more information, see your WordPerfect for Windows Reference guide.*

CHANGE RELATIVE FONT SIZE

■ Relative font sizes are a percentage of the current font size. For example, **Large** is 120 percent larger than the current font size.

1 In the **Font** dialog box, click the box beside the desired size option (example: **Large**) and ☐ becomes ☒.

Note: Depending on the printer and printer driver selected, the size you choose may not appear any different than the current font size.

For more information, see your WordPerfect for Windows Reference guide.

48

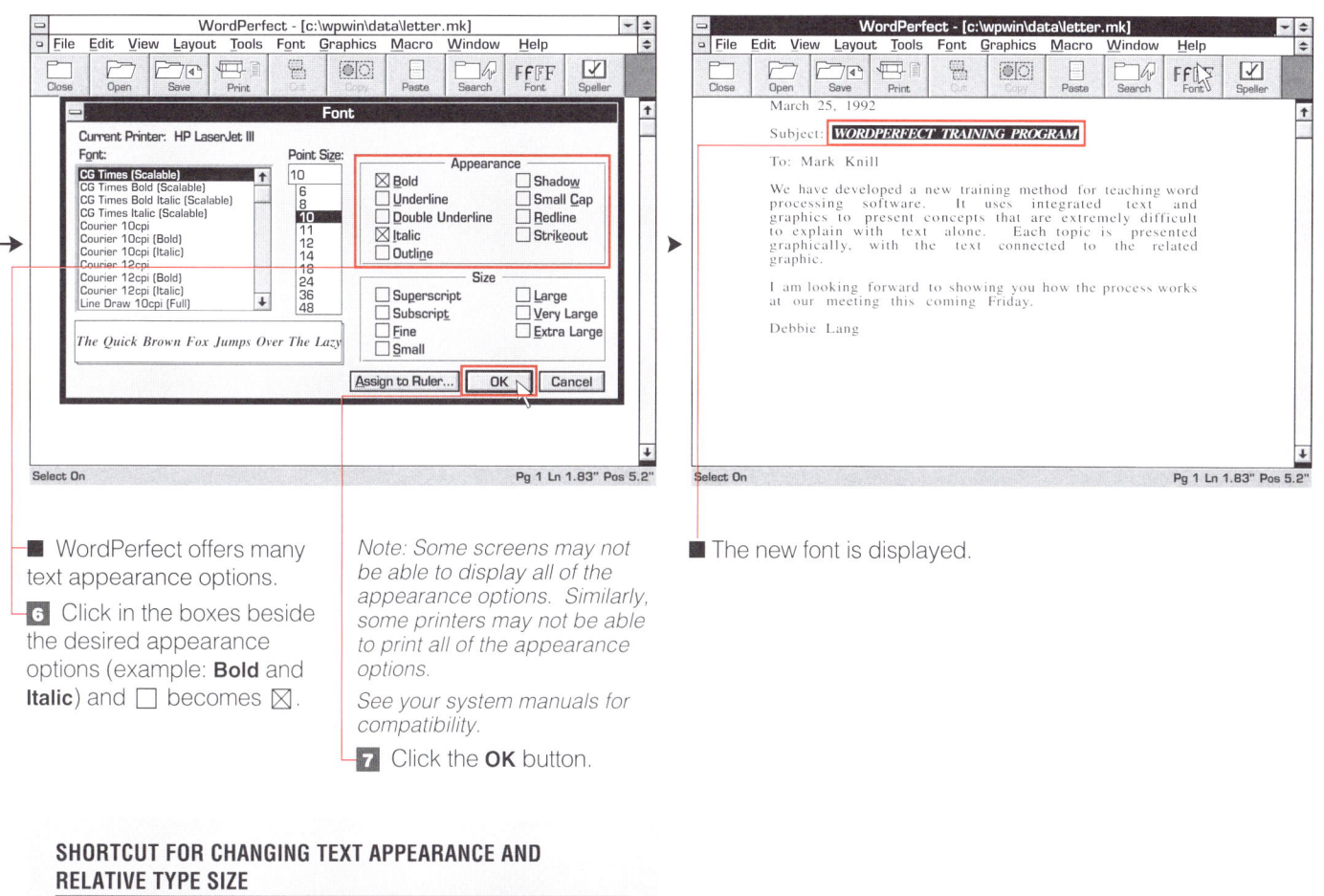

| VIEW THE RULER | ALIGN TEXT | CHANGE LINE SPACING | INDENT A PARAGRAPH | CHANGE MARGINS | SETTING TABS | **CHANGE FONTS** | PAGE BREAKS | CENTER TEXT ON A PAGE | AUTOMATIC PAGE NUMBERING | HEADERS AND FOOTERS | FOOTNOTES AND ENDNOTES |

- WordPerfect offers many text appearance options.

6 Click in the boxes beside the desired appearance options (example: **Bold** and **Italic**) and ☐ becomes ☒.

Note: Some screens may not be able to display all of the appearance options. Similarly, some printers may not be able to print all of the appearance options.

See your system manuals for compatibility.

7 Click the **OK** button.

- The new font is displayed.

SHORTCUT FOR CHANGING TEXT APPEARANCE AND RELATIVE TYPE SIZE

1 Select the text you want to change   **or**   Position the insertion point where you are about to type new text.

2 Click **Font**.

3 To change the text appearance, click one of the options in the **Font** menu.

4 To change the relative size of the text click **Subscript** or **Superscript** in the **Font** menu

or

Click **Size**, then click a **Size** option.

GETTING STARTED

THE BUTTON BAR

EDIT A DOCUMENT

SAVE FILES AND EXIT WORDPERFECT

VIEW DOCUMENTS

CHECK A DOCUMENT

FORMAT A DOCUMENT

TABLES

GRAPHICS

PRINT

MERGE AND SORT FILES

FILE MANAGER

HELP

◀ 49

PAGE BREAKS **CENTER TEXT ON A PAGE**

PAGE BREAKS

1 Position the insertion point where you want the page to end.

2 Click **Layout** to open its menu.

3 Click **Page**.

*Note: To position the insertion point below text, you may have to press **Enter** several times after the last sentence you typed.*

4 Click **Page Break**.

■ A double line appears which represents the end of the page.

5 To remove a page break, position the insertion point one line below the page break. Then press **Backspace**.

CENTER TEXT ON A PAGE

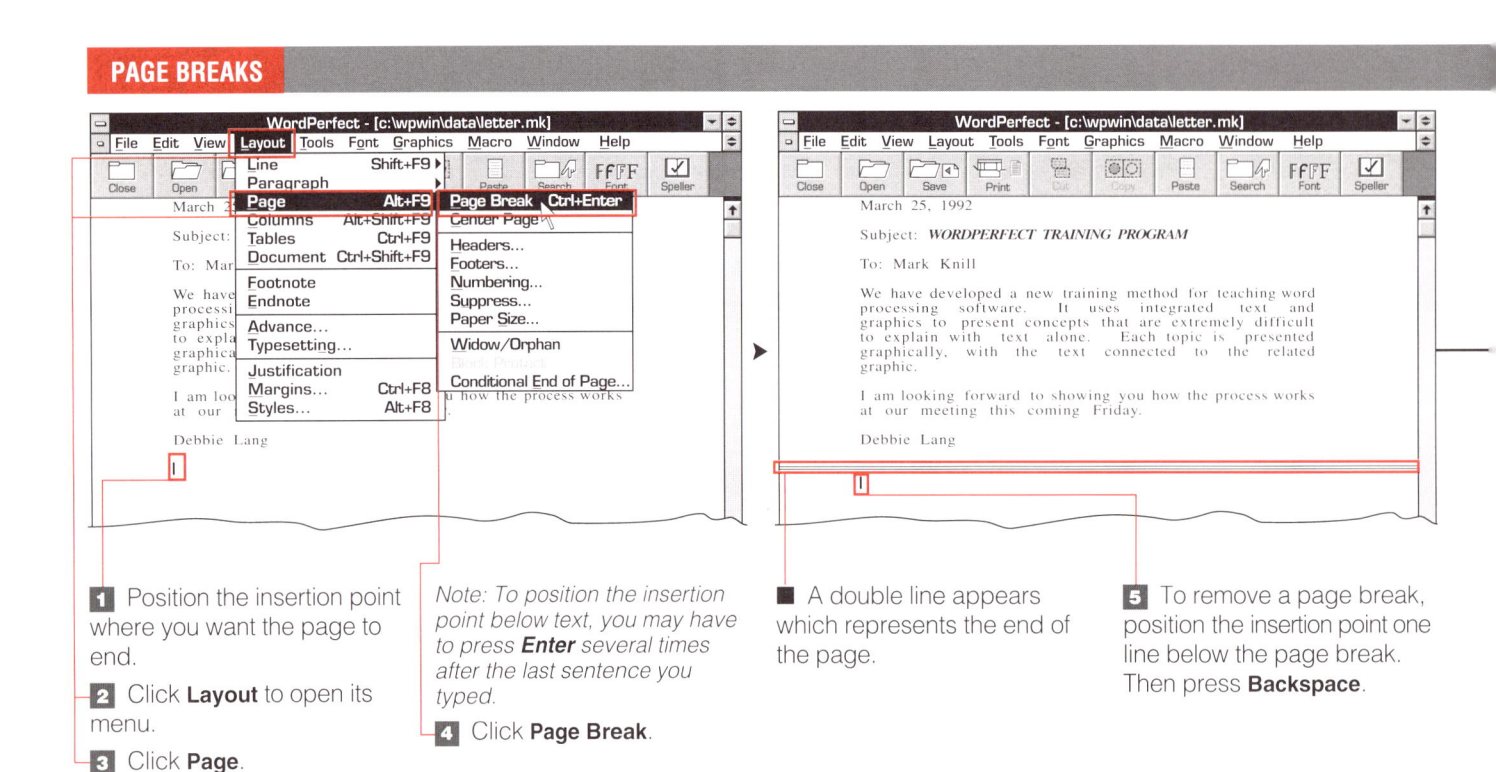

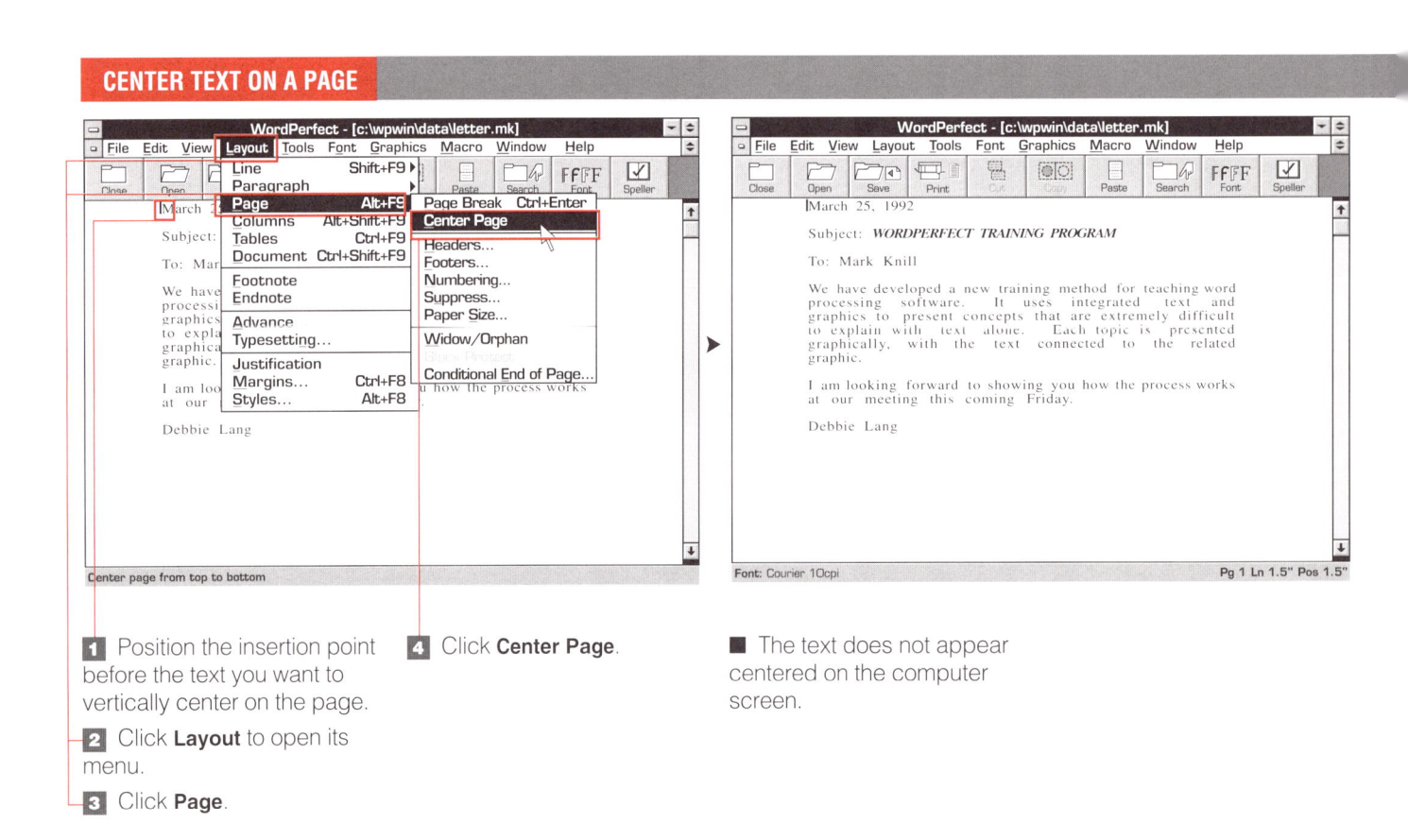

1 Position the insertion point before the text you want to vertically center on the page.

2 Click **Layout** to open its menu.

3 Click **Page**.

4 Click **Center Page**.

■ The text does not appear centered on the computer screen.

50

| VIEW THE RULER | ALIGN TEXT | CHANGE LINE SPACING | INDENT A PARAGRAPH | CHANGE MARGINS | SETTING TABS | CHANGE FONTS | **PAGE BREAKS** | **CENTER TEXT ON A PAGE** | AUTOMATIC PAGE NUMBERING | HEADERS AND FOOTERS | FOOTNOTES AND ENDNOTES |

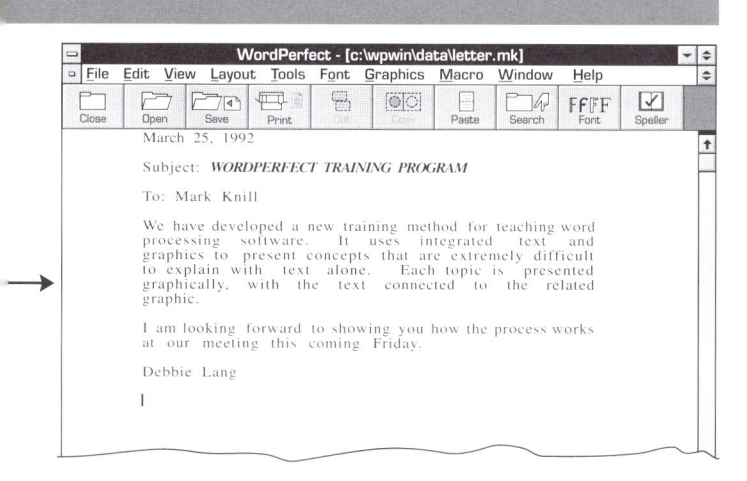

■ The page break is removed.

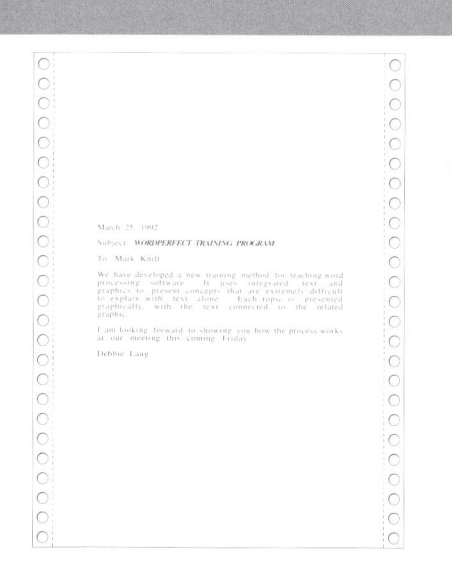

■ When printed, the text is vertically centered on the page.

Note: To preview a document before printing, refer to page 68.

TURN OFF CENTER PAGE

1 Position the insertion point before the text you want to remove the centering from.

2 Click **Layout** to open its menu. Then click **Page**.

3 A checkmark √ is displayed in front of the Center Page command indicating it is on.

√ Center Page

To turn off center page, click **Center Page**.

GETTING STARTED

THE BUTTON BAR

EDIT A DOCUMENT

SAVE FILES AND EXIT WORDPERFECT

VIEW DOCUMENTS

CHECK A DOCUMENT

FORMAT A DOCUMENT

TABLES

GRAPHICS

PRINT

MERGE AND SORT FILES

FILE MANAGER

HELP

◀ 51

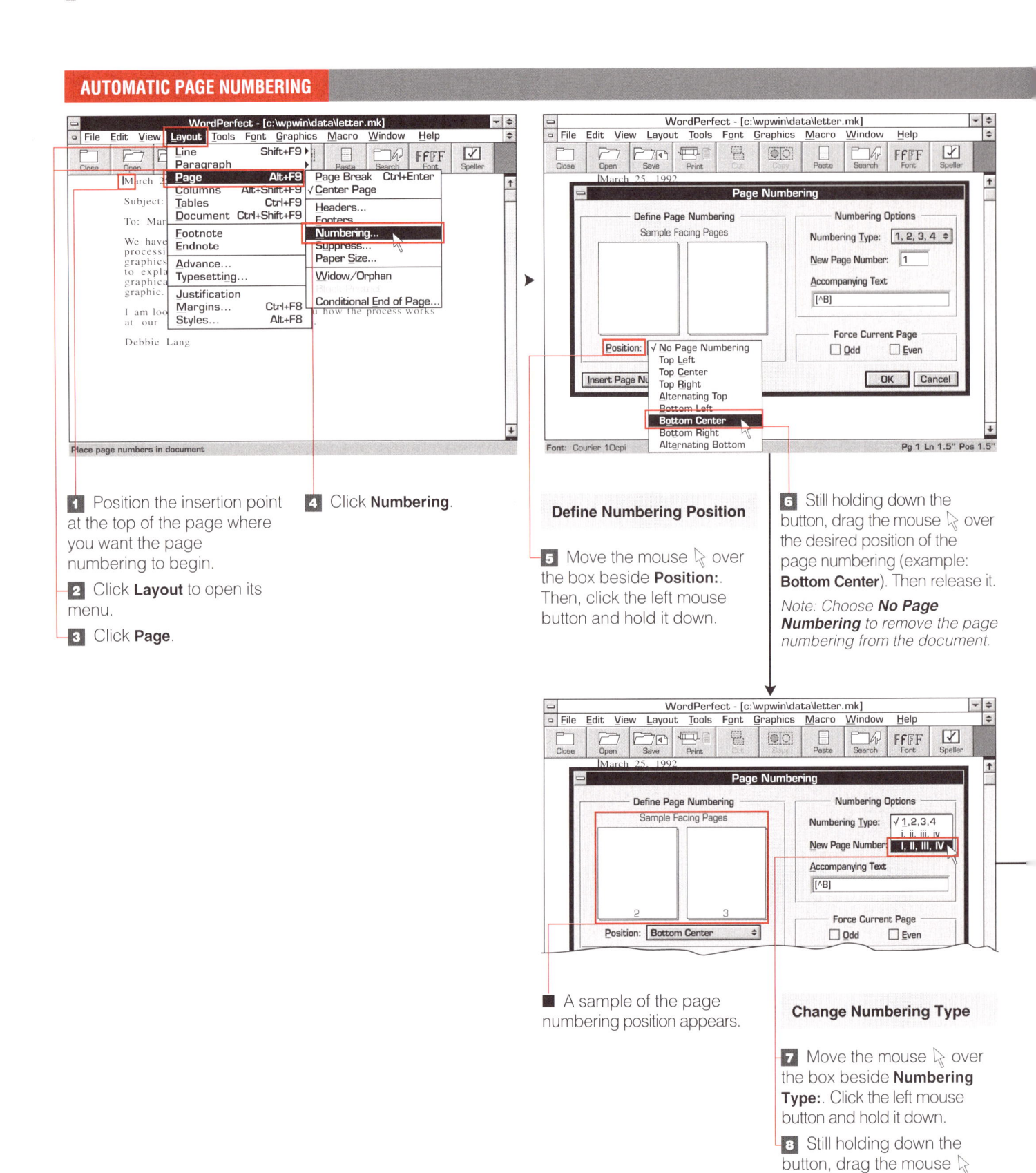

AUTOMATIC PAGE NUMBERING

AUTOMATIC PAGE NUMBERING

1 Position the insertion point at the top of the page where you want the page numbering to begin.

2 Click **Layout** to open its menu.

3 Click **Page**.

4 Click **Numbering**.

Define Numbering Position

5 Move the mouse over the box beside **Position:**. Then, click the left mouse button and hold it down.

6 Still holding down the button, drag the mouse over the desired position of the page numbering (example: **Bottom Center**). Then release it.

*Note: Choose **No Page Numbering** to remove the page numbering from the document.*

■ A sample of the page numbering position appears.

Change Numbering Type

7 Move the mouse over the box beside **Numbering Type:**. Click the left mouse button and hold it down.

8 Still holding down the button, drag the mouse over the desired number type (example: **I, II, III, IV**). Then release the button.

52

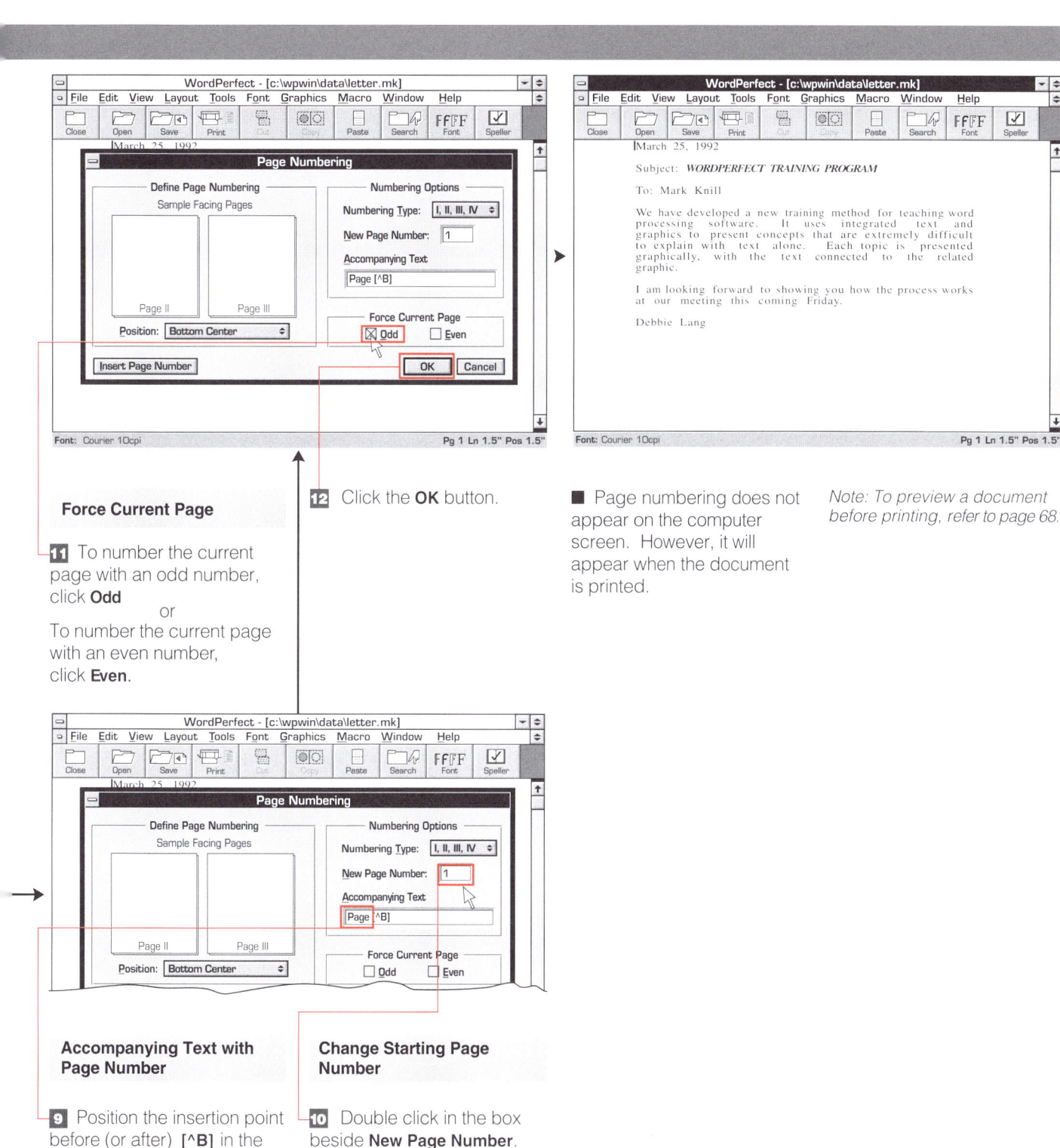

| VIEW THE RULER | ALIGN TEXT | CHANGE LINE SPACING | INDENT A PARAGRAPH | CHANGE MARGINS | SETTING TABS | CHANGE FONTS | PAGE BREAKS | CENTER TEXT ON A PAGE | **AUTOMATIC PAGE NUMBERING** | HEADERS AND FOOTERS | FOOTNOTES AND ENDNOTES |

Force Current Page

11 To number the current page with an odd number, click **Odd**
or
To number the current page with an even number, click **Even**.

12 Click the **OK** button.

■ Page numbering does not appear on the computer screen. However, it will appear when the document is printed.

Note: To preview a document before printing, refer to page 68.

Accompanying Text with Page Number

9 Position the insertion point before (or after) **[^B]** in the box under **Accompanying Text:**. Then type the text (example: **Page**).

*Note: [^B] represents the page number. For example, on page two the page will display **Page 2**.*

Change Starting Page Number

10 Double click in the box beside **New Page Number**. Then type the number you want the page number sequence to begin with (example: **1**).

53

HEADERS AND FOOTERS

HEADERS AND FOOTERS

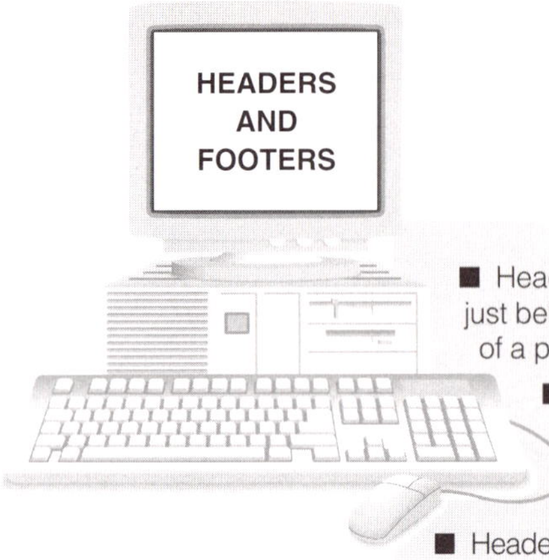

- Headers are printed just below the top margin of a page.
- Footers are printed just above the bottom margin of a page.
- Headers and footers do not appear on the computer screen. However, they are displayed when the document is printed.

Note: To preview a document before printing, see page 68.

CREATE A HEADER OR FOOTER

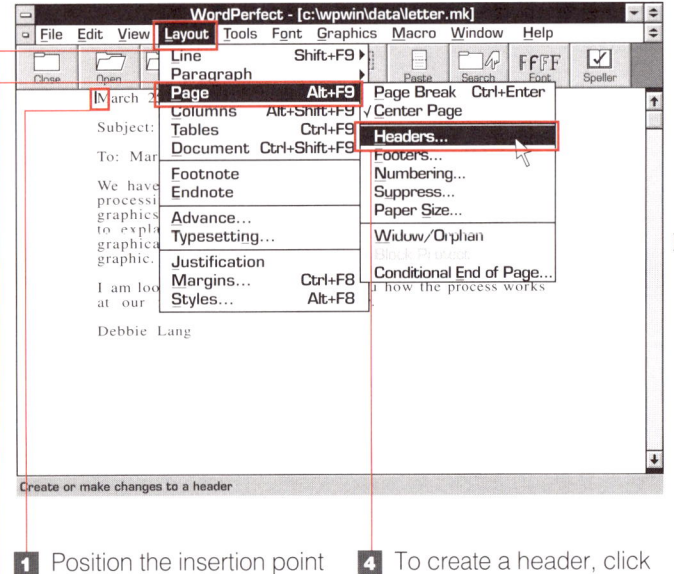

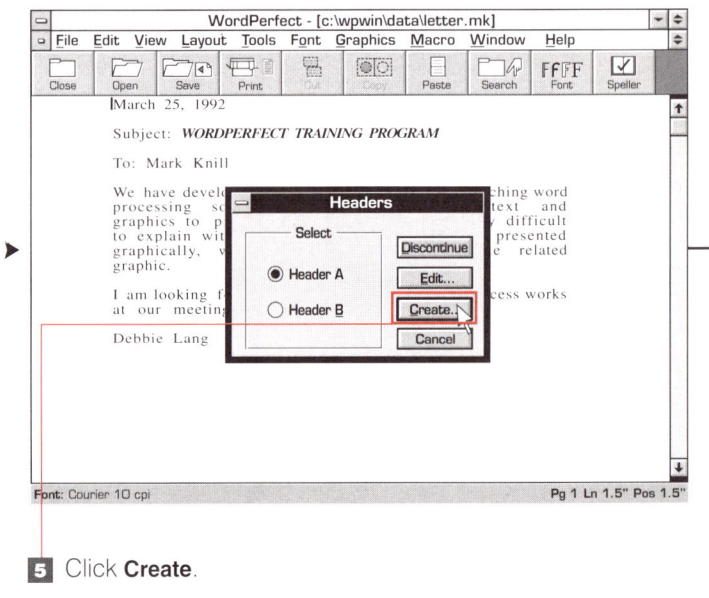

1 Position the insertion point at the top of the page where you want the header or footer to begin.

2 Click **Layout**.

3 Click **Page**.

4 To create a header, click **Headers**

or

To create a footer, click **Footers**.

5 Click **Create**.

54

| VIEW THE RULER | ALIGN TEXT | CHANGE LINE SPACING | INDENT A PARAGRAPH | CHANGE MARGINS | SETTING TABS | CHANGE FONTS | PAGE BREAKS | CENTER TEXT ON A PAGE | AUTOMATIC PAGE NUMBERING | **HEADERS AND FOOTERS** | FOOTNOTES AND ENDNOTES |

Header

Footer

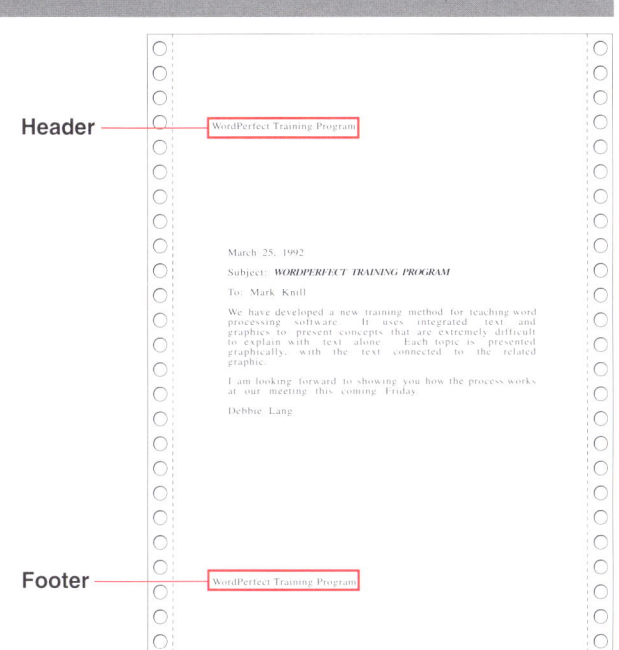

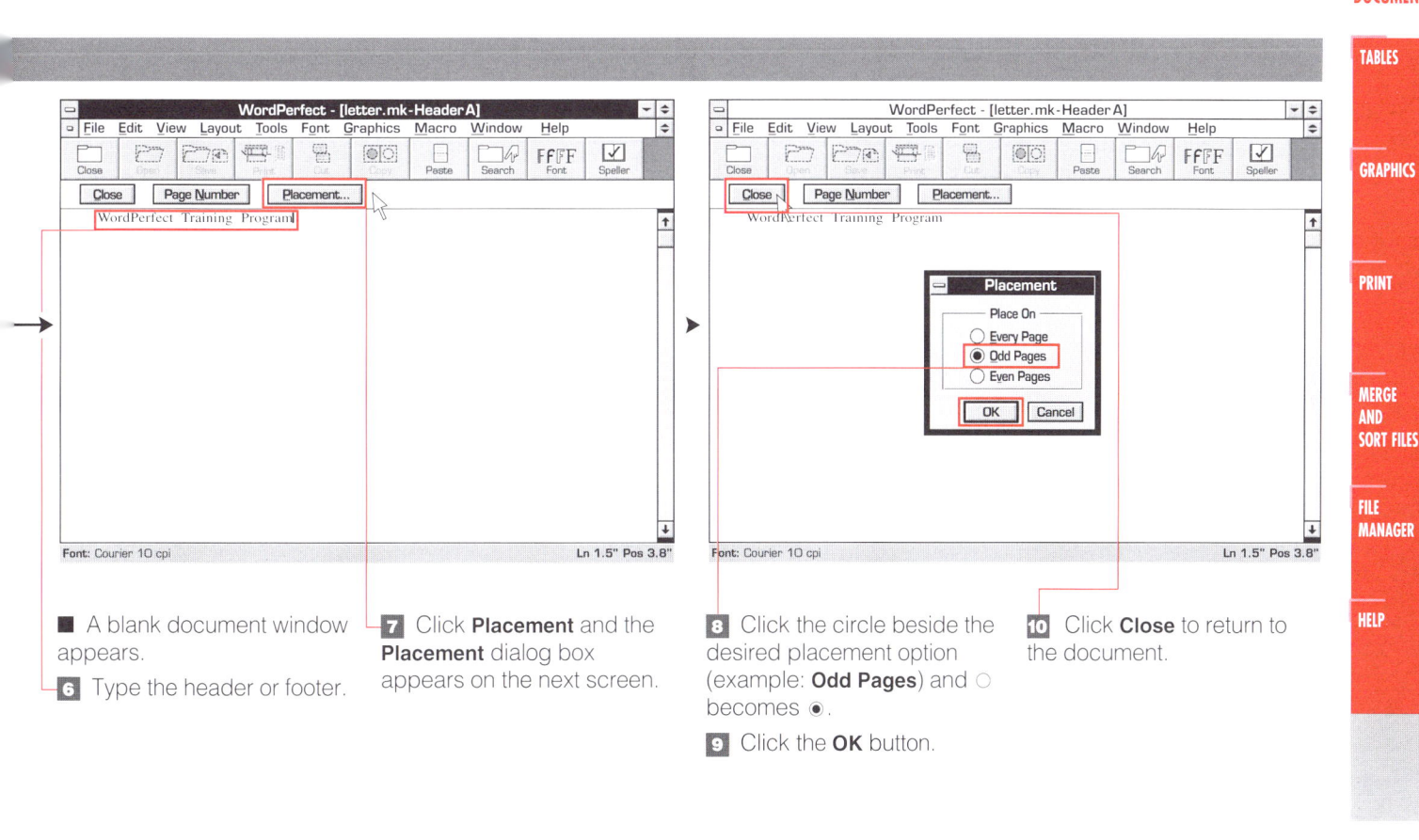

- A blank document window appears.

6 Type the header or footer.

7 Click **Placement** and the **Placement** dialog box appears on the next screen.

8 Click the circle beside the desired placement option (example: **Odd Pages**) and ○ becomes ●.

9 Click the **OK** button.

10 Click **Close** to return to the document.

GETTING STARTED

THE BUTTON BAR

EDIT A DOCUMENT

SAVE FILES AND EXIT WORDPERFECT

VIEW DOCUMENTS

CHECK A DOCUMENT

FORMAT A DOCUMENT

TABLES

GRAPHICS

PRINT

MERGE AND SORT FILES

FILE MANAGER

HELP

◀ 55

FOOTNOTES AND ENDNOTES

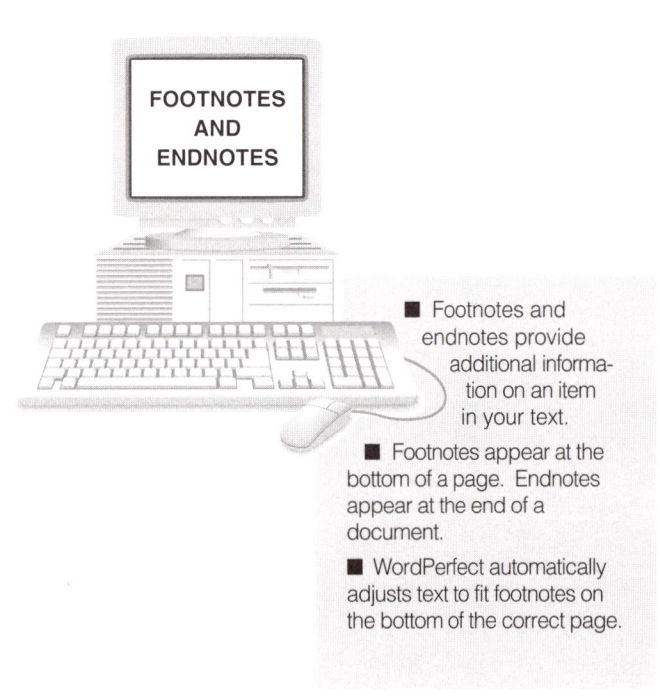

- Footnotes and endnotes provide additional information on an item in your text.

- Footnotes appear at the bottom of a page. Endnotes appear at the end of a document.

- WordPerfect automatically adjusts text to fit footnotes on the bottom of the correct page.

CREATE A FOOTNOTE OR ENDNOTE

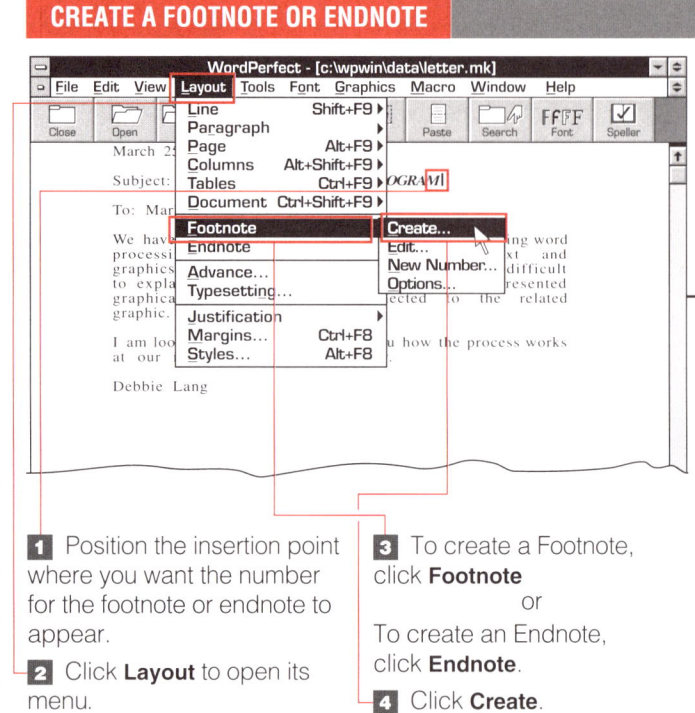

1 Position the insertion point where you want the number for the footnote or endnote to appear.

2 Click **Layout** to open its menu.

3 To create a Footnote, click **Footnote**
or
To create an Endnote, click **Endnote**.

4 Click **Create**.

EDIT A FOOTNOTE OR ENDNOTE

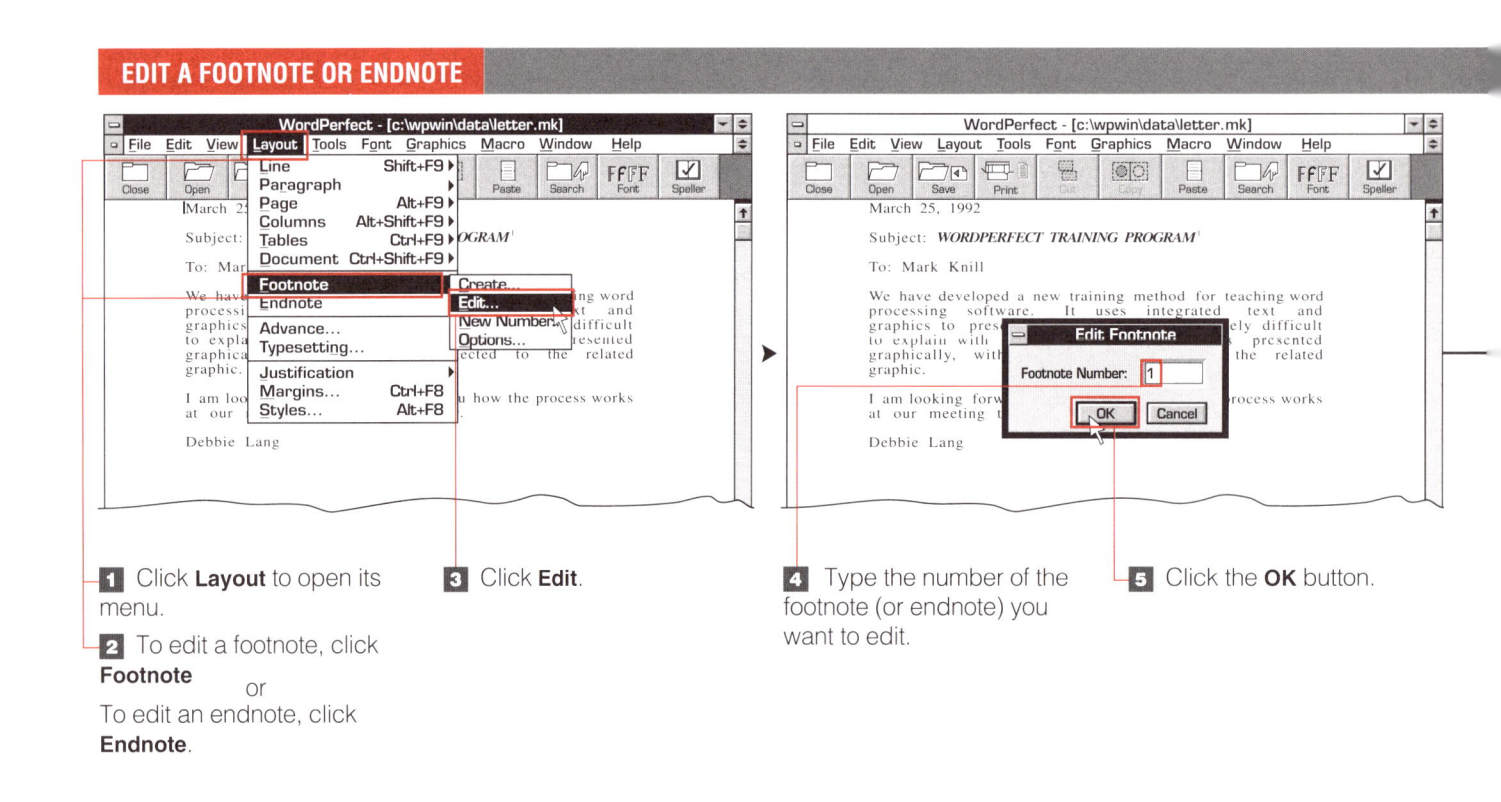

1 Click **Layout** to open its menu.

2 To edit a footnote, click **Footnote**
or
To edit an endnote, click **Endnote**.

3 Click **Edit**.

4 Type the number of the footnote (or endnote) you want to edit.

5 Click the **OK** button.

56

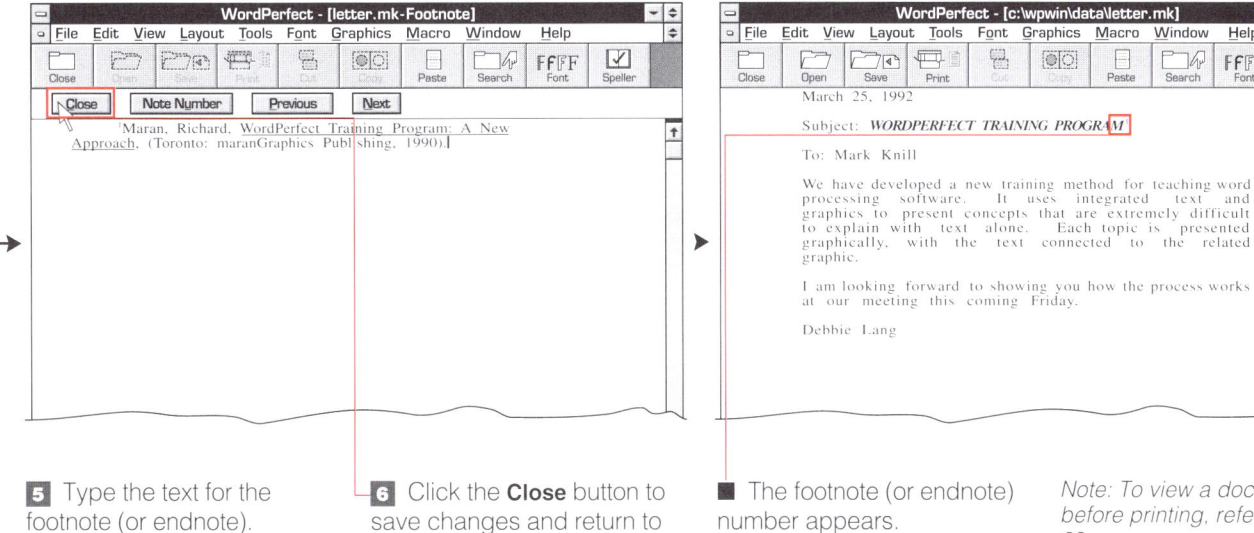

| VIEW THE RULER | ALIGN TEXT | CHANGE LINE SPACING | INDENT A PARAGRAPH | CHANGE MARGINS | SETTING TABS | CHANGE FONTS | PAGE BREAKS | CENTER TEXT ON A PAGE | AUTOMATIC PAGE NUMBERING | HEADERS AND FOOTERS | **FOOTNOTES AND ENDNOTES** |

5 Type the text for the footnote (or endnote).

Note: Format your footnote (or endnote) using the same skills you learned when formatting a document.

6 Click the **Close** button to save changes and return to the document.

■ The footnote (or endnote) number appears.

Note: Footnotes and endnotes do not appear on the computer screen. However, they do appear when the document is printed.

Note: To view a document before printing, refer to page 68.

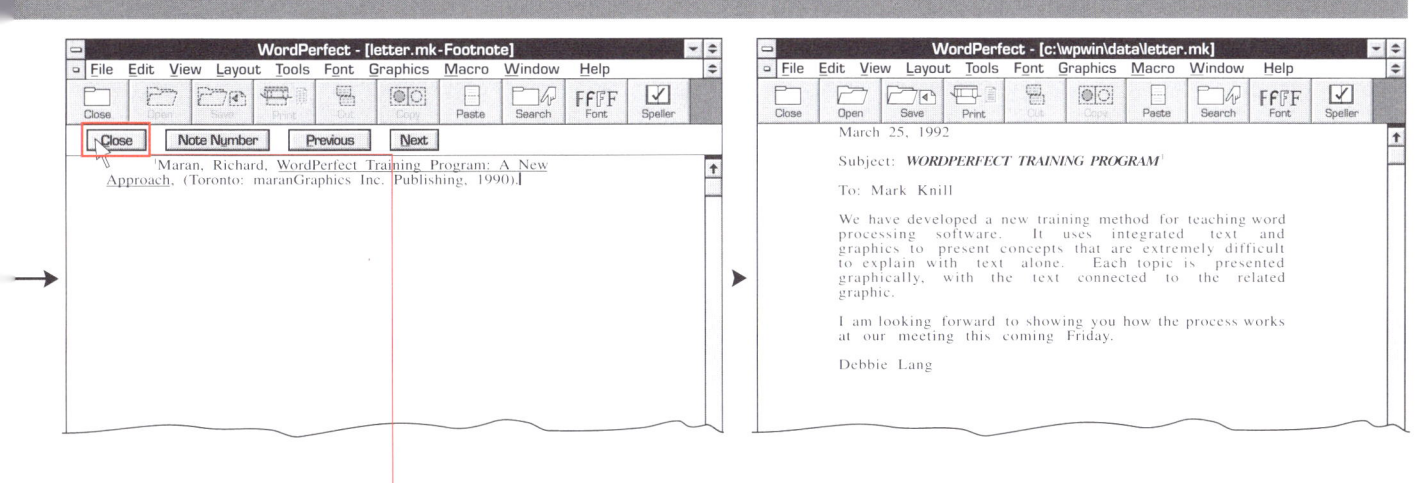

6 Edit the footnote (or endnote) using the same skills you learned when editing a document.

*Note: To view the next note, click **Next**.*

*To view the previous note, click **Previous**.*

If you insert a footnote (or endnote) between existing ones, WordPerfect automatically changes the numbering scheme.

7 Click the **Close** button.

■ Changes to the footnote (or endnote) information do not appear on the computer screen. However, they do appear when the document is printed.

Note: To view a document before printing, refer to page 68.

GETTING STARTED

THE BUTTON BAR

EDIT A DOCUMENT

SAVE FILES AND EXIT WORDPERFECT

VIEW DOCUMENTS

CHECK A DOCUMENT

FORMAT A DOCUMENT

TABLES

GRAPHICS

PRINT

MERGE AND SORT FILES

FILE MANAGER

HELP

◀ 57

CREATE A TABLE | **SELECT CELLS** | **JOIN CELLS**

CREATE A TABLE

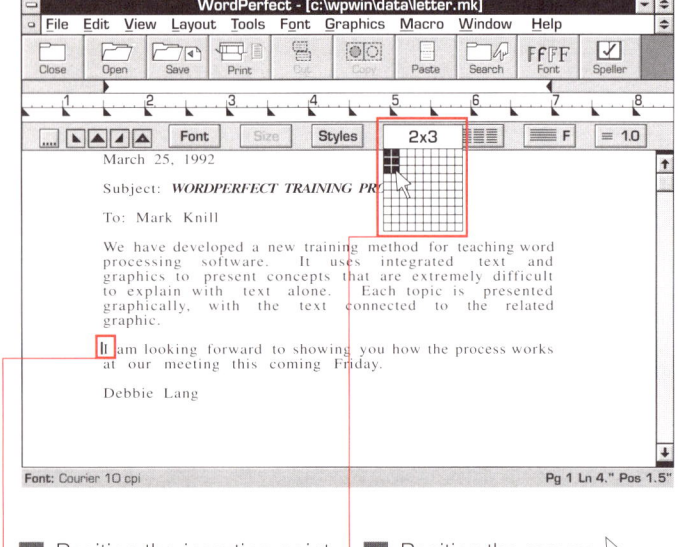

1 Position the insertion point where you want the table to appear.

*Note: To view the ruler, click **View**. Then click **Ruler**.*

2 Position the mouse over the Tables button. Click and hold down the left mouse button.

3 Still holding down the button, drag the mouse over the desired table size (example: **2x3**).

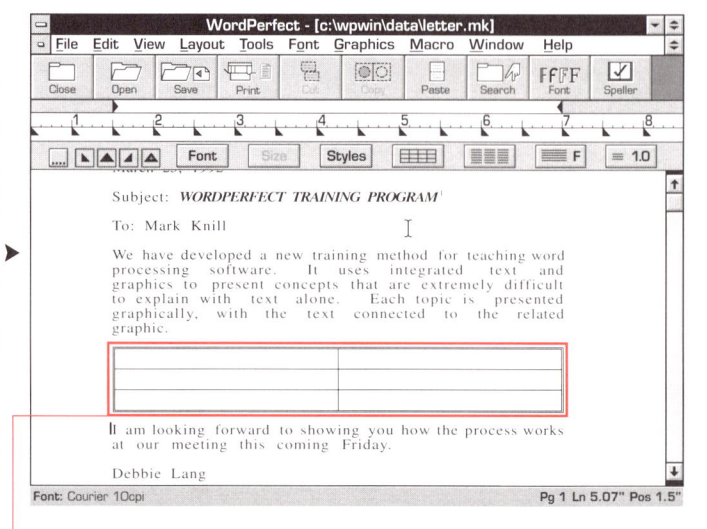

4 Release the button and the table is created.

*Note: To leave one blank line between the table and the paragraph below it, position the insertion point at the beginning of the paragraph, then press **Enter**.*

JOIN CELLS

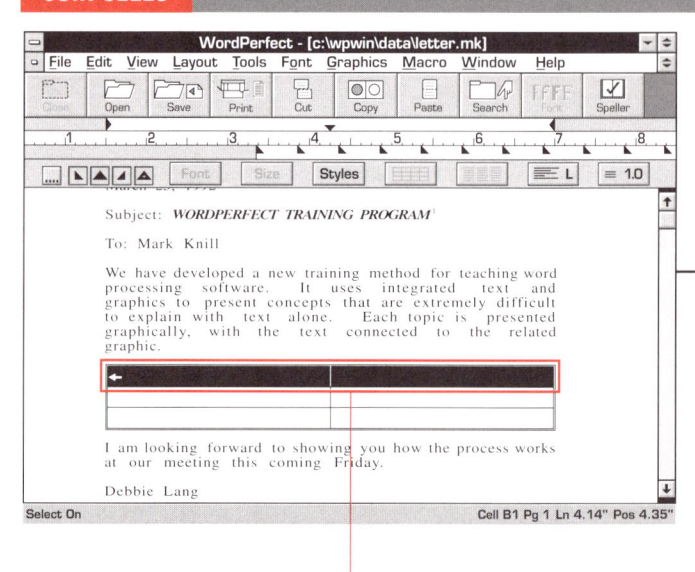

Two or more cells in a table can be combined to make one large cell.

1 Select the cells you want to join together.

CREATE A TABLE | SELECT CELLS | JOIN CELLS | ENTER TEXT IN A TABLE | RESIZE COLUMNS | INSERT A ROW OR COLUMN | DELETE A ROW OR COLUMN

SELECT CELLS

To select a cell
1. Move the I beam to the left edge of a cell and it becomes ⇐.
2. Click the mouse once.

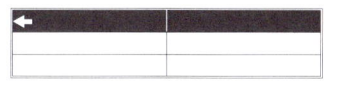

To select a row
1. Move the I beam to the left edge of a cell and it becomes ⇐.
2. Click the mouse twice.

To select a column
1. Move the I beam to the top edge of a cell and it becomes ⇑.
2. Click the mouse twice.

To select the entire table
1. Move the I beam to the left edge of a cell and it becomes ⇐.
2. Click the mouse three times.

To deselect cells:
Click anywhere outside the table.

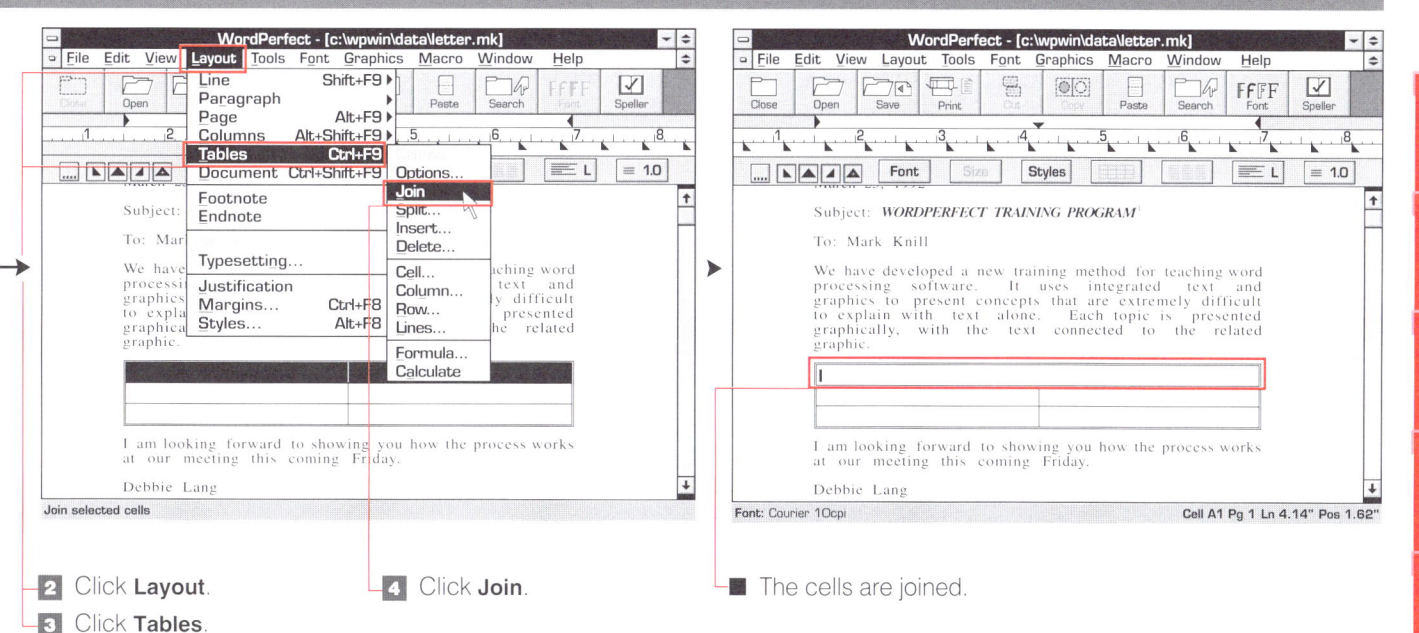

2. Click **Layout**.
3. Click **Tables**.

4. Click **Join**.

■ The cells are joined.

GETTING STARTED

THE BUTTON BAR

EDIT A DOCUMENT

SAVE FILES AND EXIT WORDPERFECT

VIEW DOCUMENTS

CHECK A DOCUMENT

FORMAT A DOCUMENT

TABLES

GRAPHICS

PRINT

MERGE AND SORT FILES

FILE MANAGER

HELP

◀ 59

ENTER TEXT IN A TABLE / RESIZE COLUMNS

ENTER TEXT IN A TABLE

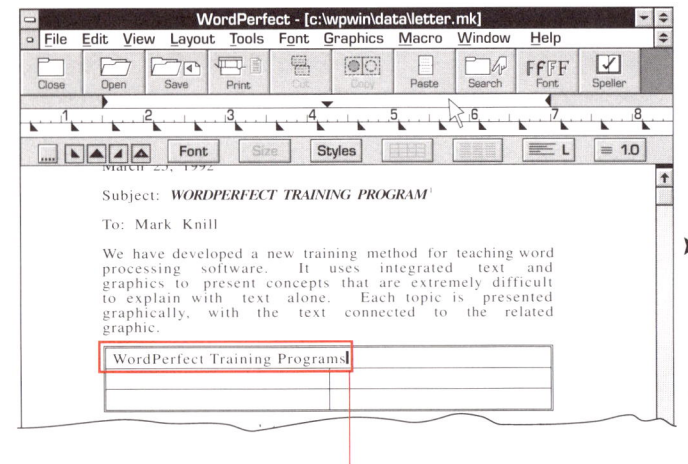

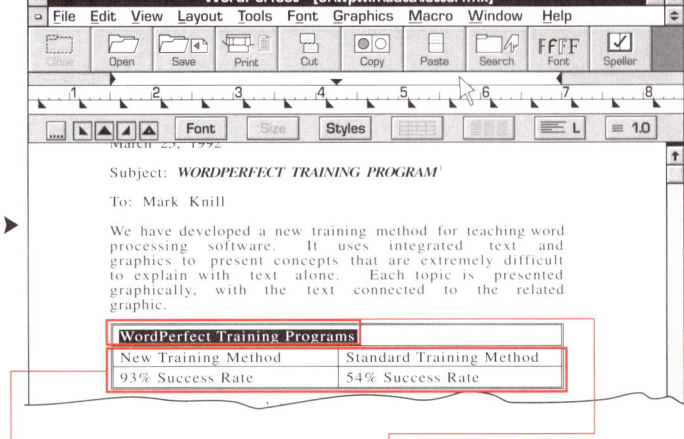

When entering, editing and formatting text in a table, use the same methods that you learned when entering text in a document.

1 Click in the first cell you want to enter text into.

2 Type the text.

3 Click in the next cell you want to enter text into.

4 Type the text.

5 Type the remaining text.

*Note: Do not press **Enter** after typing text in a table. This will increase the row height. To immediately undo this action, press **Backspace**.*

6 To format text in a table select the text you want to format.

Note: For more information on selecting text, refer to page 6.

RESIZE COLUMNS

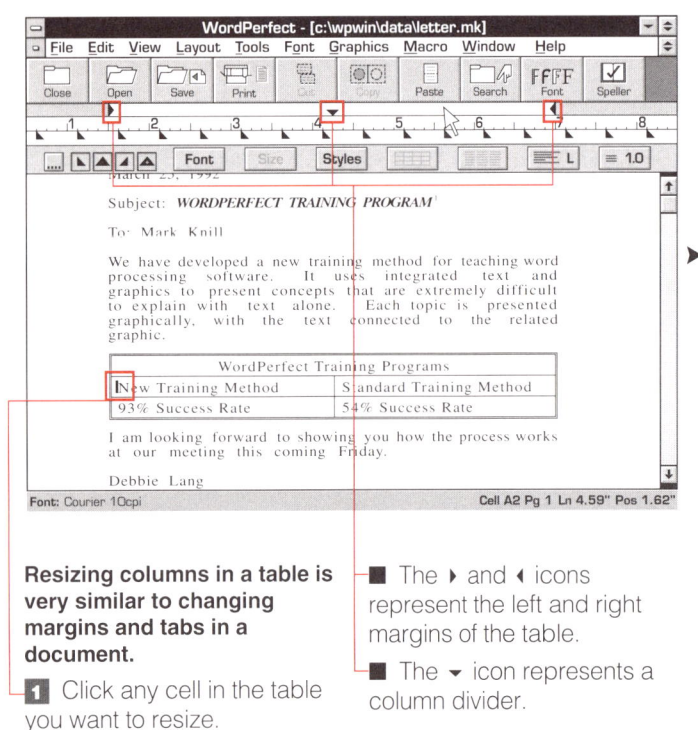

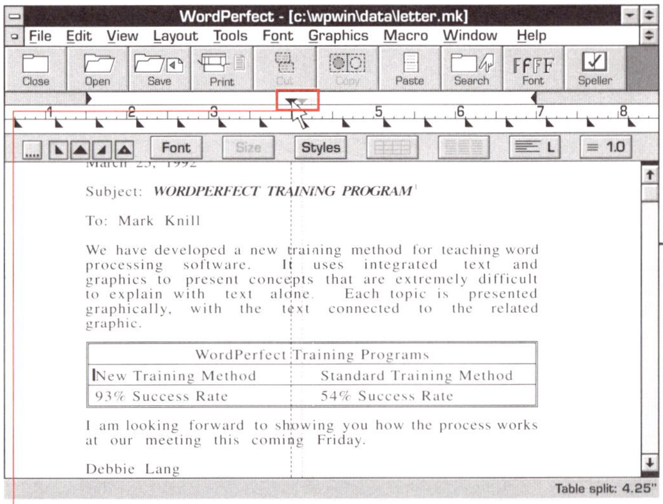

Resizing columns in a table is very similar to changing margins and tabs in a document.

1 Click any cell in the table you want to resize.

- The ▶ and ◀ icons represent the left and right margins of the table.

- The ▼ icon represents a column divider.

2 Position the mouse over the table column width icon (▶ or ▼ or ◀) you want to change. Click and hold down the left mouse button.

Note: A dotted line appears which displays the current column width setting.

3 Still holding down the button, drag the icon to a new position.

60

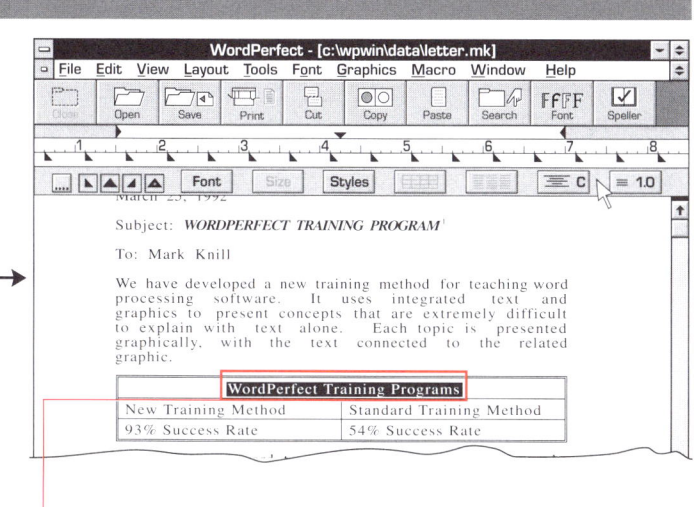

| CREATE A TABLE | SELECT CELLS | JOIN CELLS | **ENTER TEXT IN A TABLE** | **RESIZE COLUMNS** | INSERT A ROW OR COLUMN | DELETE A ROW OR COLUMN |

MOVE ONE CELL IN ANY DIRECTION

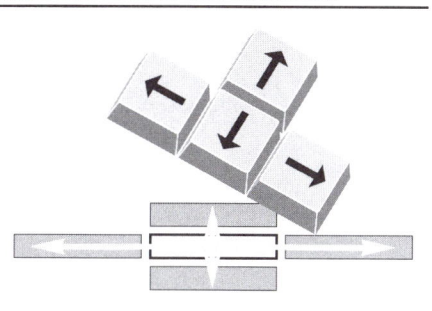

Press ↑ to move one cell up.
Press ← to move one cell left.
Press ↓ to move one cell down.
Press → to move one cell right.

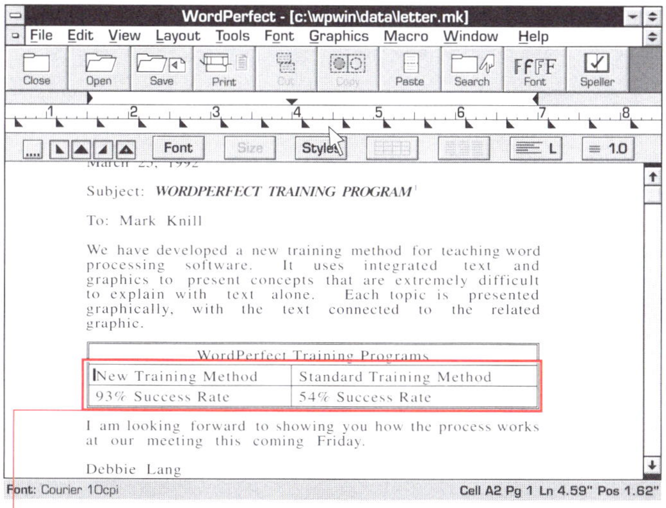

7 Format the text (example: center).

Note: For more information on formatting text, refer to page 40 and 48.

4 Release the button and the columns are resized.

Note: To hide the ruler, click **View**. *Then click* **Ruler**.

GETTING STARTED

THE BUTTON BAR

EDIT A DOCUMENT

SAVE FILES AND EXIT WORDPERFECT

VIEW DOCUMENTS

CHECK A DOCUMENT

FORMAT A DOCUMENT

TABLES

GRAPHICS

PRINT

MERGE AND SORT FILES

FILE MANAGER

HELP

◀ 61

INSERT A ROW OR COLUMN / DELETE A ROW OR COLUMN

INSERT A ROW OR COLUMN

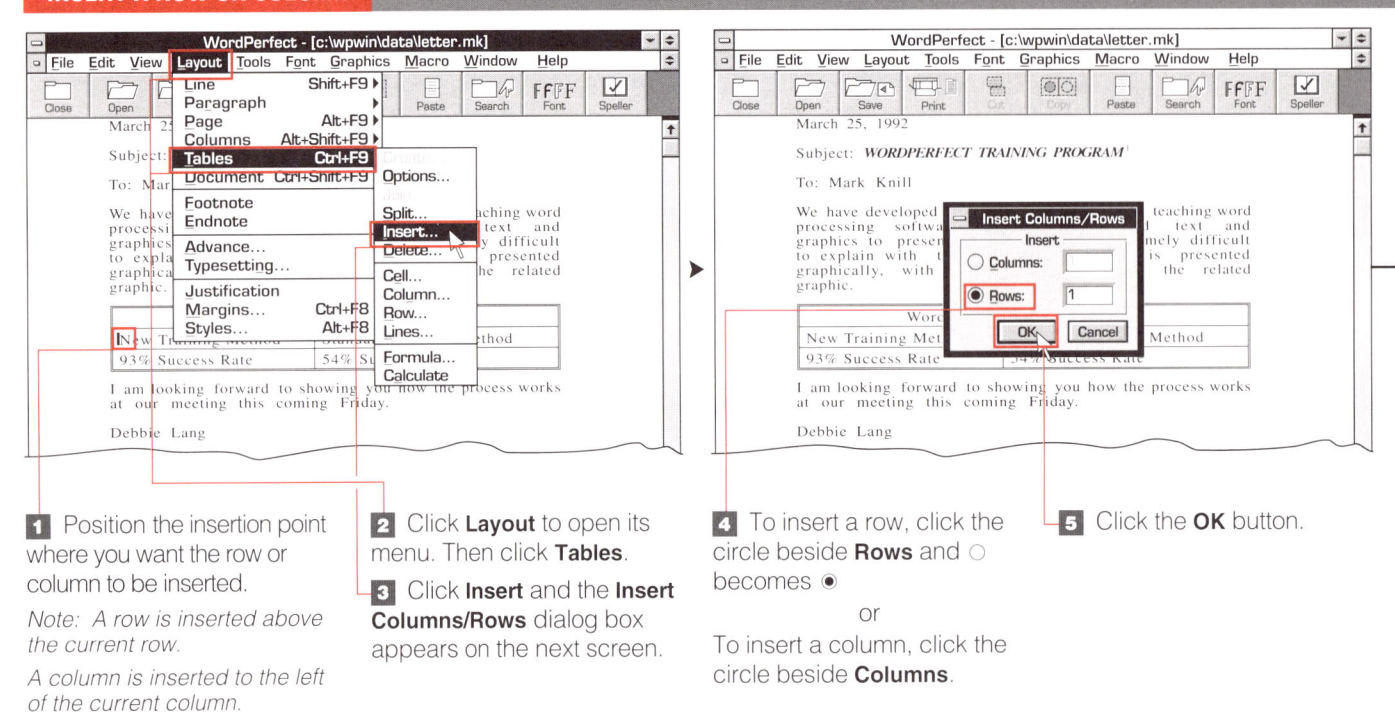

1 Position the insertion point where you want the row or column to be inserted.

Note: A row is inserted above the current row.

A column is inserted to the left of the current column.

2 Click **Layout** to open its menu. Then click **Tables**.

3 Click **Insert** and the **Insert Columns/Rows** dialog box appears on the next screen.

4 To insert a row, click the circle beside **Rows** and ○ becomes ●

or

To insert a column, click the circle beside **Columns**.

5 Click the **OK** button.

DELETE A ROW OR COLUMN

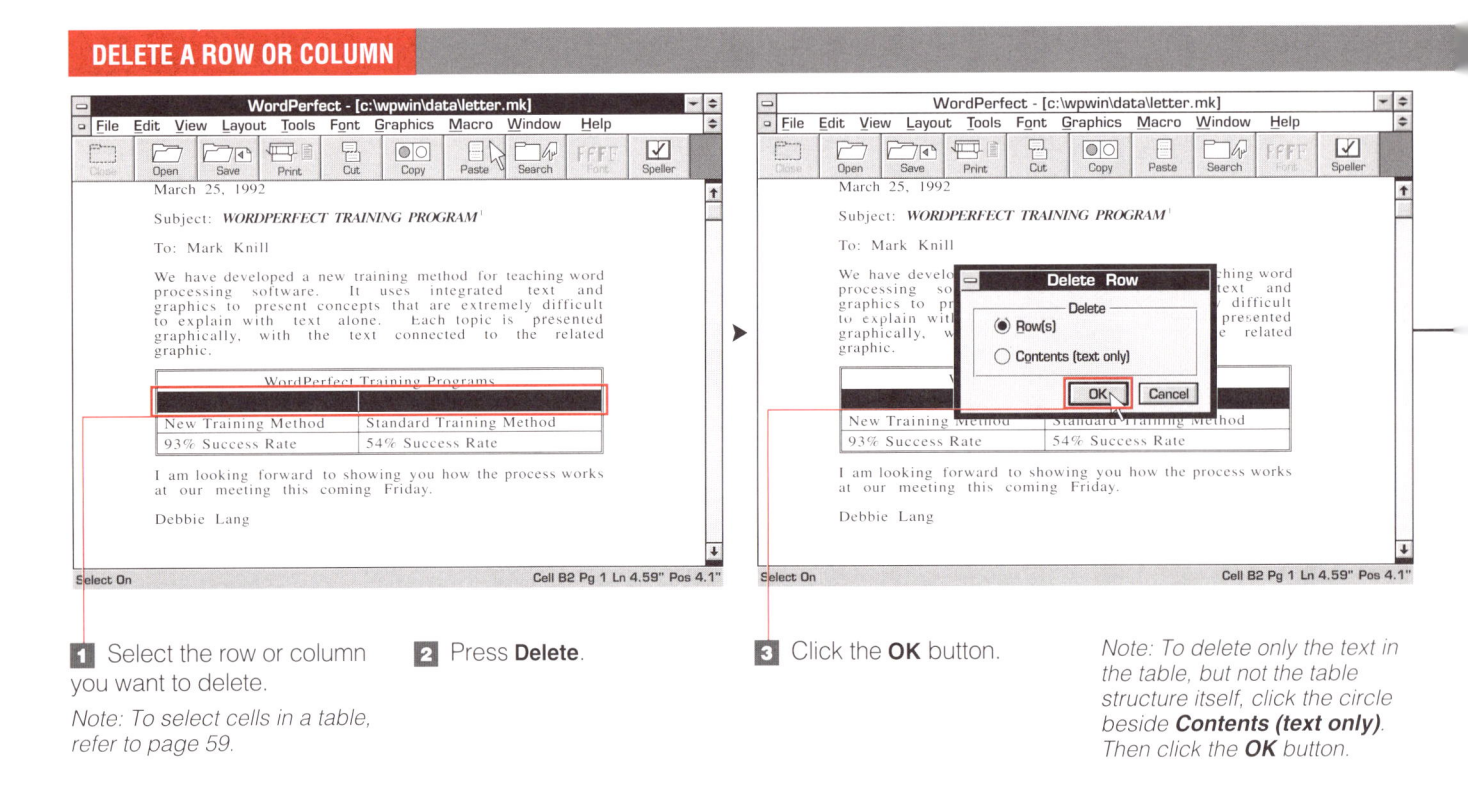

1 Select the row or column you want to delete.

Note: To select cells in a table, refer to page 59.

2 Press **Delete**.

3 Click the **OK** button.

*Note: To delete only the text in the table, but not the table structure itself, click the circle beside **Contents (text only)**. Then click the **OK** button.*

62

CREATE A TABLE | SELECT CELLS | JOIN CELLS | ENTER TEXT IN A TABLE | RESIZE COLUMNS | **INSERT A ROW OR COLUMN** | **DELETE A ROW OR COLUMN**

GETTING STARTED

THE BUTTON BAR

EDIT A DOCUMENT

SAVE FILES AND EXIT WORDPERFECT

VIEW DOCUMENTS

CHECK A DOCUMENT

FORMAT A DOCUMENT

TABLES

GRAPHICS

PRINT

MERGE AND SORT FILES

FILE MANAGER

HELP

■ The row (or column) is inserted.

Note: To resize columns in a table, refer to page 60.

DELETE A TABLE

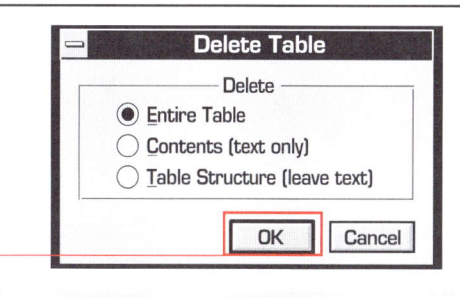

1 Select the entire table you want to delete.

Note: To select the entire table, refer to page 59.

2 Press **Delete**.

3 To delete the table structure and the text within the table, click the **OK** button.

*Note: To delete only the text in the table, click the circle beside **Contents (text only)**. Then click the **OK** button.*

*To delete only the table structure, but not the text, click the circle beside **Table Structure (leave text)**. Then click the **OK** button.*

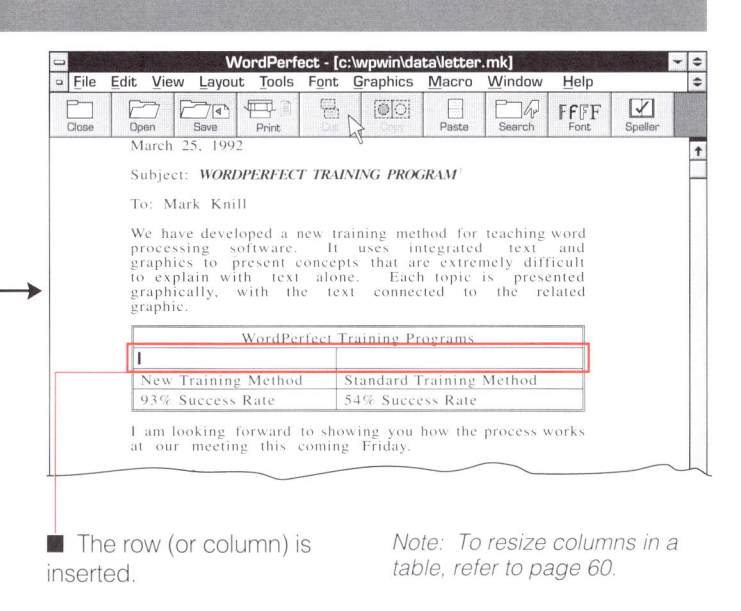

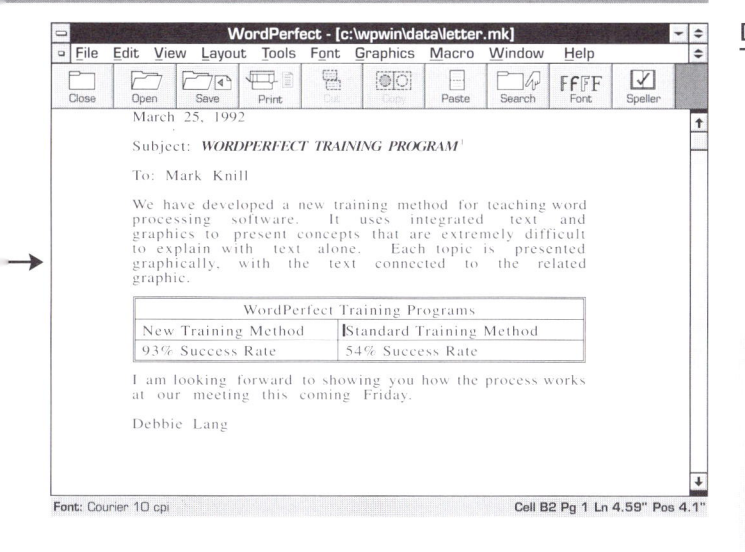

■ The row (or column) is deleted.

◀ 63

RETRIEVE A GRAPHIC IMAGE

SIZE A GRAPHIC

RETRIEVE A GRAPHIC IMAGE

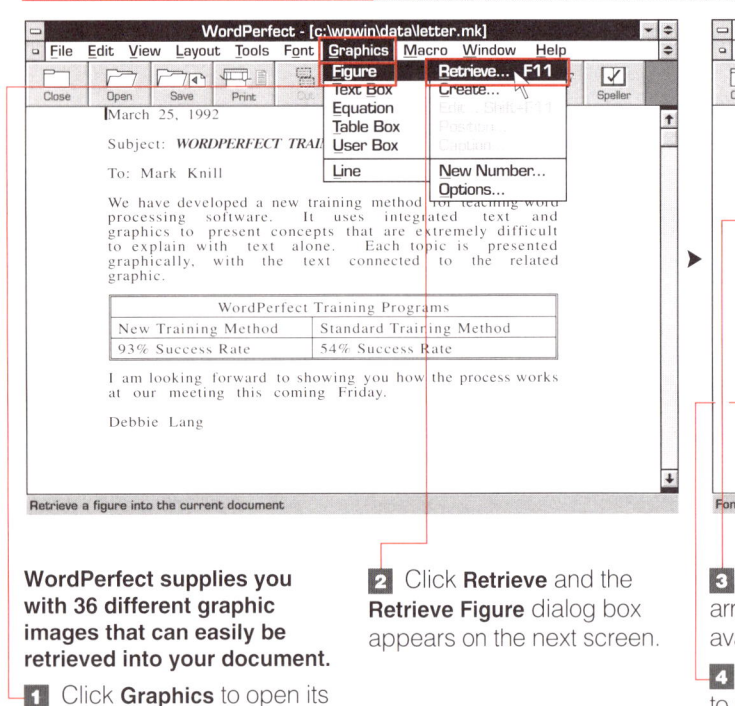

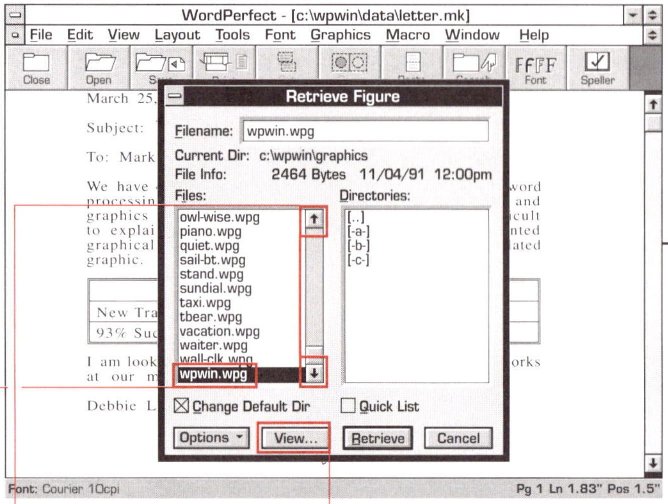

WordPerfect supplies you with 36 different graphic images that can easily be retrieved into your document.

1 Click **Graphics** to open its menu. Then click **Figure**.

2 Click **Retrieve** and the **Retrieve Figure** dialog box appears on the next screen.

3 Click the up or down scroll arrows to view more of the available graphics.

4 Click the graphic you want to retrieve into the current document (example: **wpwin.wpg**).

5 Click the **View** button to view the graphic before retrieving it into the document.

SIZE A GRAPHIC

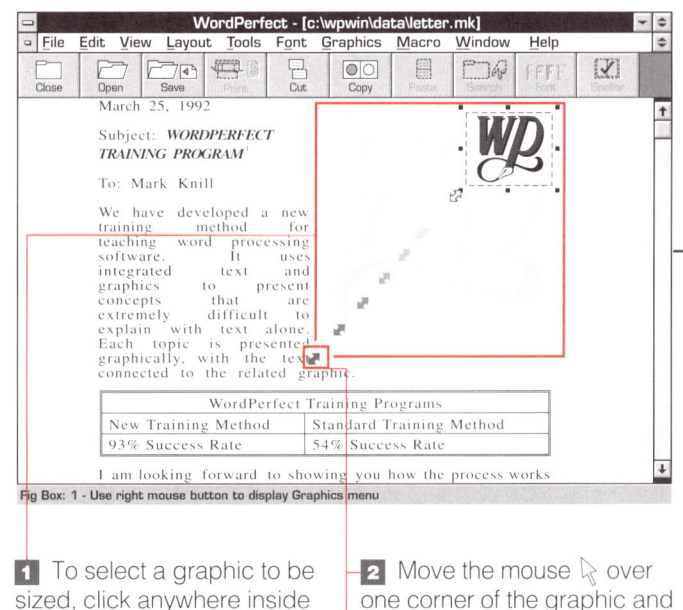

1 To select a graphic to be sized, click anywhere inside the box surrounding the graphic.

2 Move the mouse over one corner of the graphic and it turns into.

3 Click and hold down the left mouse button as you drag the edge of the graphic to the desired size.

64

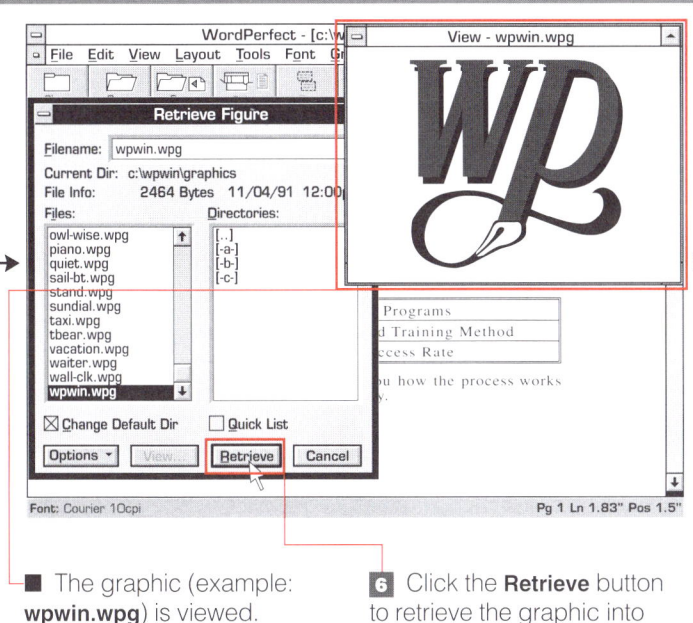

RETRIEVE A GRAPHIC IMAGE | SIZE A GRAPHIC | MOVE A GRAPHIC | CREATE A TEXT BOX

■ The graphic (example: **wpwin.wpg**) is viewed.

6 Click the **Retrieve** button to retrieve the graphic into the document.

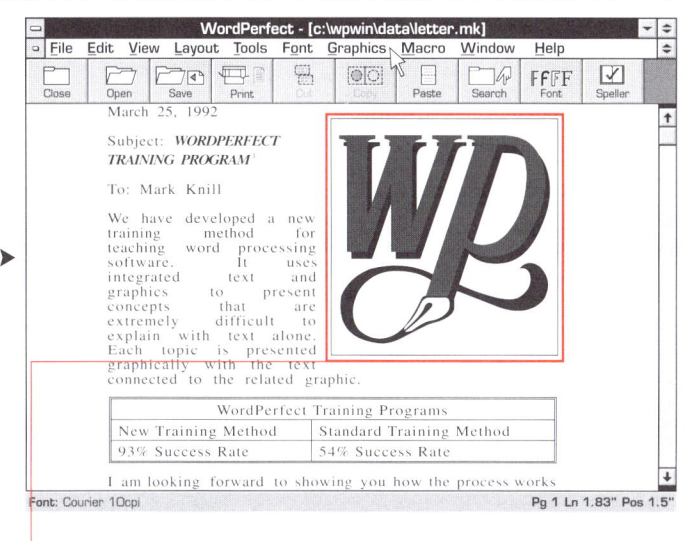

■ The graphic is retrieved into the document.

*Note: If a box appears with the statement **Fig Box: 1**, the **Graphics** mode is not on. Click **View**, then click **Graphics** to turn on the graphic mode and view the retrieved graphic.*

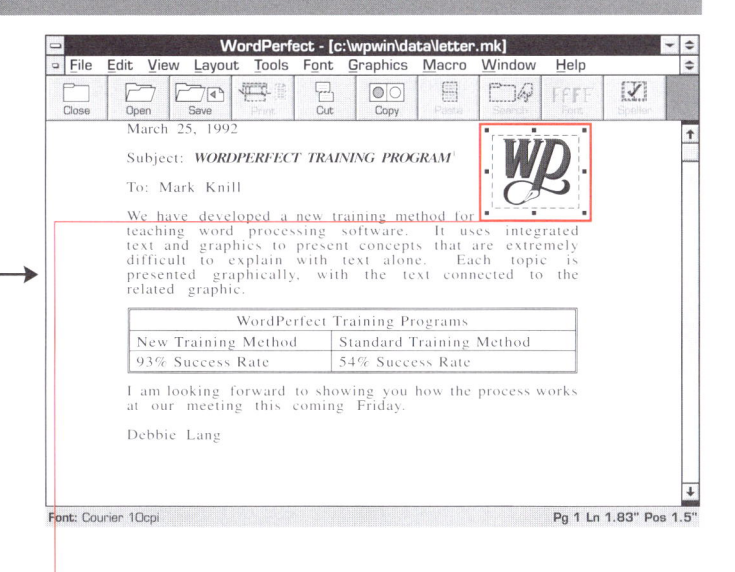

DELETE A GRAPHIC

1 Select the graphic.

2 Press **Delete**.

4 Release the button and the graphic is sized.

GETTING STARTED

THE BUTTON BAR

EDIT A DOCUMENT

SAVE FILES AND EXIT WORDPERFECT

VIEW DOCUMENTS

CHECK A DOCUMENT

FORMAT A DOCUMENT

TABLES

GRAPHICS

PRINT

MERGE AND SORT FILES

FILE MANAGER

HELP

◀ 65

MOVE A GRAPHIC / CREATE A TEXT BOX

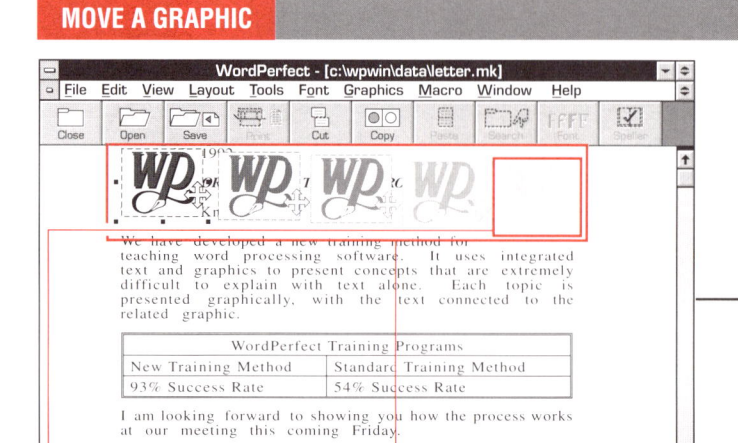

MOVE A GRAPHIC

1 To select a graphic to be moved, click anywhere inside the box surrounding the graphic and the I beam changes to ✥.

2 Click and hold down the left mouse button as you drag the graphic to the desired position.

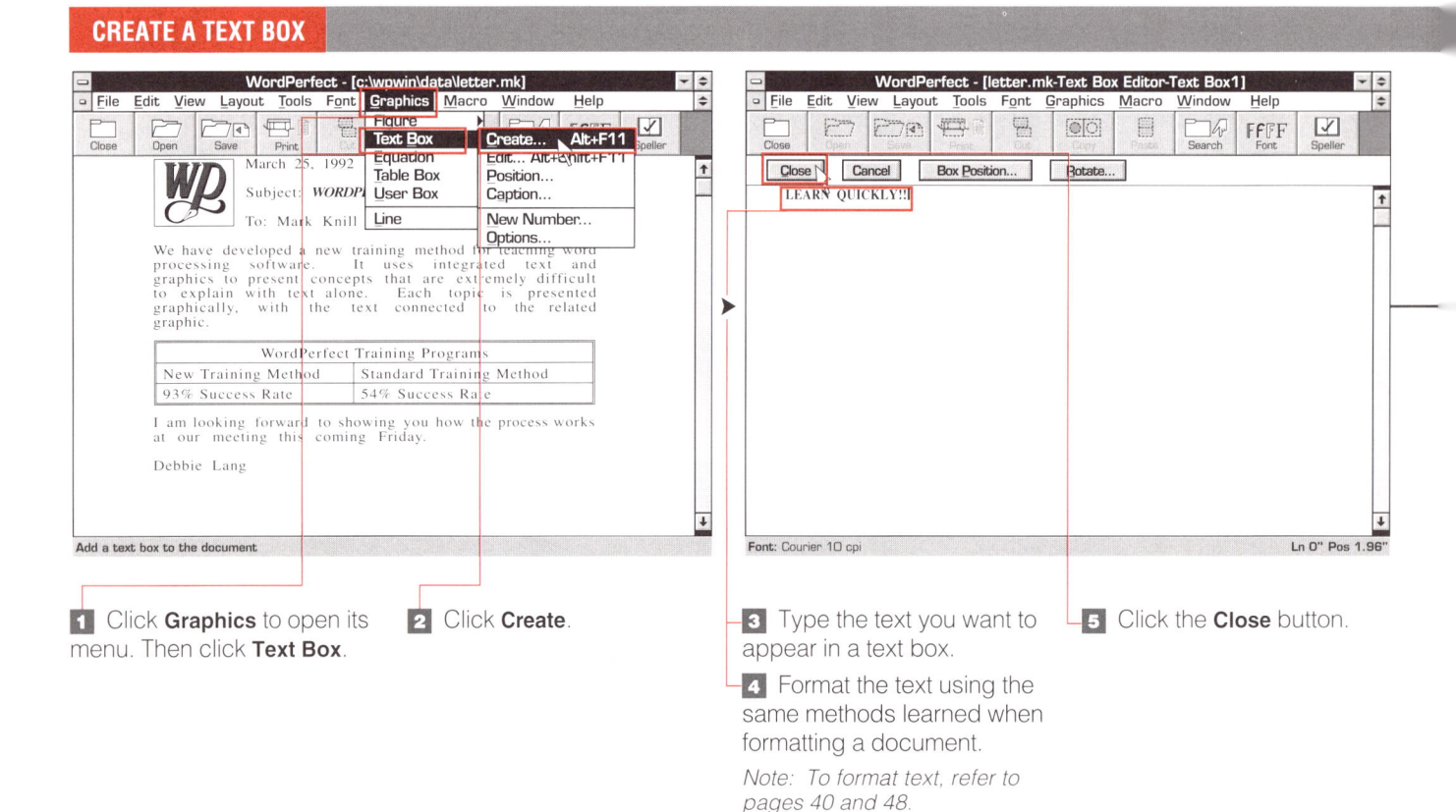

CREATE A TEXT BOX

1 Click **Graphics** to open its menu. Then click **Text Box**.

2 Click **Create**.

3 Type the text you want to appear in a text box.

4 Format the text using the same methods learned when formatting a document.

Note: To format text, refer to pages 40 and 48.

5 Click the **Close** button.

66 ▶

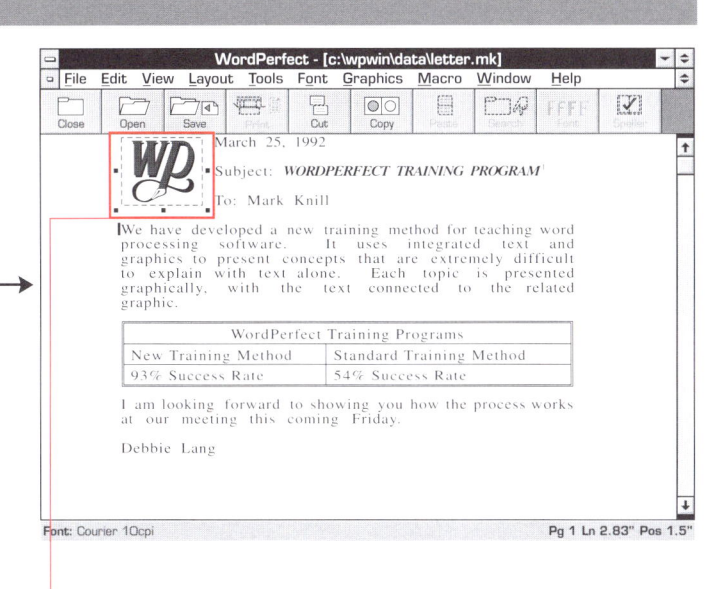

RETRIEVE A GRAPHIC IMAGE | SIZE A GRAPHIC | **MOVE A GRAPHIC** | **CREATE A TEXT BOX**

3 Release the button and the graphic is moved.

Note: To deselect a graphic, click anywhere outside the graphic box.

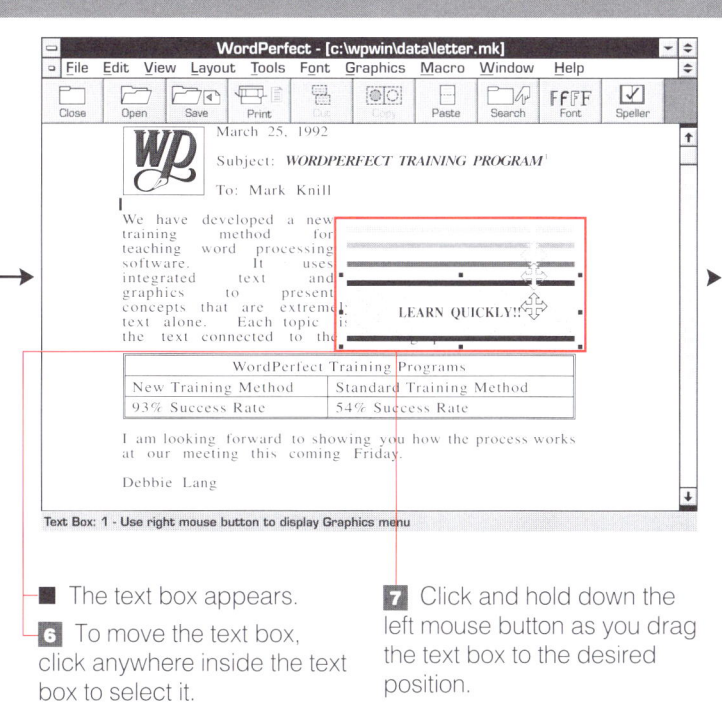

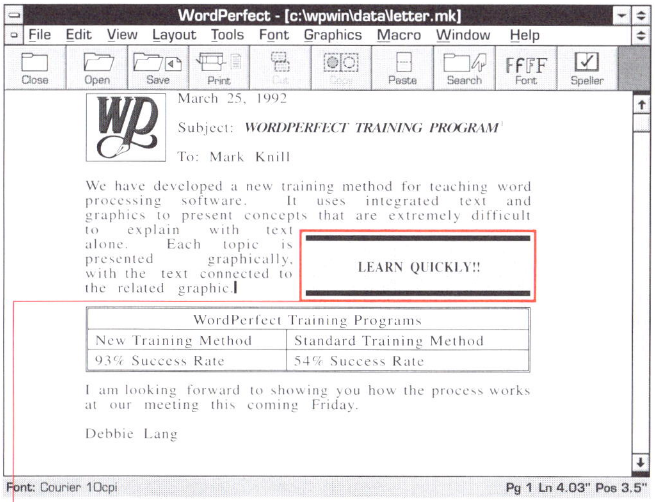

- The text box appears.

6 To move the text box, click anywhere inside the text box to select it.

7 Click and hold down the left mouse button as you drag the text box to the desired position.

8 Release the button and the text box is moved.

Note: To deselect a text box, click anywhere outside the text box.

Note: You can size a text box using the same methods learned when sizing a graphic. Refer to page 64.

GETTING STARTED

THE BUTTON BAR

EDIT A DOCUMENT

SAVE FILES AND EXIT WORDPERFECT

VIEW DOCUMENTS

CHECK A DOCUMENT

FORMAT A DOCUMENT

TABLES

GRAPHICS

PRINT

MERGE AND SORT FILES

FILE MANAGER

HELP

◀ 67

PREVIEW A DOCUMENT

PREVIEW A DOCUMENT BEFORE PRINTING

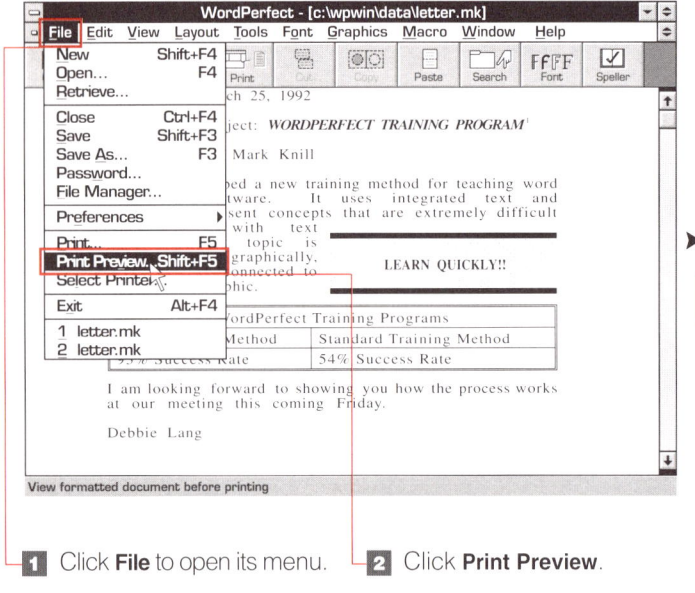

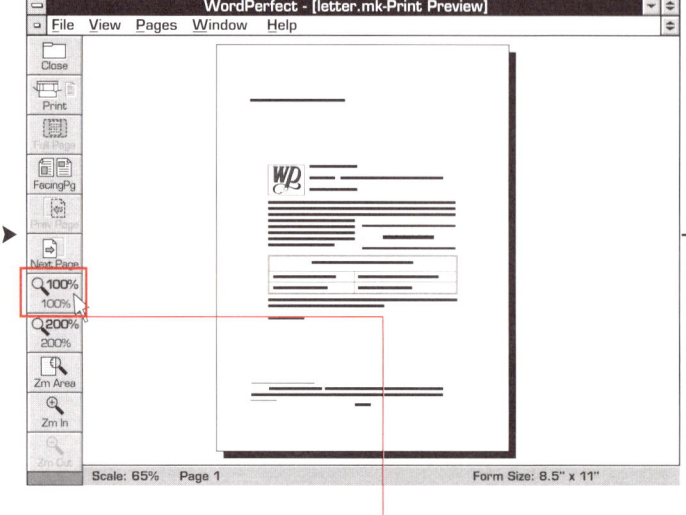

1 Click **File** to open its menu.

2 Click **Print Preview**.

■ The **Print Preview** window appears.

Note: You cannot make changes to the document in the Print Preview window.

3 Click a print preview option (example: **100%**).

PRINT PREVIEW OPTIONS

Close
Click this button to return to the document.

FacingPg
Click this button to display two consecutive pages.

Note: If no facing page exists, only one page is displayed.

Print
Click this button to return to the document and display the Print dialog box.

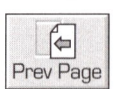

Prev Page
Click this button to display the page before the current page.

Full Page
Click this button to display the entire page.

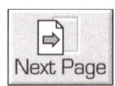

Next Page
Click this button to display the page after the current page.

68

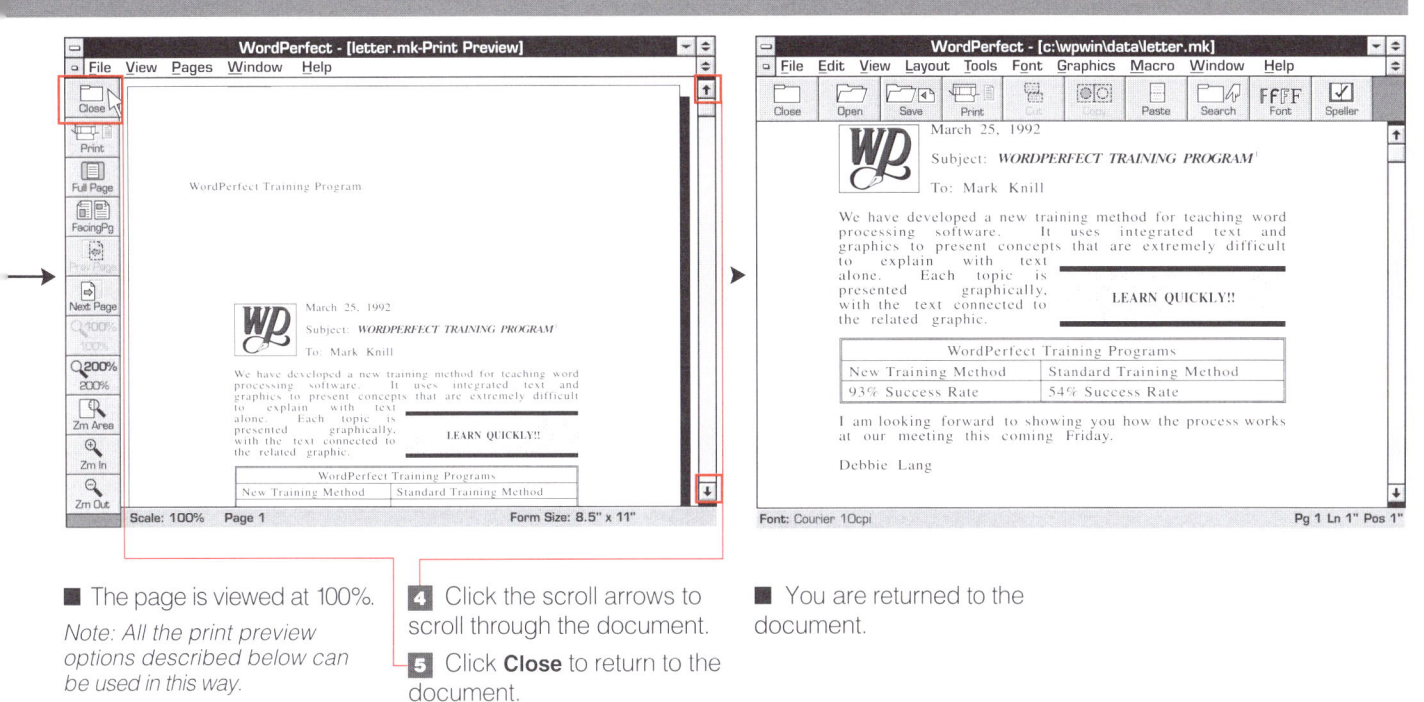

PREVIEW A DOCUMENT

- The page is viewed at 100%.

Note: All the print preview options described below can be used in this way.

4 Click the scroll arrows to scroll through the document.

5 Click **Close** to return to the document.

- You are returned to the document.

100%
Click this button to view the page at its actual printed size.

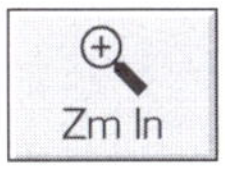

Zm In
Click this button to enlarge the viewing size of the document by 25%.

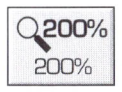

200%
Click this button to view the page at twice its actual printed size.

Zm Out
Click this button to reduce the viewing size of the document by 25%.

Note: When a button is not currently operational, it appears dimmed.

Zm Area
Click this button then move the mouse over one corner of the area you want to view enlarged.

Click and hold down the mouse as you drag to form a box around the area.

Release the button.

GETTING STARTED

THE BUTTON BAR

EDIT A DOCUMENT

SAVE FILES AND EXIT WORDPERFECT

VIEW DOCUMENTS

CHECK A DOCUMENT

FORMAT A DOCUMENT

TABLES

GRAPHICS

PRINT

MERGE AND SORT FILES

FILE MANAGER

HELP

◀ 69

PRINT A DOCUMENT

PRINT THE CURRENT PAGE OR ALL PAGES

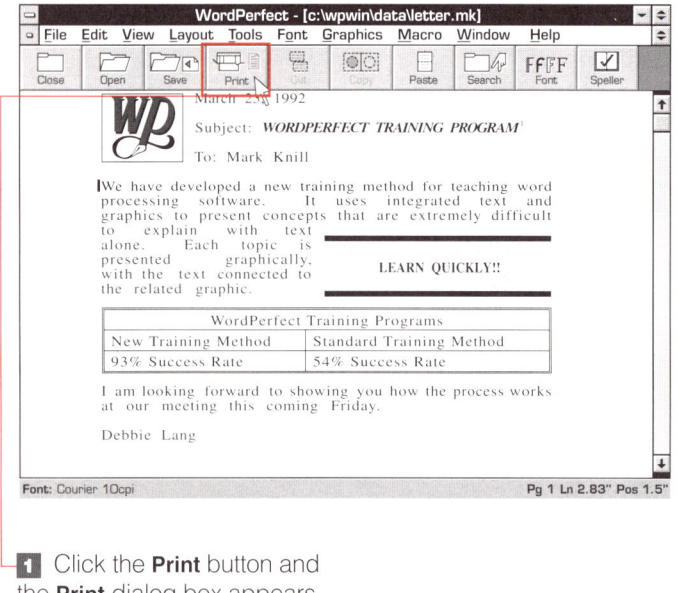

1 Click the **Print** button and the **Print** dialog box appears on the next screen.

2 To print the page the insertion point is currently on, click the circle beside **Current Page** and ○ becomes ●

or

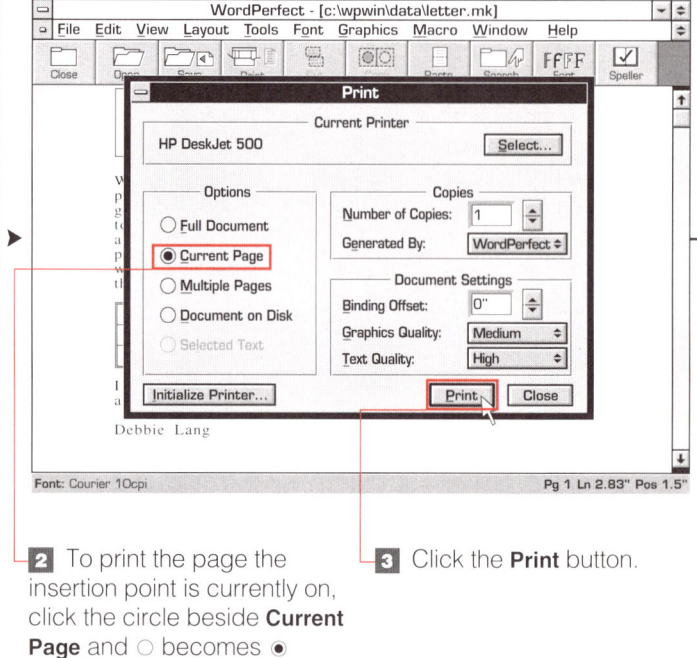

To print the entire document, click the circle beside **Full Document**.

3 Click the **Print** button.

PRINT SPECIFIC PAGES

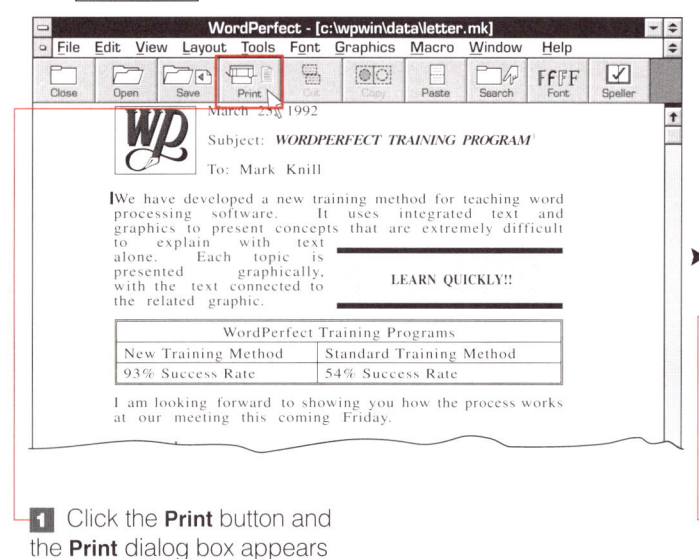

1 Click the **Print** button and the **Print** dialog box appears on the next screen.

2 Click the circle beside **Multiple Pages** and ○ becomes ●.

3 Click the **Print** button and the **Multiple Pages** dialog box appears on the next screen.

PREVIEW A DOCUMENT

PRINT A DOCUMENT

PRINT SELECTED TEXT

1 Select the text you want to print.

Note: To select text, refer to page 6.

2 Click [Print] and the **Print** dialog box appears.

3 Click [Print].

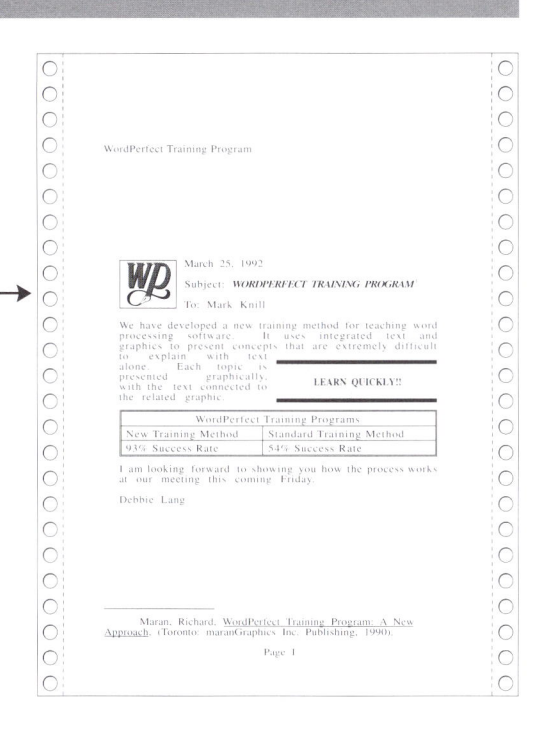

■ The page is printed.

PRINT THE FOLLOWING PAGES:	EXAMPLE:
A	1
A, B and C	1,3,5
A to end of document	3-
Start of document to A	-3
A to B	3-5

Note: A, B, and C are pages in a document.

4 Type the pages you want to print (example: **1**).

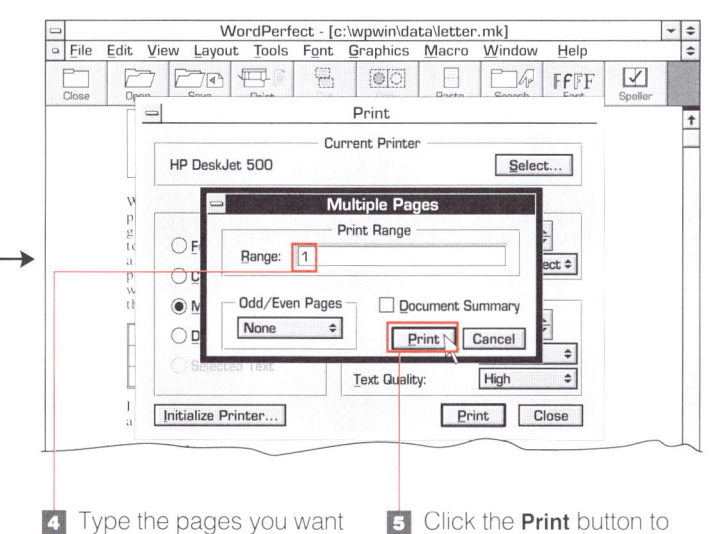

5 Click the **Print** button to print the page(s) you specified.

GETTING STARTED

THE BUTTON BAR

EDIT A DOCUMENT

SAVE FILES AND EXIT WORDPERFECT

VIEW DOCUMENTS

CHECK A DOCUMENT

FORMAT A DOCUMENT

TABLES

GRAPHICS

PRINT

MERGE AND SORT FILES

FILE MANAGER

HELP

◀ 71

PRINT A DOCUMENT

PRINT A DOCUMENT STORED ON A DISK

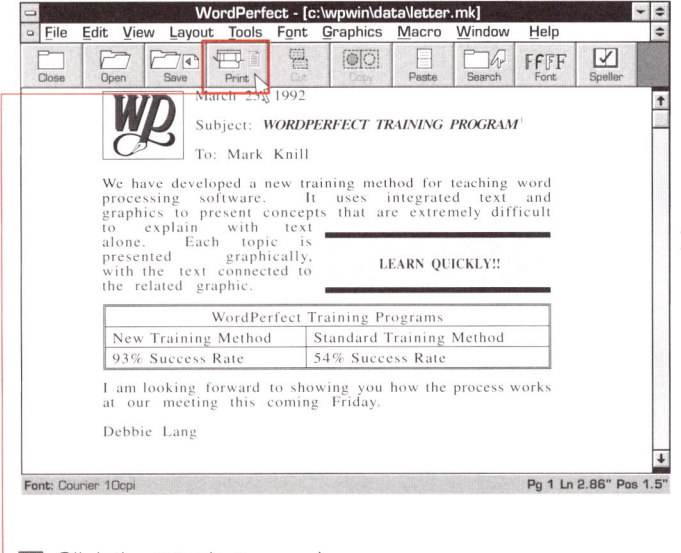

1 Click the **Print** button and the **Print** dialog box appears on the next screen.

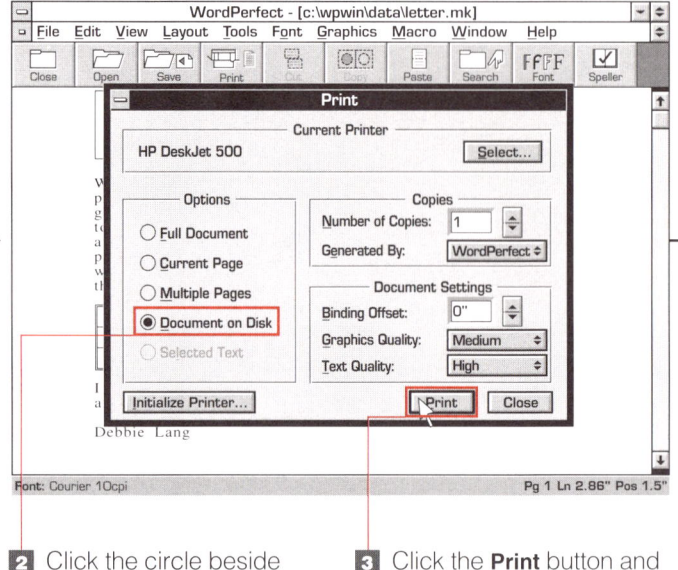

2 Click the circle beside **Document on Disk** and ○ becomes ⊙.

3 Click the **Print** button and the **Document on Disk** dialog box appears on the next screen.

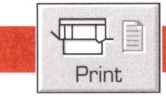

CHANGE TEXT AND GRAPHICS PRINT QUALITY

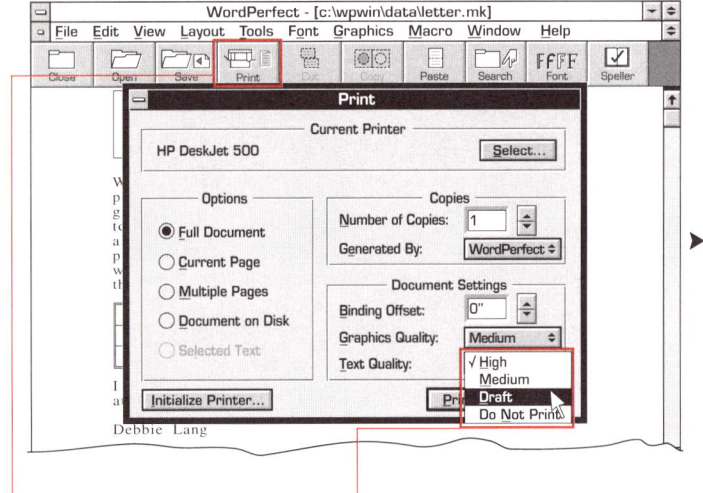

As the print quality decreases, the printer produces a faster lower quality image.

1 Click the **Print** button.

2 Move the mouse over the box beside the print quality you want to change (example: **Text Quality**).

3 Click and hold down the left mouse button as you drag the mouse over the desired quality (example: **Draft**).

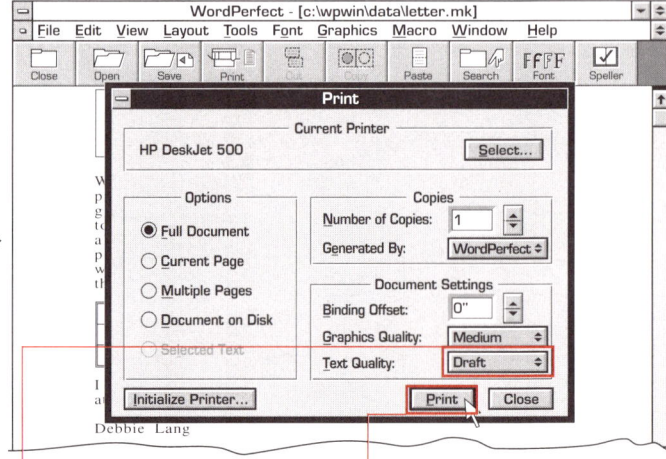

4 Release the button and the print quality is changed.

5 To print the document, click the **Print** button.

Note: Your printer may only have two print qualities, therefore, the medium print quality may look identical to the high print quality.

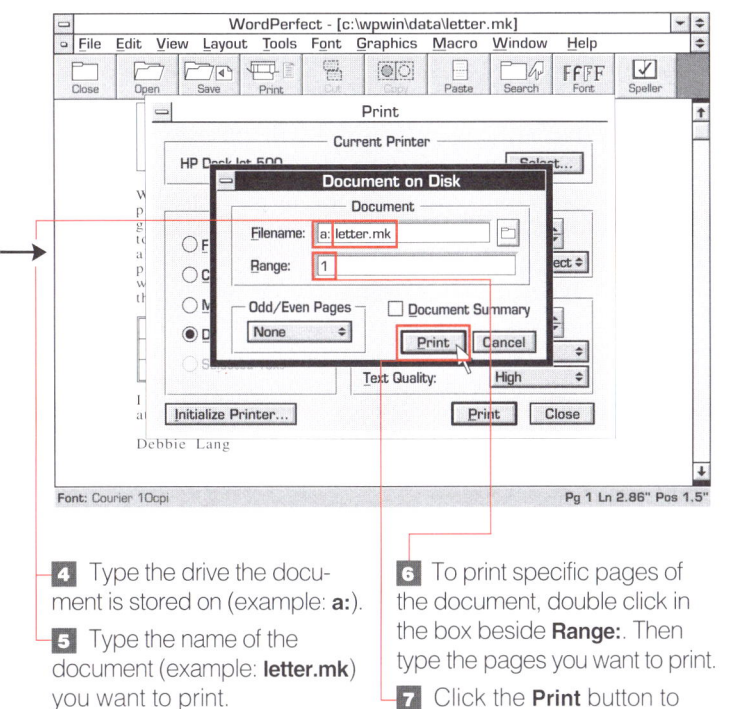

PRINT THE FOLLOWING PAGES:	EXAMPLE:
A	1
A, B and C	1,3,5
A to end of document	3-
Start of document to A	-3
A to B	3-5

Note: A, B, and C are pages in a document.

4 Type the drive the document is stored on (example: **a:**).

5 Type the name of the document (example: **letter.mk**) you want to print.

6 To print specific pages of the document, double click in the box beside **Range:**. Then type the pages you want to print.

7 Click the **Print** button to print the document.

PRINT MULTIPLE COPIES

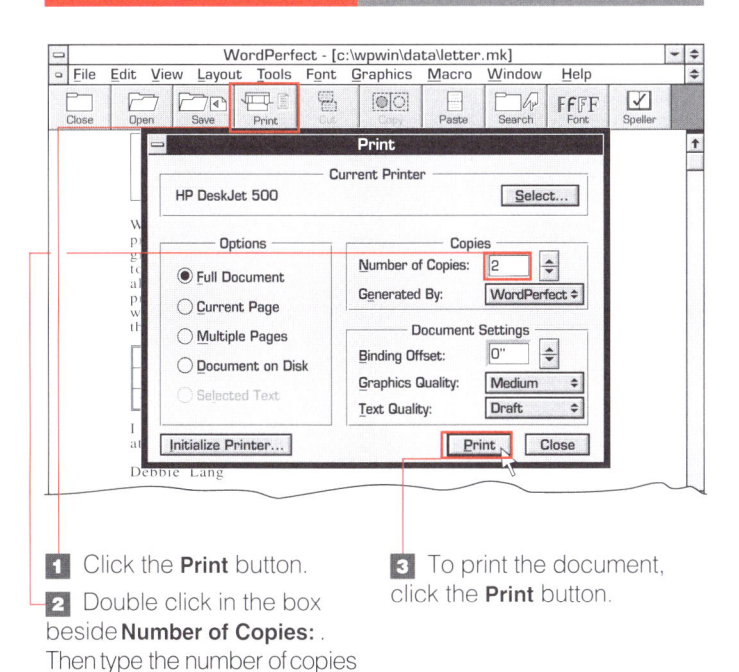

1 Click the **Print** button.

2 Double click in the box beside **Number of Copies:** . Then type the number of copies you want printed (example: **2**).

3 To print the document, click the **Print** button.

MERGE FILES OVERVIEW

MERGE FILES OVERVIEW

PRIMARY FILE

April 2, 1992

{FIELD}1~
{FIELD}2~
Dear {FIELD}3~,

On behalf of our company, I would like to invite you to attend our Open House on May 1, 1992. Coffee and donuts will be served, and our staff will be available to answer any questions you may have.

Sincerely,

Kari Steinburg
Manager

{FIELD}1~
{FIELD}2~
       {FIELD}3~,

This file contains the standard text of the letter and the merge commands to tell WordPerfect where to insert the customized information.

Note: This file does not have to use all the fields in the Secondary file.

SECONDARY FILE

The information in each **record** is broken down into different **fields**. For example, a customer's name may be in one field, the address in another, etc.

RECORD 1
- FIELD 1 | Glen Jones
- FIELD 2 | 12 Willow Avenue / Buffalo, NY 14386
- FIELD 3 | Glen

RECORD 2
- FIELD 1 | Ross Anderson
- FIELD 2 | 212 Lakeshore Road / Atlanta, GA 30354
- FIELD 3 | Ross

RECORD 3
- FIELD 1 | Martha Hunter
- FIELD 2 | 432 Linton Street / Fullerton, CA 92740
- FIELD 3 | Martha

This file contains the customized information (names, addresses, etc.) to go into each letter. Each group of information is called a record and contains the data for each separate customer.

When creating the Secondary file, each field **must** contain the same information in every record.

For example, if the first field of one record contains the customer name, the first field of **every** record must contain the customer name.

Note: The secondary file must contain all the fields used in the primary file.

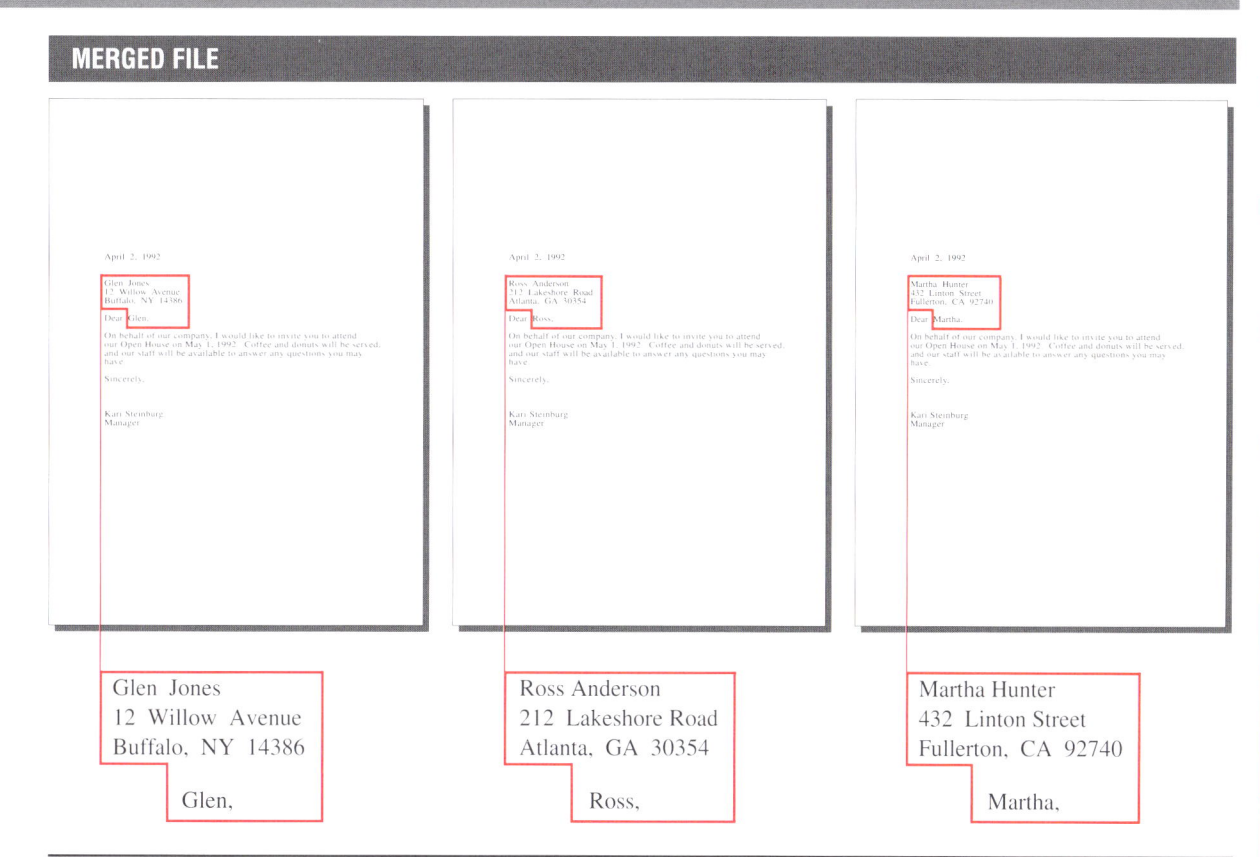

| MERGE FILES OVERVIEW | CREATE THE PRIMARY FILE | CREATE THE SECONDARY FILE | MERGE FILES | PRINT A MERGED FILE | SORT DATA |

MERGED FILE

Glen Jones
12 Willow Avenue
Buffalo, NY 14386

Glen,

Ross Anderson
212 Lakeshore Road
Atlanta, GA 30354

Ross,

Martha Hunter
432 Linton Street
Fullerton, CA 92740

Martha,

This file contains documents generated from the merging of the primary and secondary files.

◀ 75

CREATE THE PRIMARY FILE

CREATE THE SECONDARY FILE

Before creating the primary and secondary file, decide on how the information will be split into different fields. For example, the entire address may be treated as one field, or it may be broken down into 'address', 'city', 'state', and 'zip code' (this may be of benefit later on if only parts of the address are required in a merge).

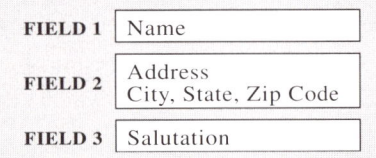

FIELD 1	Name
FIELD 2	Address City, State, Zip Code
FIELD 3	Salutation

CREATE THE PRIMARY FILE

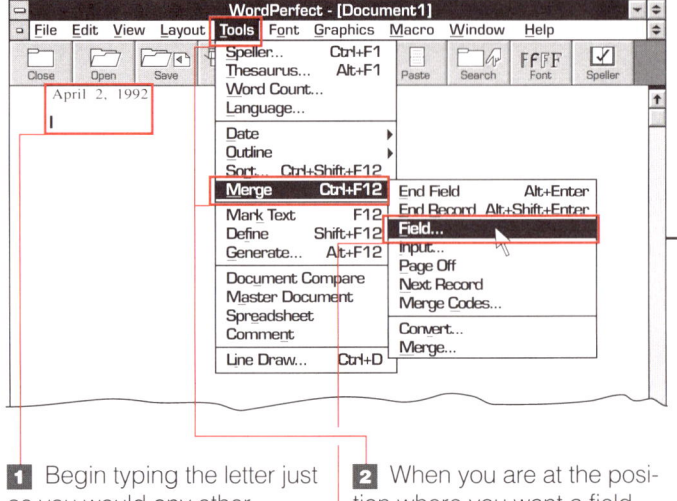

1 Begin typing the letter just as you would any other document in WordPerfect.

*Note: To open a new file, click **File**. Then click **New**.*

2 When you are at the position where you want a field (example: the customer's name) to be inserted, click **Tools**. Then click **Merge**.

3 Click **Field** and the **Insert Merge Code** dialog box appears.

CREATE THE SECONDARY FILE

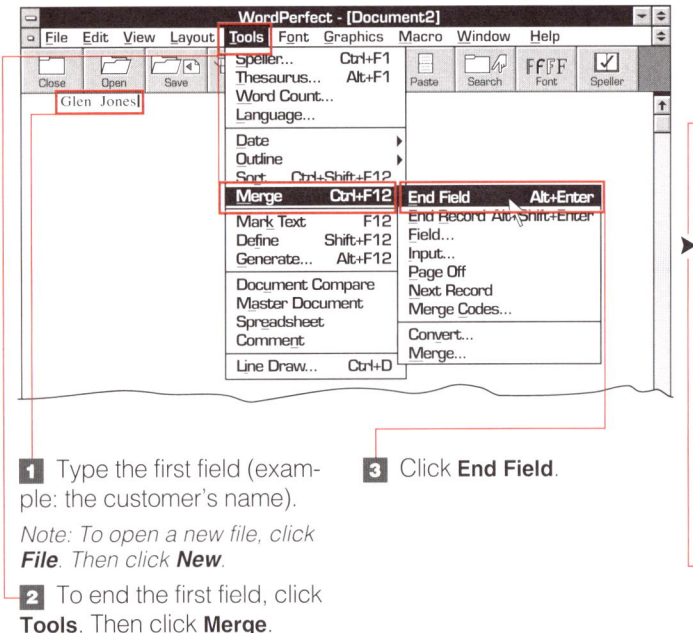

1 Type the first field (example: the customer's name).

*Note: To open a new file, click **File**. Then click **New**.*

2 To end the first field, click **Tools**. Then click **Merge**.

3 Click **End Field**.

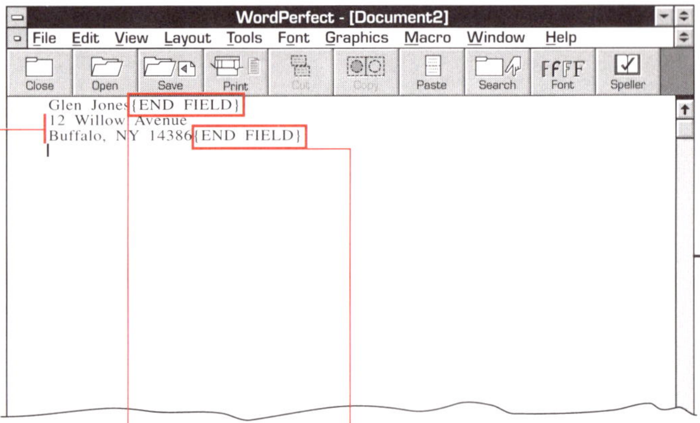

■ The code **{END FIELD}** appears, and the insertion point moves to the next line.

4 Type the next field (example: the customer's address).

5 To end the field, press **Alt+Enter**.

■ The code **{END FIELD}** appears, and the insertion point moves to the next line.

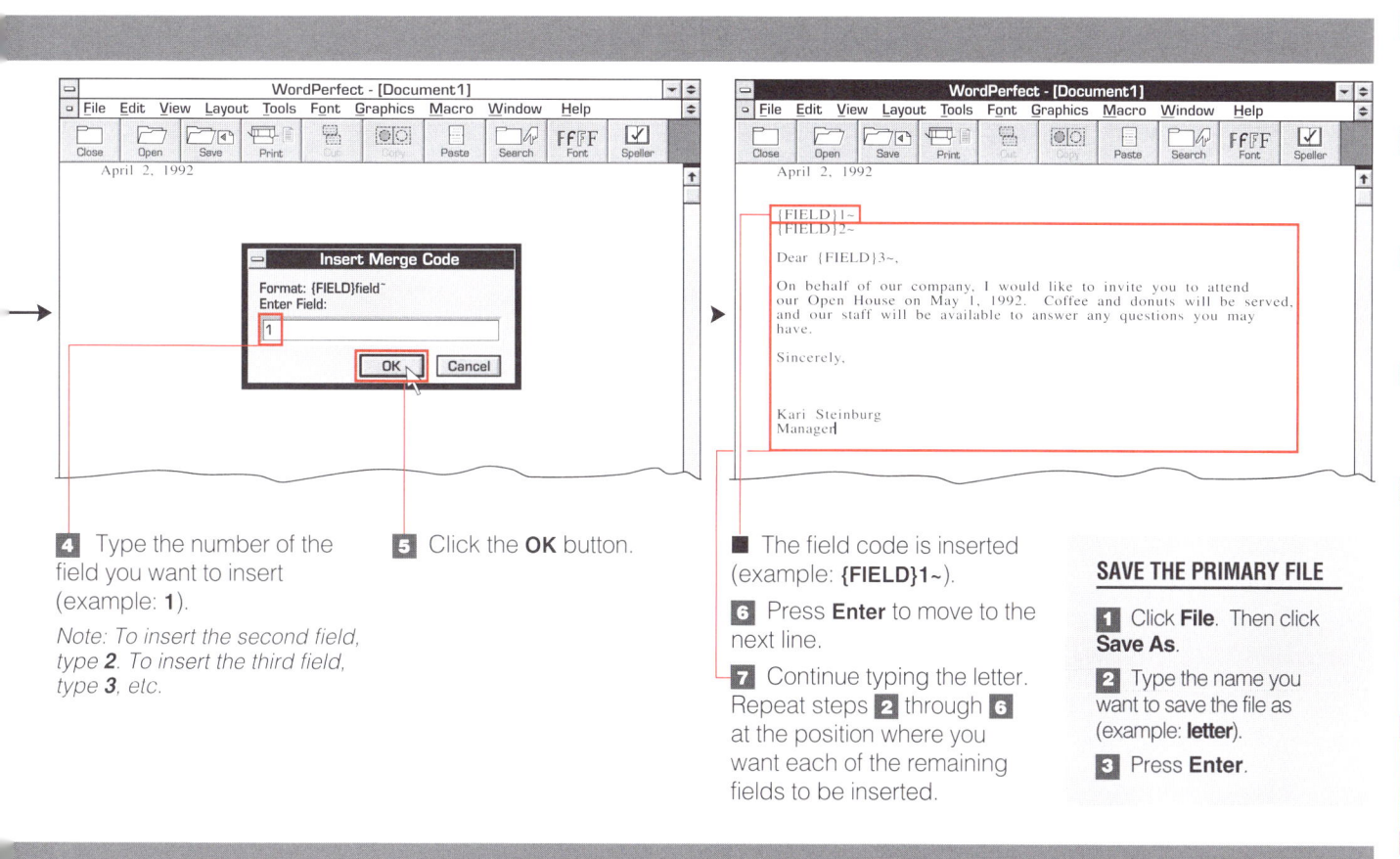

| MERGE FILES OVERVIEW | **CREATE THE PRIMARY FILE** | **CREATE THE SECONDARY FILE** | MERGE FILES | PRINT A MERGED FILE | SORT DATA |

4 Type the number of the field you want to insert (example: **1**).

Note: To insert the second field, type **2**. To insert the third field, type **3**, etc.

5 Click the **OK** button.

■ The field code is inserted (example: **{FIELD}1~**).

6 Press **Enter** to move to the next line.

7 Continue typing the letter. Repeat steps **2** through **6** at the position where you want each of the remaining fields to be inserted.

SAVE THE PRIMARY FILE

1 Click **File**. Then click **Save As**.

2 Type the name you want to save the file as (example: **letter**).

3 Press **Enter**.

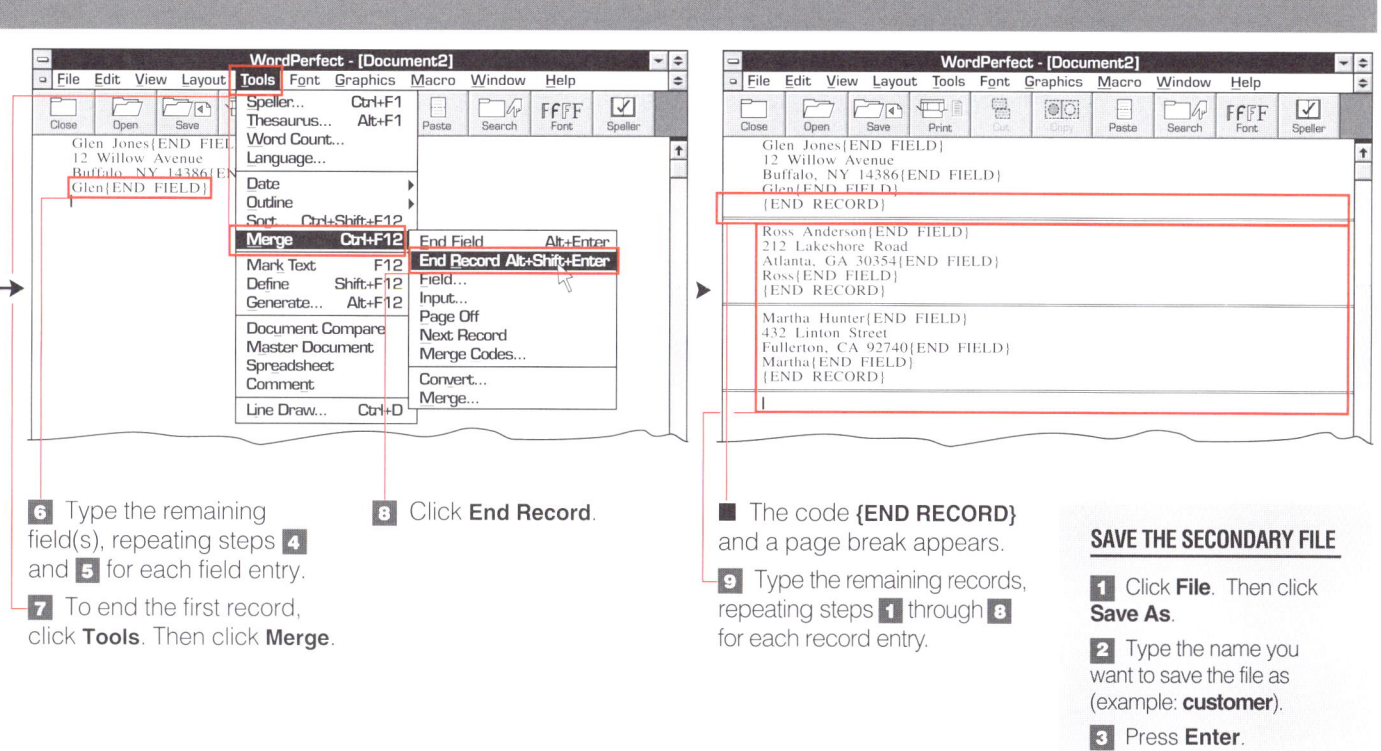

---

6 Type the remaining field(s), repeating steps **4** and **5** for each field entry.

7 To end the first record, click **Tools**. Then click **Merge**.

8 Click **End Record**.

■ The code **{END RECORD}** and a page break appears.

9 Type the remaining records, repeating steps **1** through **8** for each record entry.

SAVE THE SECONDARY FILE

1 Click **File**. Then click **Save As**.

2 Type the name you want to save the file as (example: **customer**).

3 Press **Enter**.

◀ 77

MERGE FILES / PRINT A MERGED FILE

MERGE FILES

1 Click **Tools**. Then click **Merge**.

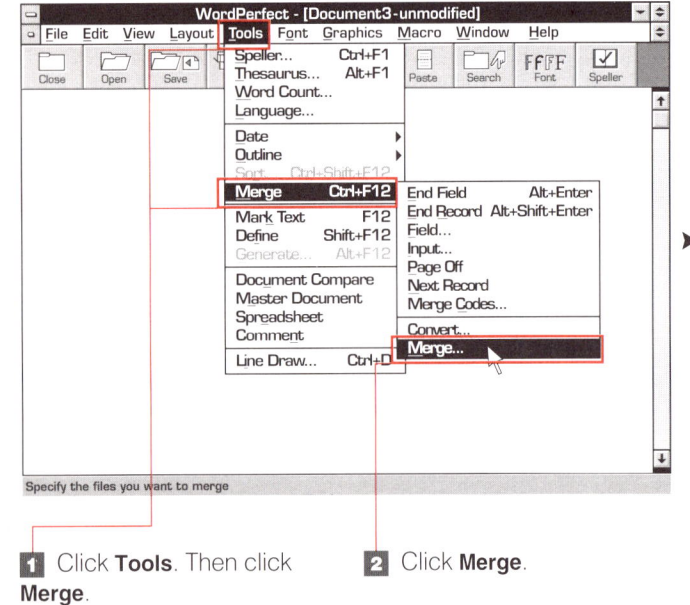

*Note: Make sure you open a new file before merging files. To open a new file, click **File**. Then click **New**.*

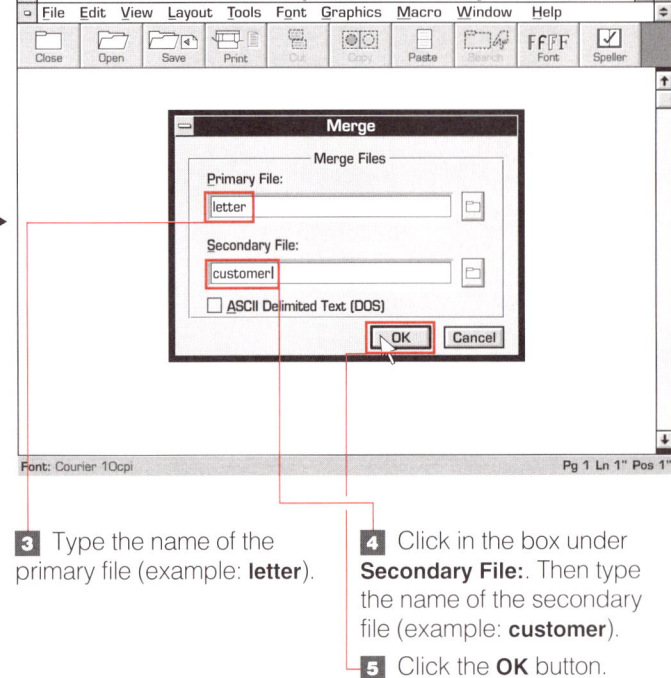

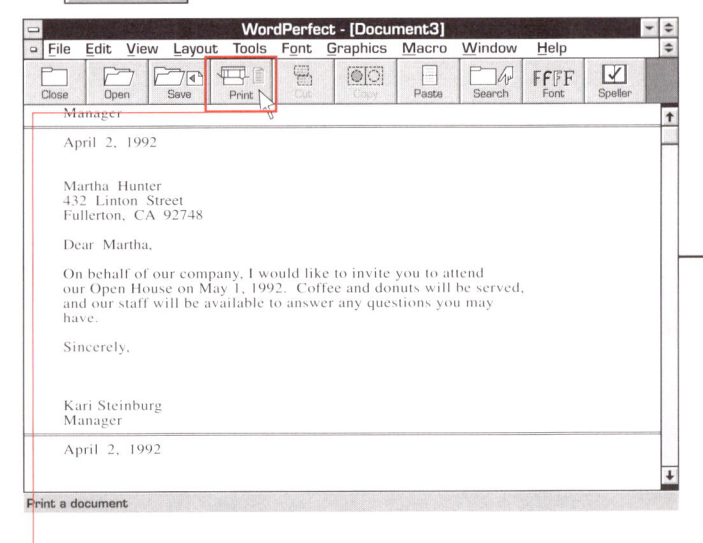

2 Click **Merge**.

3 Type the name of the primary file (example: **letter**).

4 Click in the box under **Secondary File:**. Then type the name of the secondary file (example: **customer**).

5 Click the **OK** button.

PRINT A MERGED FILE

1 Click **Print** and the **Print** dialog box appears on the next screen.

78

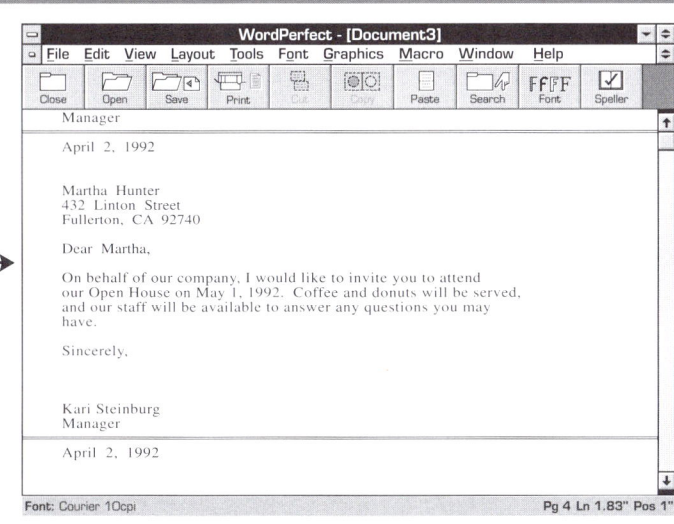

| MERGE FILES OVERVIEW | CREATE THE PRIMARY FILE | CREATE THE SECONDARY FILE | **MERGE FILES** | **PRINT A MERGED FILE** | SORT DATA |

■ The files are merged.

SAVE A MERGED DOCUMENT

1 Click **File**. Then click **Save As**.

2 Type the name you want to save the document as (example: **merged.lt**). Then press **Enter**.

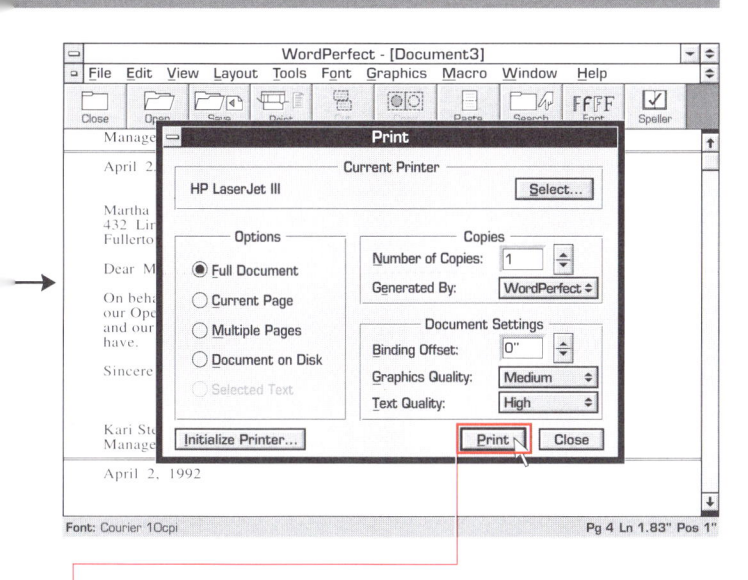

2 To print the entire document, click the **Print** button.

Note: For more information on printing a document, refer to page 70.

◀ 79

SORT DATA

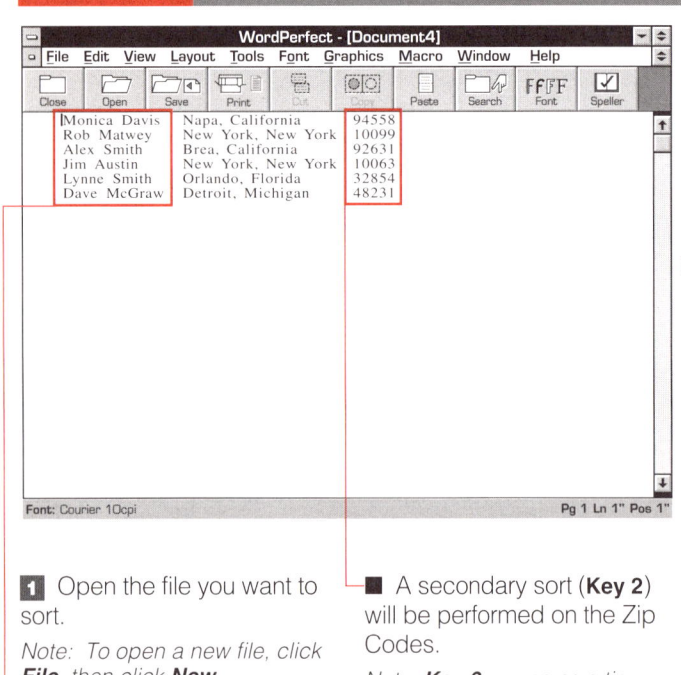

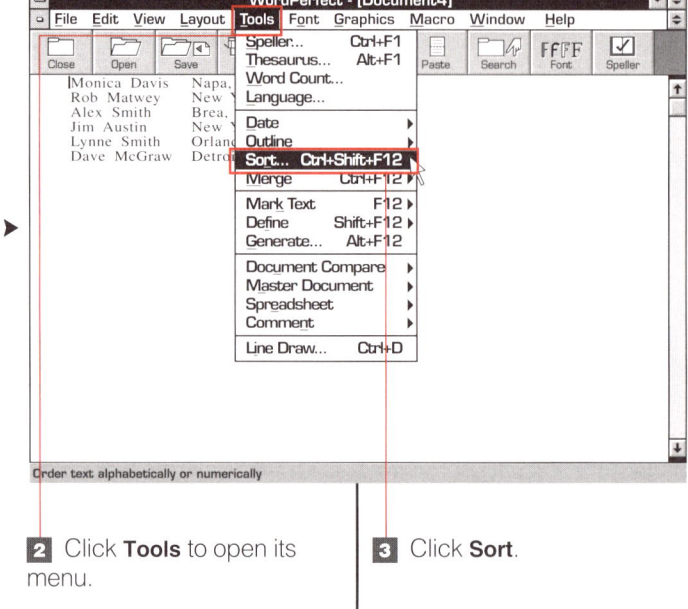

SORT DATA

1 Open the file you want to sort.

Note: To open a new file, click **File**, then click **New**.

■ In this example, a primary sort (**Key 1**) will be performed on the Last Names.

■ A secondary sort (**Key 2**) will be performed on the Zip Codes.

Note: **Key 2** serves as a tie-breaker if **Key 1** has matching entries.

2 Click **Tools** to open its menu.

3 Click **Sort**.

Data is divided into **Fields**. Each field is **Numeric** or **Alphanumeric** and may contain more than one **Word**.

Note: **Fields** are separated by <u>one</u> tab. **Words** are separated by <u>one</u> blank space.

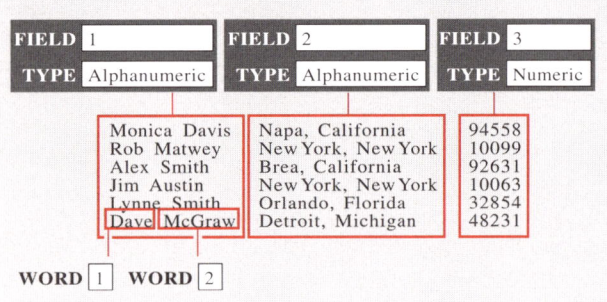

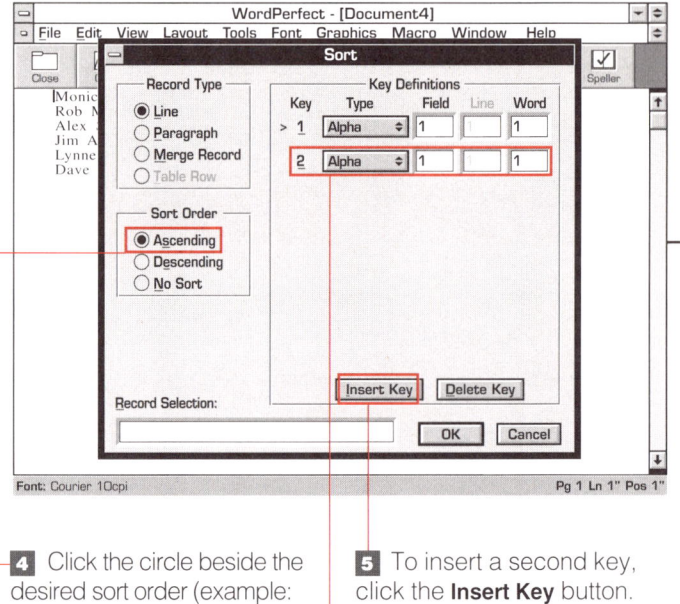

4 Click the circle beside the desired sort order (example: **Ascending**) and ○ becomes ⦿.

Note: Ascending sorts A through Z, 0 through 9. Descending sorts Z through A, 9 through 0.

5 To insert a second key, click the **Insert Key** button.

■ **Key 2** is inserted.

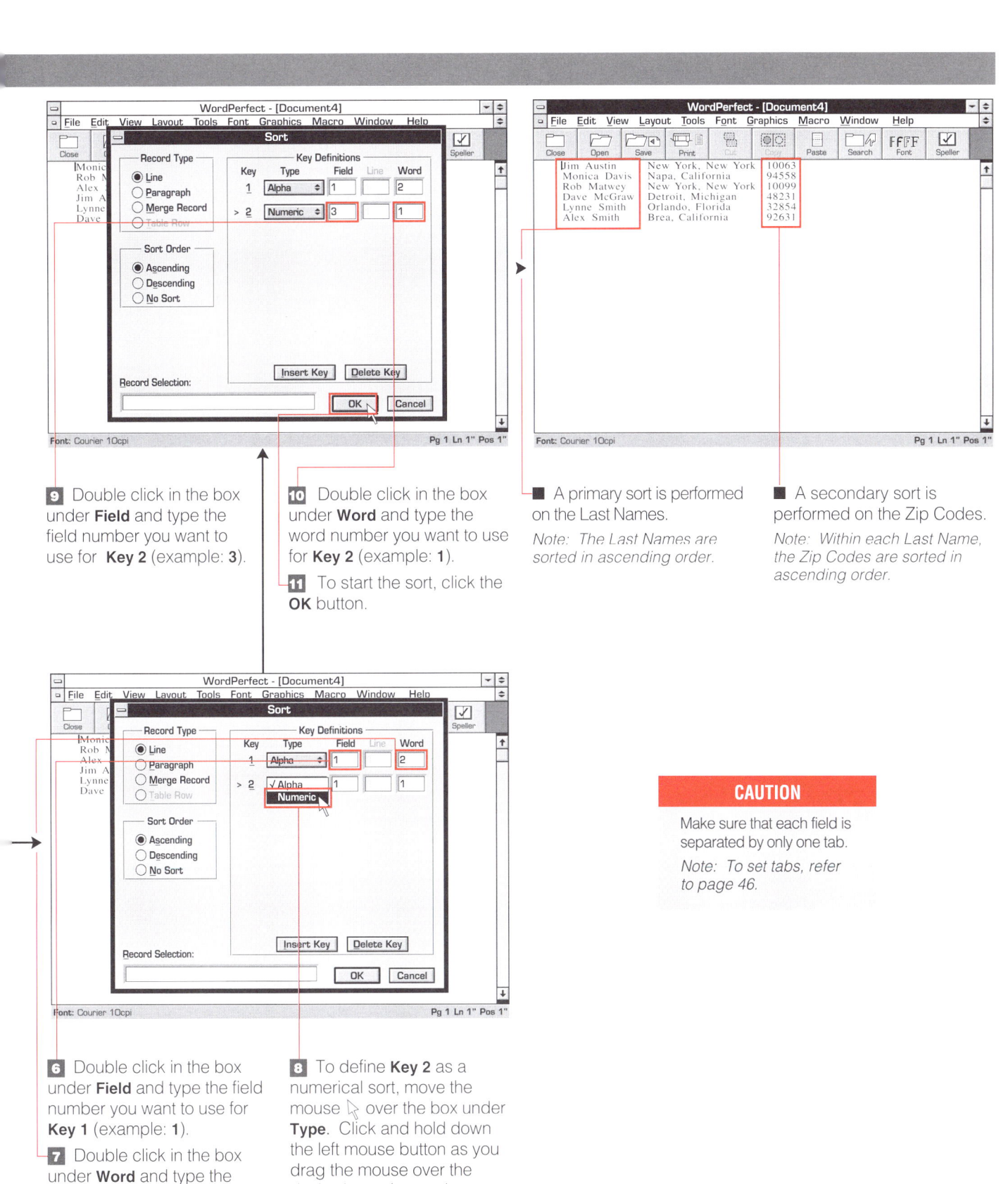

| MERGE FILES OVERVIEW | CREATE THE PRIMARY FILE | CREATE THE SECONDARY FILE | MERGE FILES | PRINT A MERGED FILE | **SORT DATA** |

9 Double click in the box under **Field** and type the field number you want to use for **Key 2** (example: **3**).

10 Double click in the box under **Word** and type the word number you want to use for **Key 2** (example: **1**).

11 To start the sort, click the **OK** button.

■ A primary sort is performed on the Last Names.
Note: The Last Names are sorted in ascending order.

■ A secondary sort is performed on the Zip Codes.
Note: Within each Last Name, the Zip Codes are sorted in ascending order.

CAUTION

Make sure that each field is separated by only one tab.

Note: To set tabs, refer to page 46.

6 Double click in the box under **Field** and type the field number you want to use for **Key 1** (example: **1**).

7 Double click in the box under **Word** and type the word number you want to use for **Key 1** (example: **2**).

8 To define **Key 2** as a numerical sort, move the mouse over the box under **Type**. Click and hold down the left mouse button as you drag the mouse over the desired type (example: **Numeric**). Release the button.

81

OPEN THE FILE MANAGER / VIEW FILES

OPEN THE FILE MANAGER

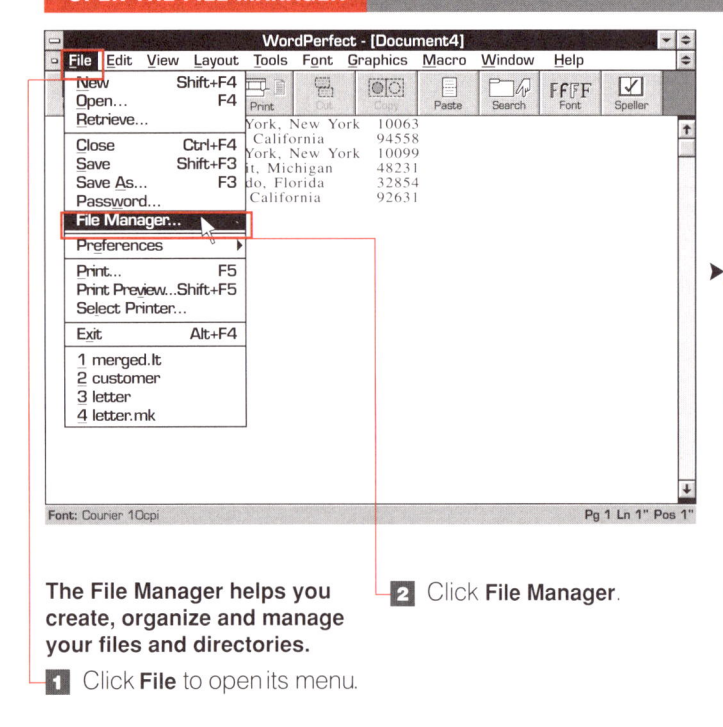

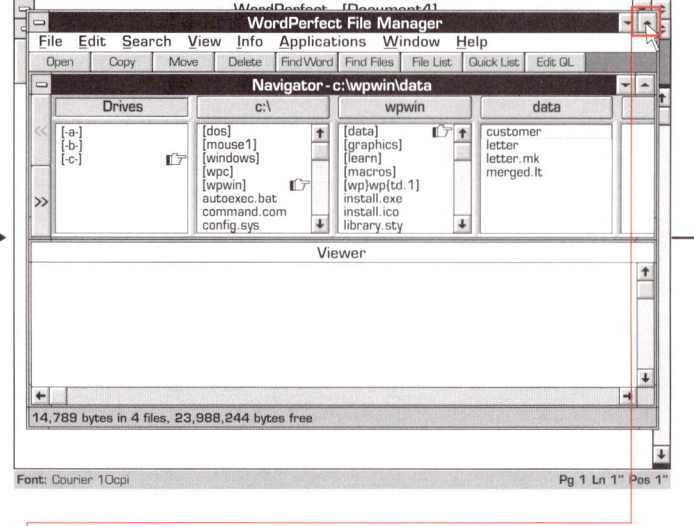

The File Manager helps you create, organize and manage your files and directories.

1 Click **File** to open its menu.

2 Click **File Manager**.

3 Click the **WordPerfect File Manager**'s maximize button to enlarge your working area.

VIEW FILES

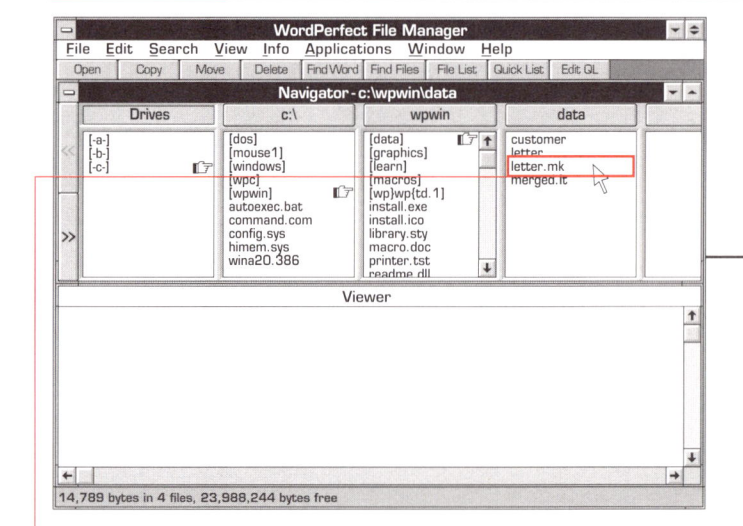

The Viewer lets you quickly view the contents of individual files.

1 Click the file you want to view (example: **letter.mk**).

*Note: If you double click a file, the **Open** dialog box appears. To open a document from the File Manager, refer to page 87.*

82

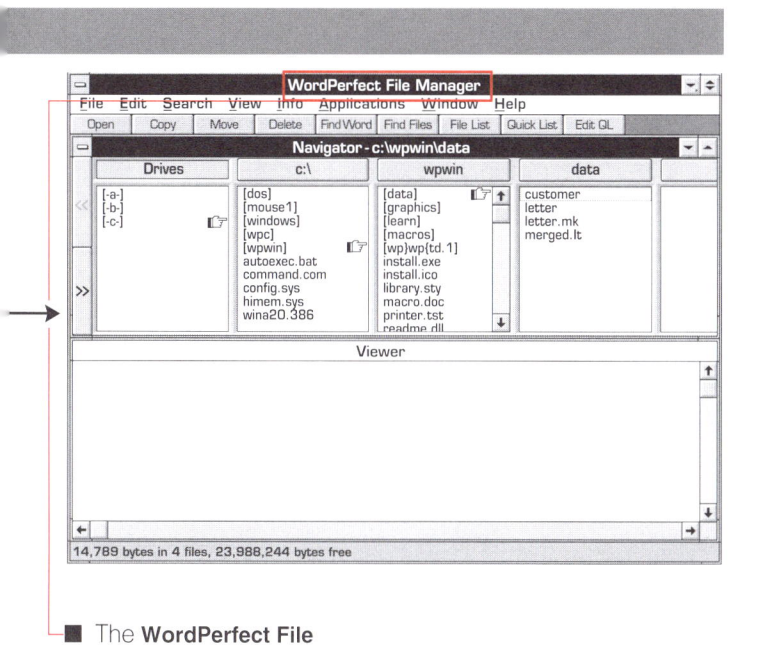

| OPEN THE FILE MANAGER | VIEW FILES | CHANGE DISK DRIVES | CHANGE DIRECTORIES | FILE LIST | CHANGE LAYOUT | COPY OR MOVE FILES | DELETE FILES | SEARCH FOR A FILE | EXIT FILE MANAGER |

■ The **WordPerfect File Manager** is enlarged to fill the entire screen.

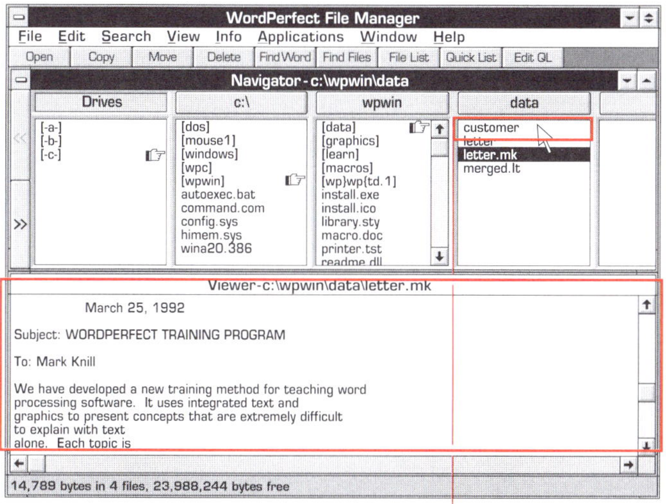

■ The file is viewed.

Note: If the viewed file contains text and graphics, only the text will be displayed.

2 Click another file you want to view (example: **customer**).

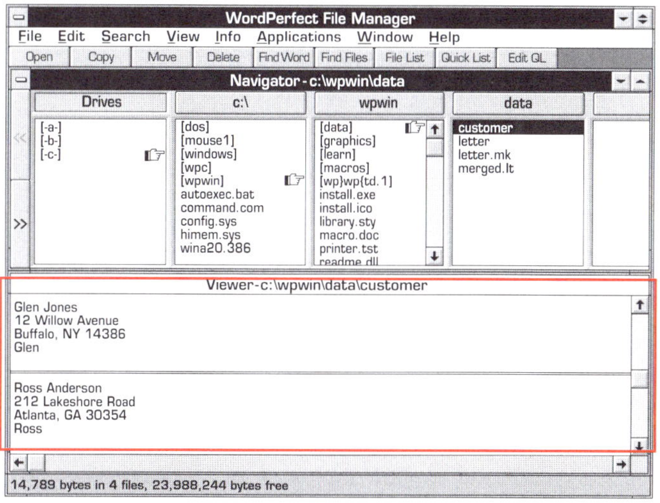

■ The file is viewed.

GETTING STARTED

THE BUTTON BAR

EDIT A DOCUMENT

SAVE FILES AND EXIT WORDPERFECT

VIEW DOCUMENTS

CHECK A DOCUMENT

FORMAT A DOCUMENT

TABLES

GRAPHICS

PRINT

MERGE AND SORT FILES

FILE MANAGER

HELP

◀ 83

CHANGE DISK DRIVES

CHANGE DIRECTORIES

This example displays a sample directory structure using cabinets, drawers and folders.

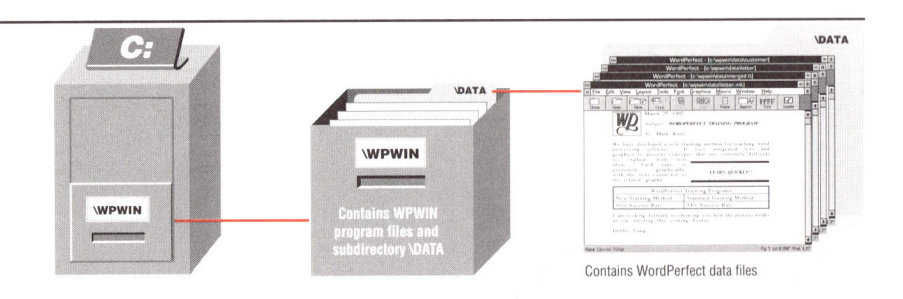

This example supplies you with the same information, but in an electronic format using the WordPerfect Navigator.

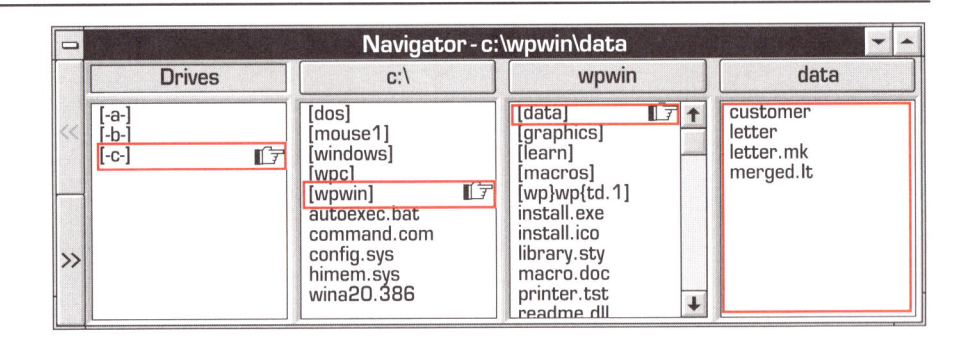

CHANGE DIRECTORIES

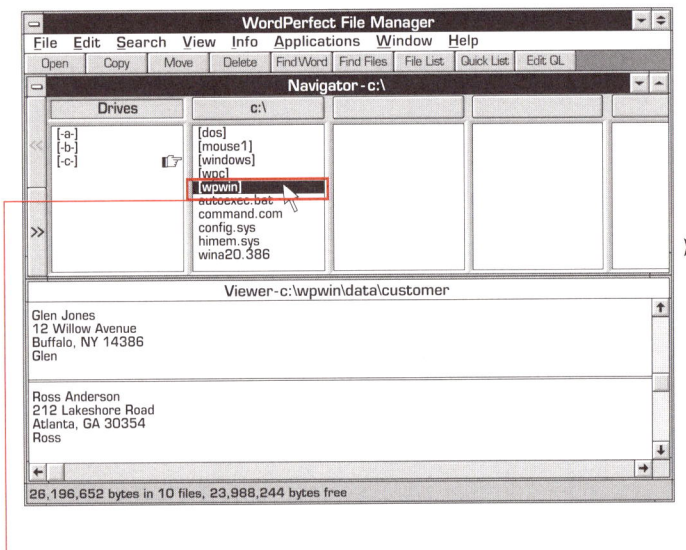

1 Double click the directory whose contents you want to view (example: **[wpwin]**).

*Note: To return to the **c** drive, double click **[-c-]**.*

*Note: Directories are shown within **[ ]** (example: **[dos]**).*

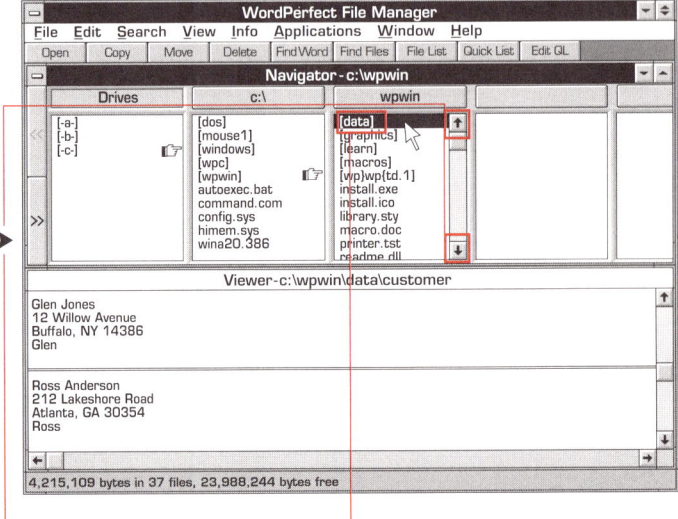

■ The contents of the directory are displayed.

2 Click the up or down scroll arrow to view more directories and files.

3 Double click the next directory whose contents you want to view (example: **[data]**).

84

| OPEN THE FILE MANAGER | VIEW FILES | **CHANGE DISK DRIVES** | CHANGE DIRECTORIES | FILE LIST | CHANGE LAYOUT | COPY OR MOVE FILES | DELETE FILES | SEARCH FOR A FILE | EXIT FILE MANAGER |

CHANGE DISK DRIVES

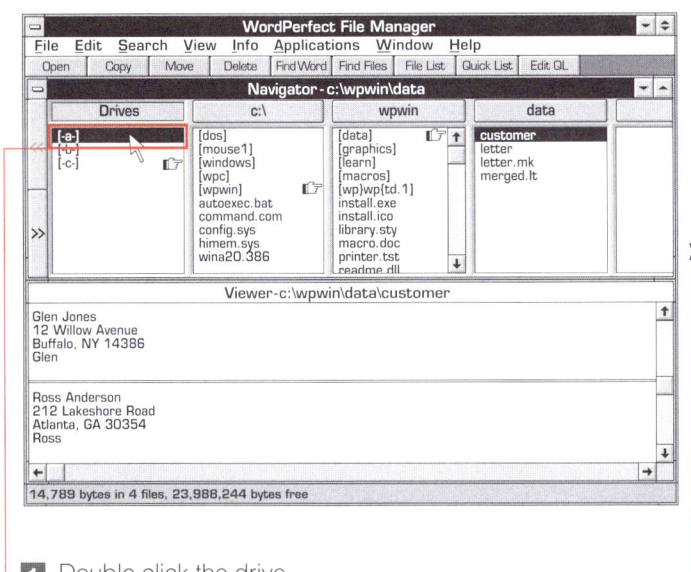

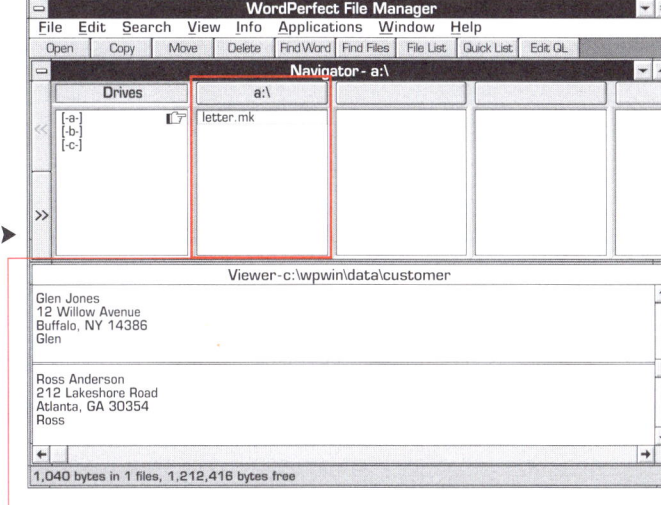

1 Double click the drive whose contents you want to view (example: **a**).

■ The contents of the drive are displayed.

Note: The pointing hand ☞ indicates which drive is current. The contents of the drive are displayed in the next column.

*Note: To view the contents of drive **c**, double click **[-c-]**.*

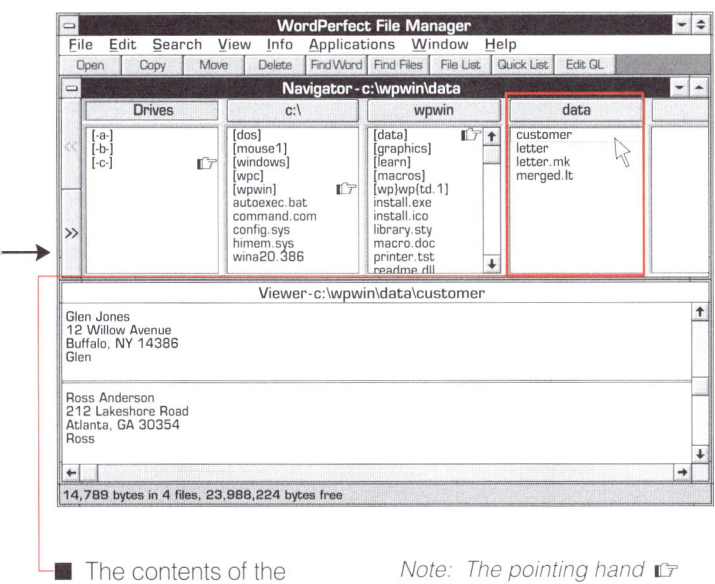

■ The contents of the directory are displayed.

Note: The pointing hand ☞ indicates which directory is current. The contents of the directory are displayed in the next column.

GETTING STARTED

THE BUTTON BAR

EDIT A DOCUMENT

SAVE FILES AND EXIT WORDPERFECT

VIEW DOCUMENTS

CHECK A DOCUMENT

FORMAT A DOCUMENT

TABLES

GRAPHICS

PRINT

MERGE AND SORT FILES

FILE MANAGER

HELP

◀ 85

FILE LIST / CHANGE LAYOUT

FILE LIST

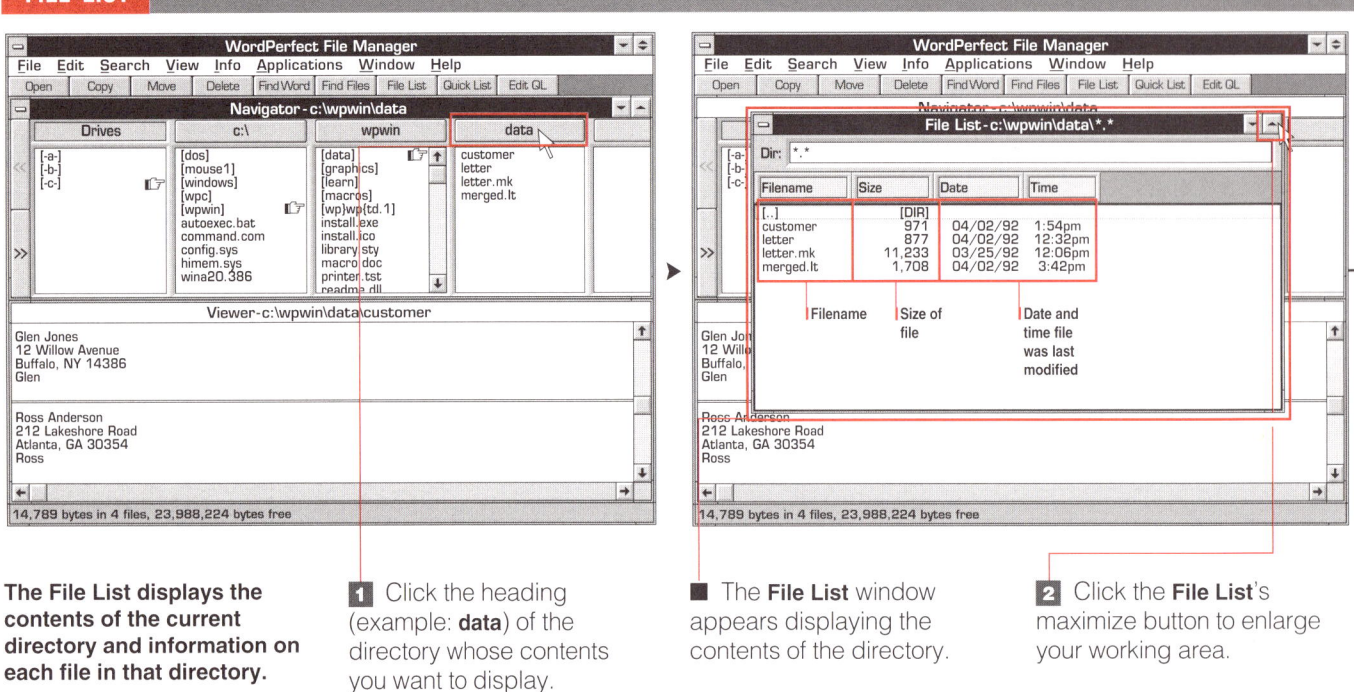

The File List displays the contents of the current directory and information on each file in that directory.

1 Click the heading (example: **data**) of the directory whose contents you want to display.

■ The **File List** window appears displaying the contents of the directory.

2 Click the **File List**'s maximize button to enlarge your working area.

CHANGE LAYOUT

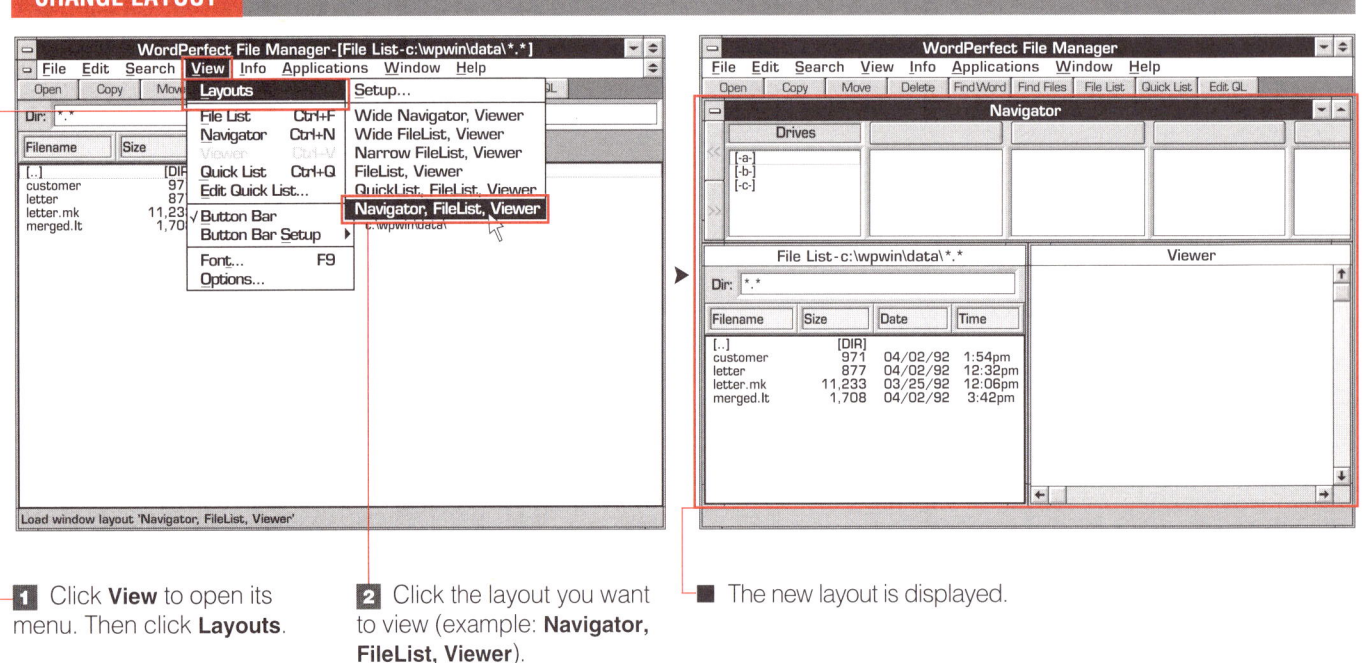

1 Click **View** to open its menu. Then click **Layouts**.

2 Click the layout you want to view (example: **Navigator, FileList, Viewer**).

■ The new layout is displayed.

86

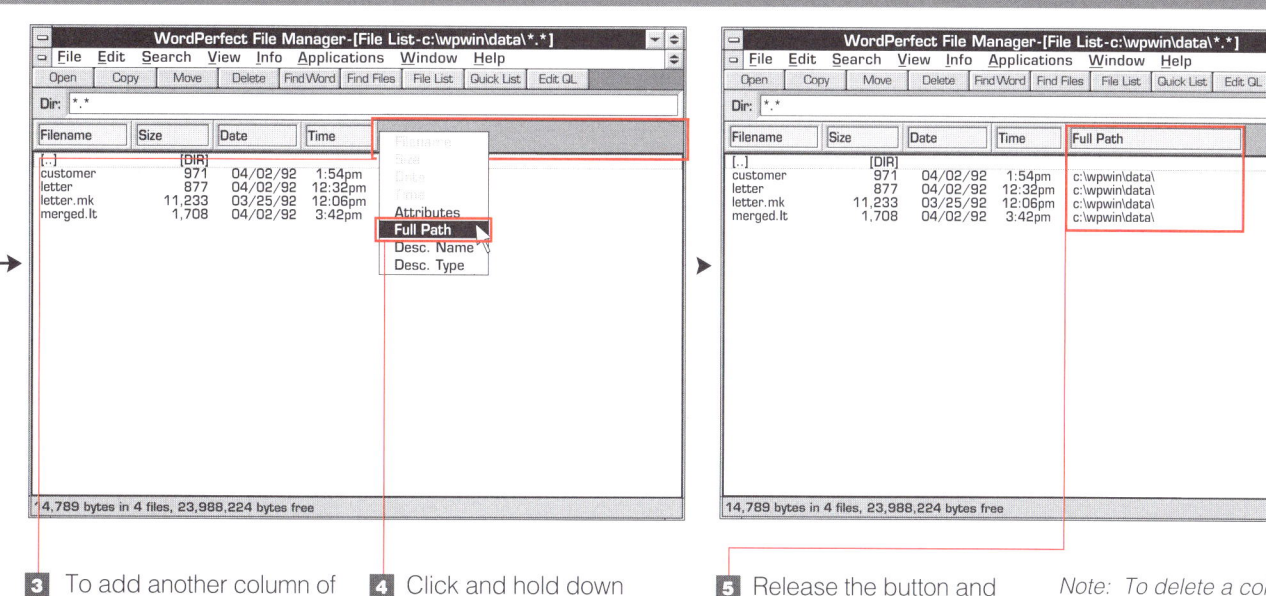

| OPEN THE FILE MANAGER | VIEW FILES | CHANGE DISK DRIVES | CHANGE DIRECTORIES | **FILE LIST** | **CHANGE LAYOUT** | COPY OR MOVE FILES | DELETE FILES | SEARCH FOR A FILE | EXIT FILE MANAGER |

3 To add another column of information to the **File List** window, move the mouse over the empty space on the heading bar.

4 Click and hold down the left mouse button as you drag the mouse over the type of information you want to add (example: **Full Path**).

5 Release the button and the information is added.

Note: To delete a column, move the mouse over the column heading you want to delete (example: Time). Click and hold down the mouse button as you drag the heading off the heading bar.

OPEN A FILE FROM THE FILE MANAGER

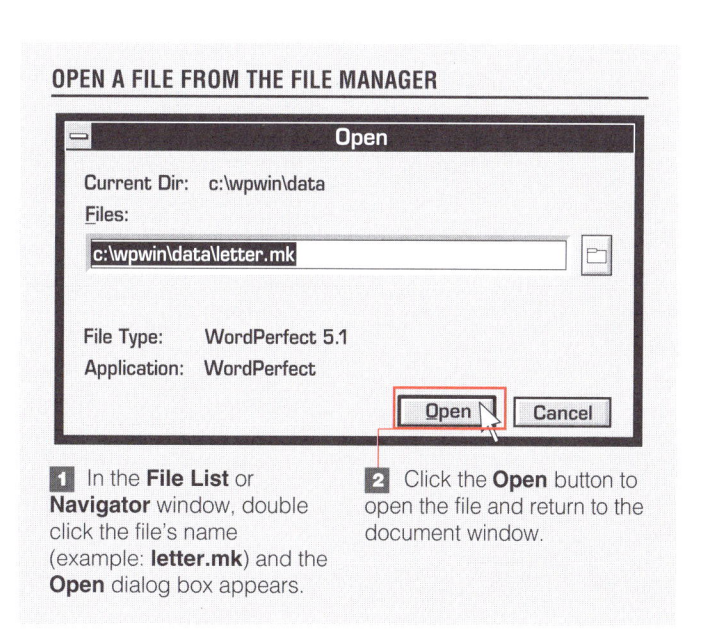

1 In the **File List** or **Navigator** window, double click the file's name (example: **letter.mk**) and the **Open** dialog box appears.

2 Click the **Open** button to open the file and return to the document window.

GETTING STARTED

THE BUTTON BAR

EDIT A DOCUMENT

SAVE FILES AND EXIT WORDPERFECT

VIEW DOCUMENTS

CHECK A DOCUMENT

FORMAT A DOCUMENT

TABLES

GRAPHICS

PRINT

MERGE AND SORT FILES

FILE MANAGER

HELP

87

COPY OR MOVE FILES

COPY OR MOVE A FILE

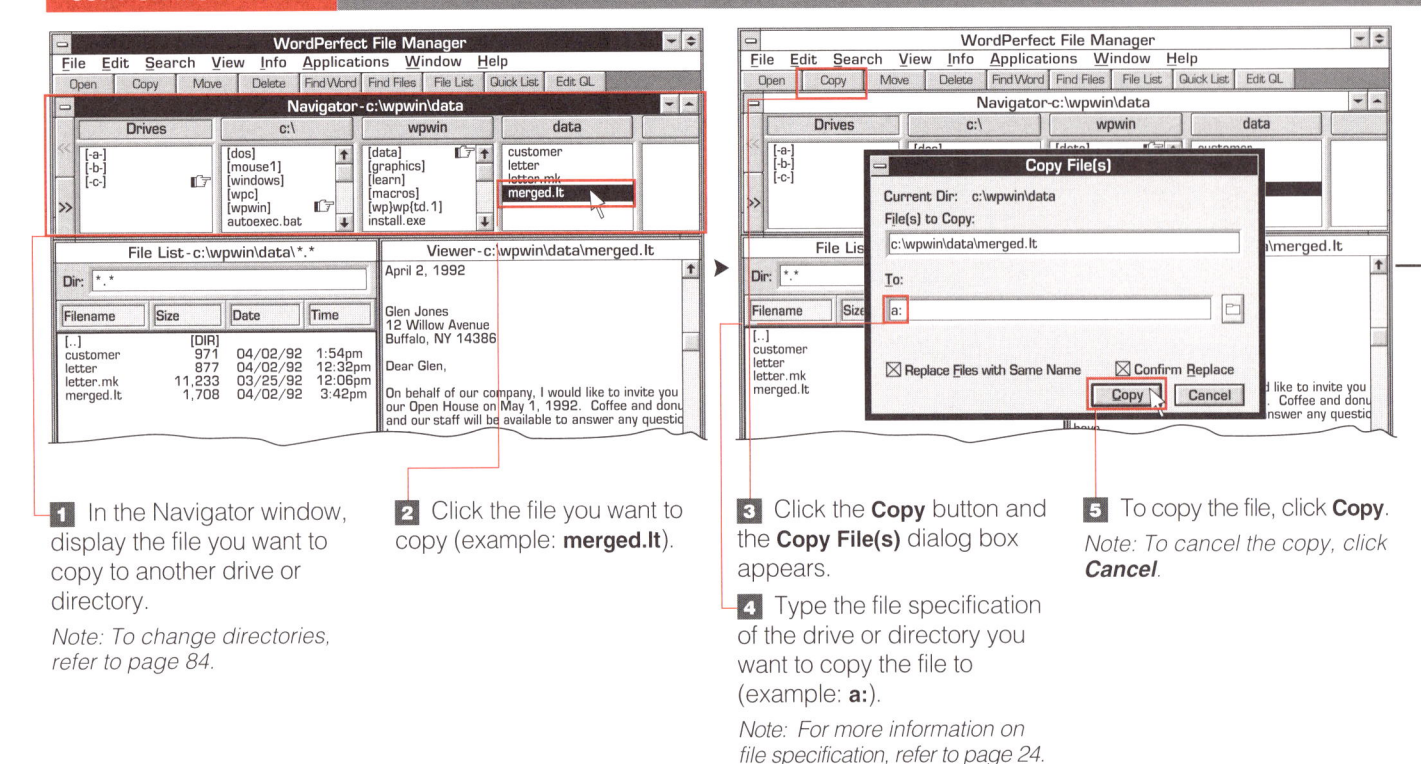

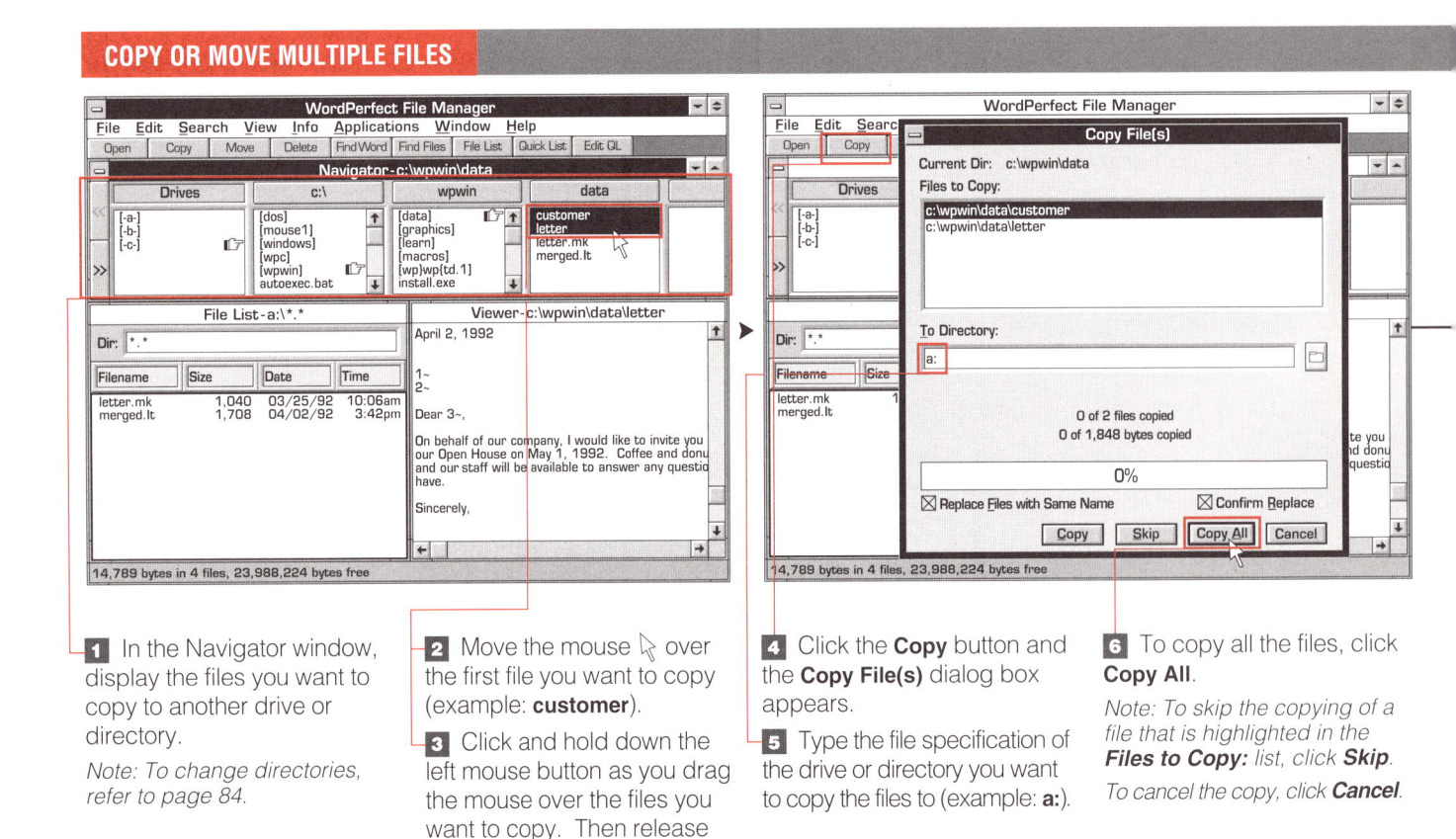

1 In the Navigator window, display the file you want to copy to another drive or directory.

Note: To change directories, refer to page 84.

2 Click the file you want to copy (example: **merged.lt**).

3 Click the **Copy** button and the **Copy File(s)** dialog box appears.

4 Type the file specification of the drive or directory you want to copy the file to (example: **a:**).

Note: For more information on file specification, refer to page 24.

5 To copy the file, click **Copy**.

*Note: To cancel the copy, click **Cancel**.*

COPY OR MOVE MULTIPLE FILES

1 In the Navigator window, display the files you want to copy to another drive or directory.

Note: To change directories, refer to page 84.

2 Move the mouse over the first file you want to copy (example: **customer**).

3 Click and hold down the left mouse button as you drag the mouse over the files you want to copy. Then release the mouse button.

4 Click the **Copy** button and the **Copy File(s)** dialog box appears.

5 Type the file specification of the drive or directory you want to copy the files to (example: **a:**).

6 To copy all the files, click **Copy All**.

*Note: To skip the copying of a file that is highlighted in the **Files to Copy:** list, click **Skip**.*

*To cancel the copy, click **Cancel**.*

88

| OPEN THE FILE MANAGER | VIEW FILES | CHANGE DISK DRIVES | CHANGE DIRECTORIES | FILE LIST | CHANGE LAYOUT | **COPY OR MOVE FILES** | DELETE FILES | SEARCH FOR A FILE | EXIT FILE MANAGER |

6 To confirm the copy, double click in the box beside **Dir:** in the **File List** window.

7 Type the file specification of the drive or directory you copied the file to (example: **a:**).

8 Press **Enter** and the copied file is displayed.

TO MOVE FILES

Click the [Move] button in step **3**.

■ The copied files are displayed.

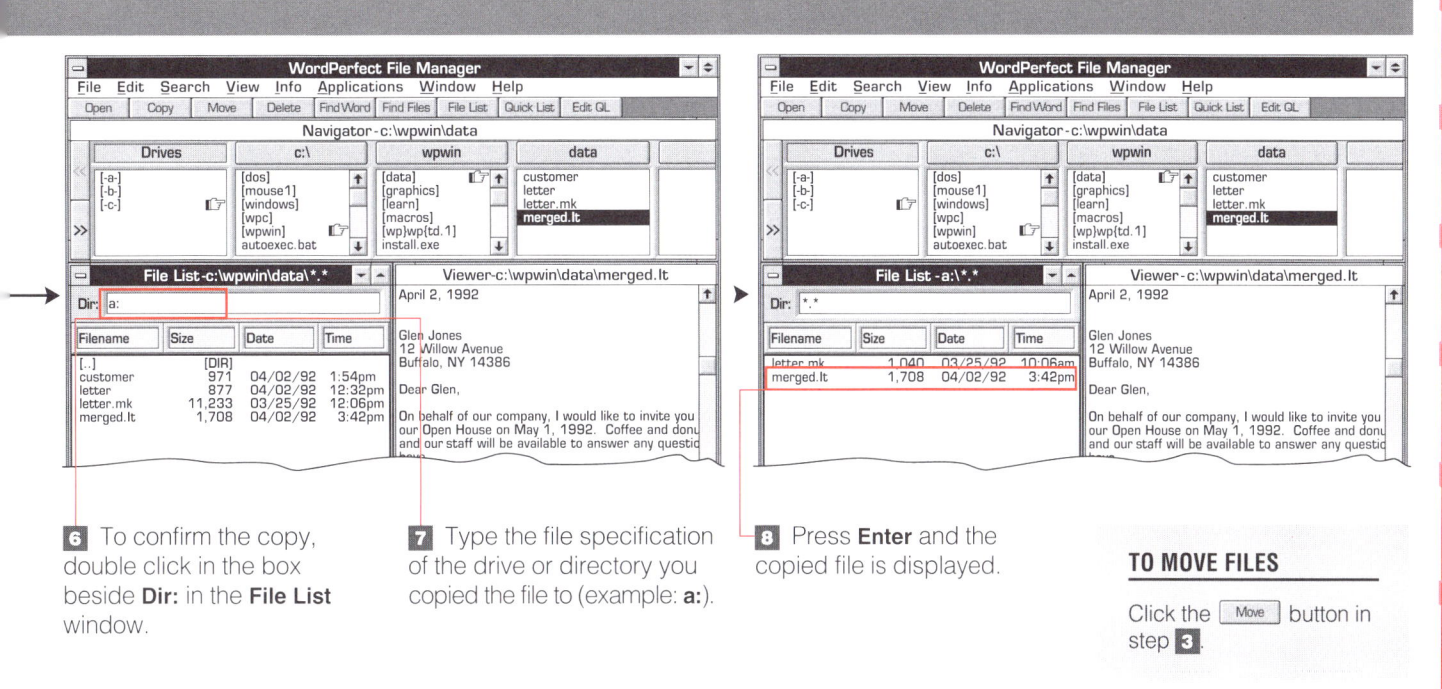

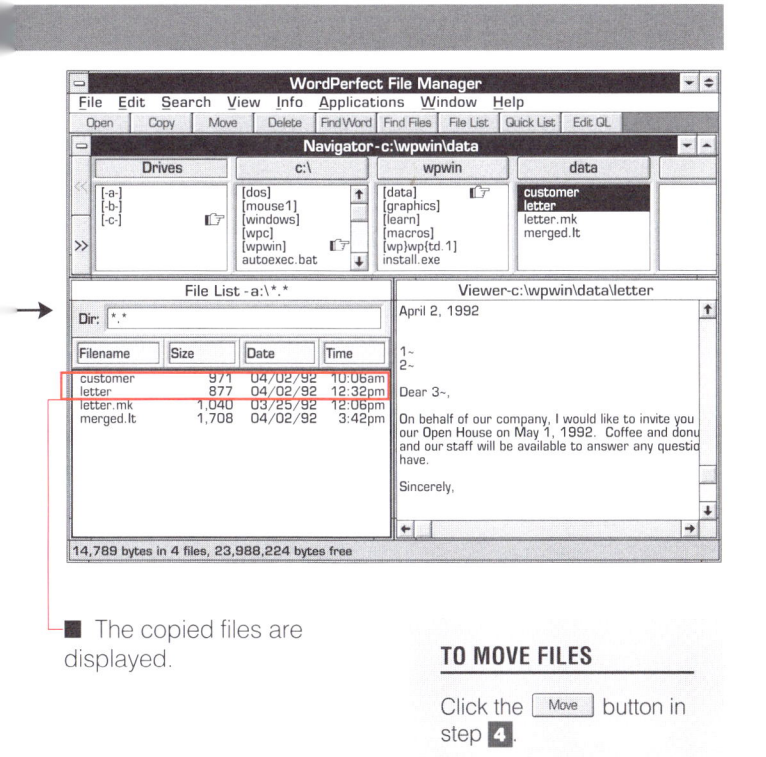

TO MOVE FILES

Click the [Move] button in step **4**.

GETTING STARTED

THE BUTTON BAR

EDIT A DOCUMENT

SAVE FILES AND EXIT WORDPERFECT

VIEW DOCUMENTS

CHECK A DOCUMENT

FORMAT A DOCUMENT

TABLES

GRAPHICS

PRINT

MERGE AND SORT FILES

FILE MANAGER

HELP

◀ 89

| DELETE FILES | SEARCH FOR A FILE | EXIT FILE MANAGER |

DELETE FILES

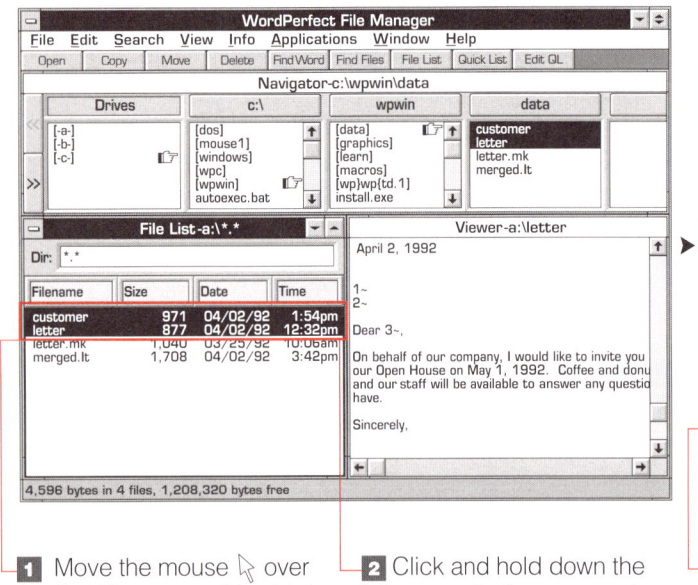

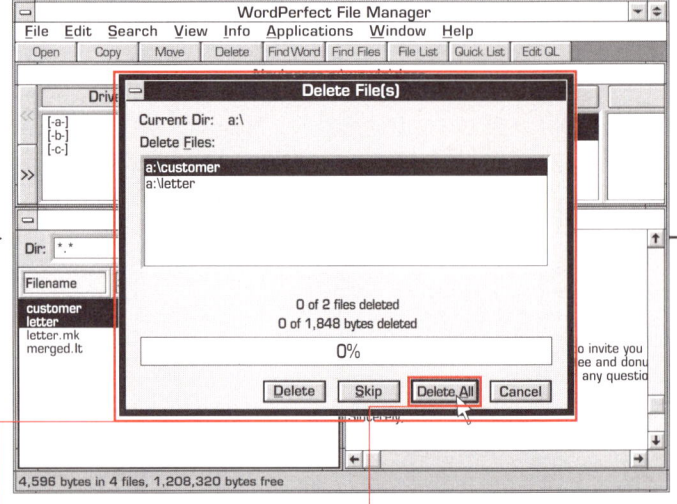

1 Move the mouse over the first file you want to delete (example: **customer**).

2 Click and hold down the left mouse button as you drag the mouse over the files you want to delete. Release the mouse button.

3 Press **Delete** and the **Delete File(s)** dialog box appears.

4 To delete all the files, click **Delete All**.

*Note: To delete only some of the files, click **Skip** to skip the deletion of a highlighted file. Click **Delete** to delete a highlighted file.*

SEARCH FOR A FILE

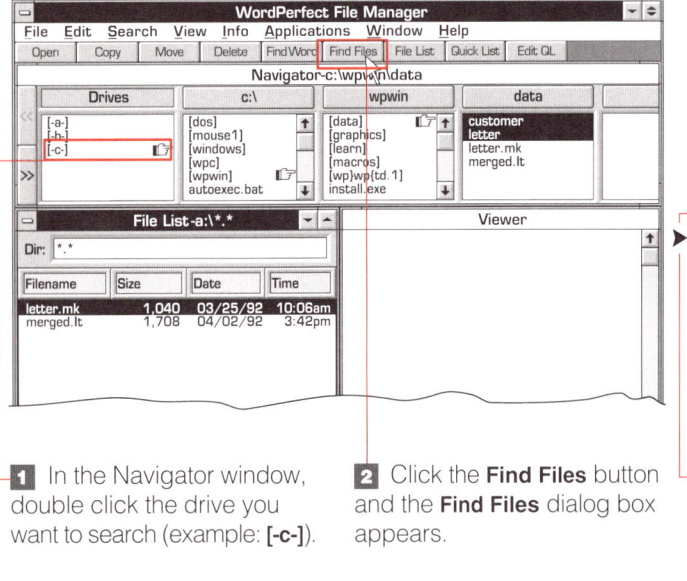

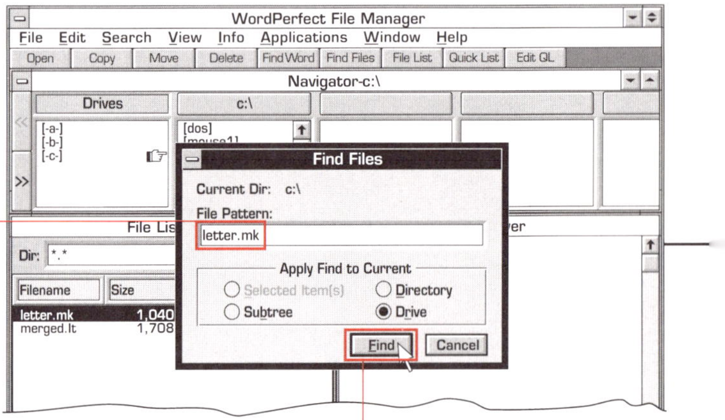

1 In the Navigator window, double click the drive you want to search (example: **[-c-]**).

2 Click the **Find Files** button and the **Find Files** dialog box appears.

3 Type the name of the file you want to search for (example: **letter.mk**).

*Note: If you use an * (asterisk) in a search name, the * is interpreted to mean any number of characters (example: **le*** matches all filenames starting with **le**).*

4 Click **Find**.

90

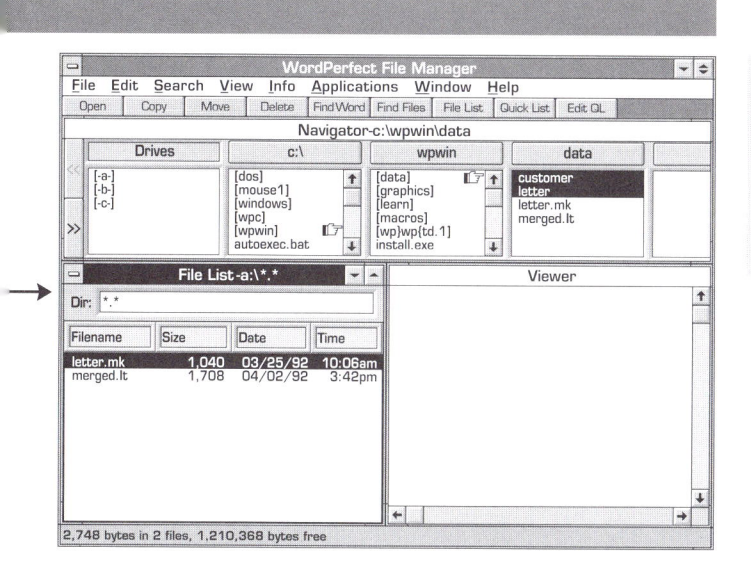

| OPEN THE FILE MANAGER | VIEW FILES | CHANGE DISK DRIVES | CHANGE DIRECTORIES | FILE LIST | CHANGE LAYOUT | COPY OR MOVE FILES | **DELETE FILES** | **SEARCH FOR A FILE** | **EXIT FILE MANAGER** |

DELETE A SINGLE FILE

1 Click the name of the file you want to delete.

2 Press **Delete** and the **Delete File(s)** dialog box appears.

3 To delete the file, click **Delete**.
Note: To cancel the deletion, click **Cancel**.

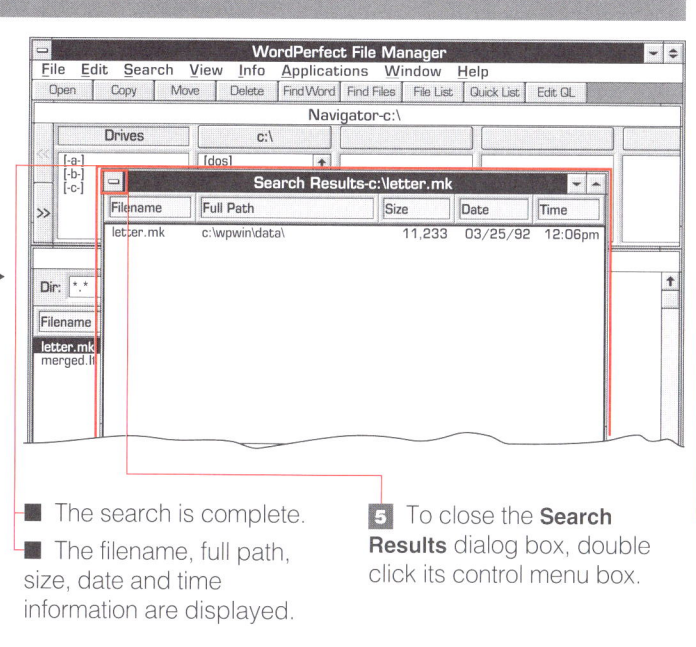

■ The files are deleted.

Note: Files can be deleted from the **File List** or **Navigator** window.

EXIT FILE MANAGER

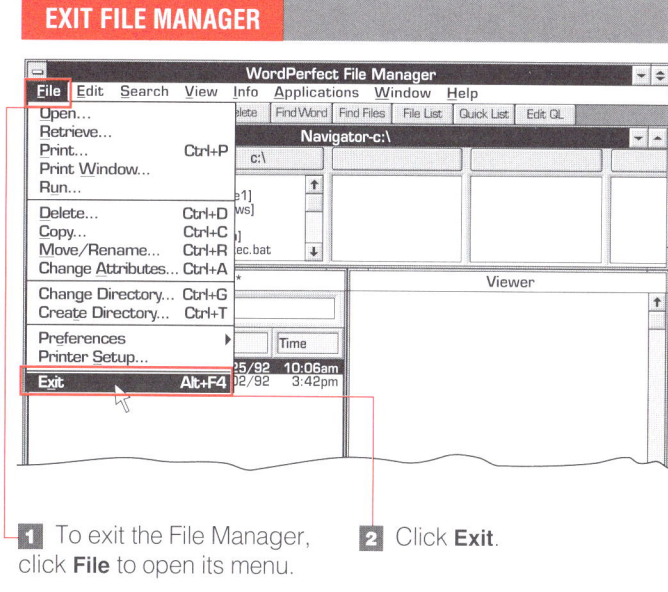

1 To exit the File Manager, click **File** to open its menu.

2 Click **Exit**.

■ The search is complete.

■ The filename, full path, size, date and time information are displayed.

5 To close the **Search Results** dialog box, double click its control menu box.

GETTING STARTED

THE BUTTON BAR

EDIT A DOCUMENT

SAVE FILES AND EXIT WORDPERFECT

VIEW DOCUMENTS

CHECK A DOCUMENT

FORMAT A DOCUMENT

TABLES

GRAPHICS

PRINT

MERGE AND SORT FILES

FILE MANAGER

HELP

◀ 91

HELP

CONTEXT SENSITIVE HELP

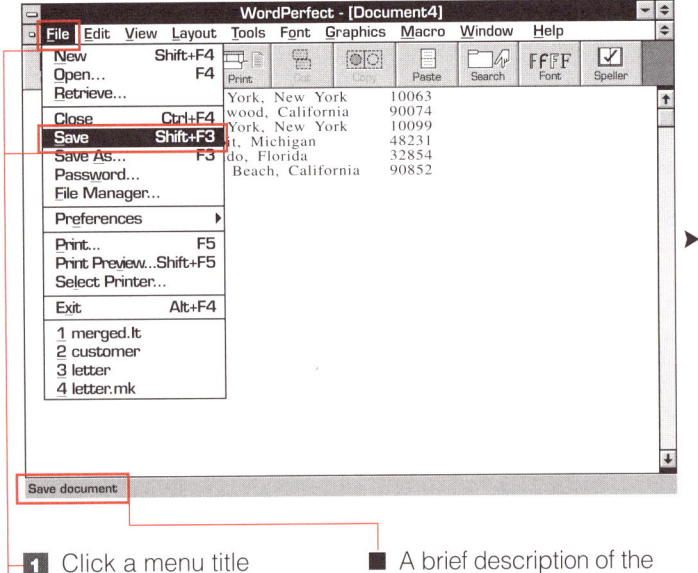

1 Click a menu title (example: **File**) to open its menu.

2 Press ↓ until the command you want help on is highlighted (example: **Save**).

■ A brief description of the command appears at the bottom of the screen.

3 For more information, press **F1**.

Note: Context sensitive help can be obtained for any command or dialog box.

4 Click the **Maximize** button to enlarge the **WordPerfect for Windows Help** window.

THE HELP MENU

HELP MENU OPTIONS	
Index	Lists help topics.
Keyboard	Displays keyboard information.
How Do I	Displays help on common tasks.
Glossary	Lists definitions of common words.
Using Help	Explains how to use Help.
What Is	Context-sensitive help using the mouse pointer.
About WordPerfect	Displays product information.

1 Click **Help** to open its menu.

2 Click the topic of interest (example: **How Do I**).

92

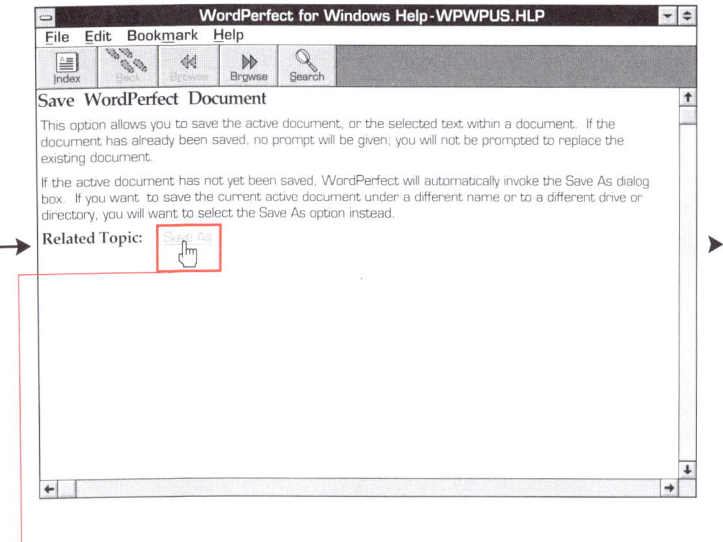

HELP

5 Move the mouse over a topic (example: **Save As**) you want more information on. The cursor turns into a pointing hand. Click the left mouse button.

Note: This only applies to dimmed/green, underlined text.

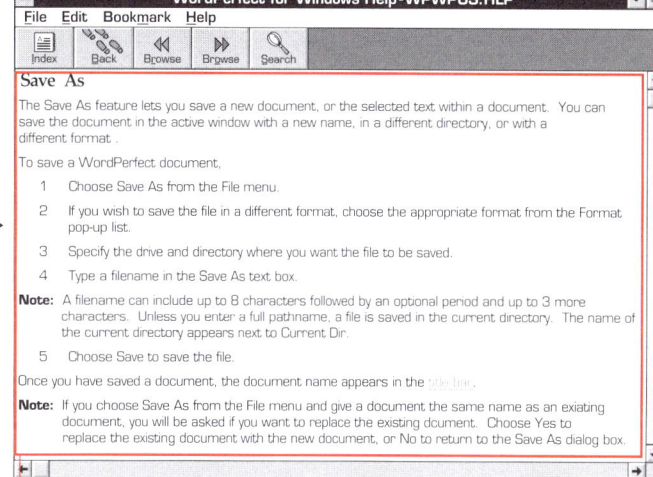

■ A detailed explanation of that topic appears.

6 Press ↓ to view more of the screen.

7 Move the mouse over the next topic of interest and click the left mouse button for more information.

*Note: To exit **Help** and return to the document, click **File**, then click **Exit**.*

ADDITIONAL NAVIGATION CHOICES

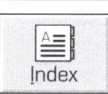

Index
Click this button to view the Help Index.

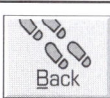

Back
Click this button to retrace your path back to the Help Index.

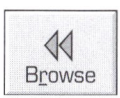

Browse (◄◄)
Click this button to move backward through a series of related topics.

Browse (►►)
Click this button to move forward through a series of related topics.

Search
Click this button to search for information on a specific word or phrase.

Note: When a button dims you have reached the first or last topic in the series.

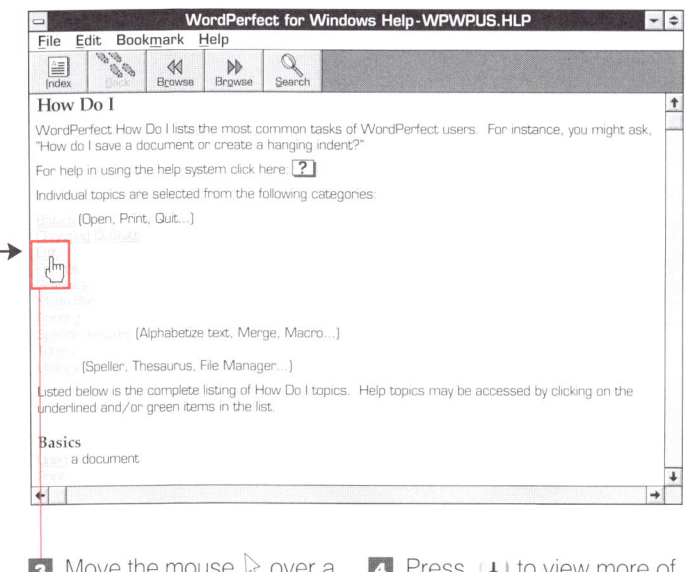

3 Move the mouse over a topic of interest (example: **Edit**) and cursor turns into a pointing hand. Click the left mouse button for more information.

4 Press ↓ to view more of the screen.

*Note: To exit **Help** and return to the document, click **File**, then click **Exit**.*

GETTING STARTED

THE BUTTON BAR

EDIT A DOCUMENT

SAVE FILES AND EXIT WORDPERFECT

VIEW DOCUMENTS

CHECK A DOCUMENT

FORMAT A DOCUMENT

TABLES

GRAPHICS

PRINT

MERGE AND SORT FILES

FILE MANAGER

HELP

◄ 93

INDEX

BUTTON BAR

	Page
Add a Button	12
Change	10
Delete a Button	12
Move a Button	13
Save	14
Select	14
View	10

DELETE

	Page
Blank Line	20
Buttons	12
Characters	20
Files	90
Page Break	50
Selected Text	21
Table	63
Tabs	47
Text	20

DIRECTORY

	Page
Change	84
Create	27
Files	24, 25

DISK DRIVES

	Page
Change	85

DOCUMENTS

	Page
Automatic Page Numbering	52
Cascade	32
Close	33
Endnotes	56
Footers	54
Footnotes	56
Headers	54
Maximize	33
Page Break	50
Save	26-28
Switch Between	31
Tile	32
View Ruler	40

EXIT

	Page
File Manager	91
WordPerfect	28

FILES

	Page
Copy	88
Delete	90
File List	86
File Manager	5, 82-91
Location	26
Merged	75, 78
Move	88
Organization	25, 26, 84
Primary	74, 76
Search	90
Secondary	74, 76
Specification	24-26
View	82

GRAPHIC

	Page
Delete	65
Move	66
Retrieve	64
Size	64
Text Box	66

HELP 92

MARGINS

	Page
Left Margin	44
Right Margin	45
Top and Bottom	44

MERGE FILES

	Page
Merge Files	75, 78
Primary File	74, 76
Print	78
Secondary File	74, 76

MOVE THROUGH A DOCUMENT 8, 9

OPEN

	Page
File from File Manager	87
File Manager	82
New Document	30
Saved Document	30

PRINT

	Page
All Pages	70
Change Print Quality	72
Current Page	70
Document Stored on Disk	72
Merged File	78
Multiple Copies	73
Preview	68
Selected Text	71
Specific Pages	70

SAVE

	Page
Button	27, 37
Button Bar	14
Document to a Floppy Disk	28
Merged Document	79
New File	26

SEARCH

	Page
For a File	90
Search	38
Search and Replace	38

SORT 80

SPELLER 5, 34

TABLE

	Page
Create	58
Delete a Row or Column	62
Delete a Table	63
Enter Text	60
Insert a Row or Column	62
Join Cells	58
Resize Columns	60
Select Cells	59

TABS

	Page
Add a Tab	47
Move a Tab	46
Remove a Tab	47
Using Tabs	46

TEXT

	Page
Align	40
Center Text on a Page	50
Copy	18
Delete	20
Draft Mode	23
Enter	6, 60
Fonts	48
Indent	42, 43
Insert	16
Line Spacing	41
Move	18
Replace	17
Select	6, 7
Split and Join Paragraphs	22
Text Box	66
Typeover	17
Upper or Lower Case	22
Word Count	36

THESAURUS 5, 36

UNDO 20